LECTURES ON JUDAISM IN THE ACADEMY
AND IN THE HUMANITIES

SOUTH FLORIDA STUDIES IN THE HISTORY OF JUDAISM

Edited by
Jacob Neusner
Ernest S. Frerichs, William Scott Green, James Strange

Number 01
Lectures on Judaism in the Academy
and in the Humanities

by
Jacob Neusner

LECTURES ON JUDAISM IN THE ACADEMY AND IN THE HUMANITIES

by

Jacob Neusner

Scholars Press
Atlanta, Georgia

LECTURES ON JUDAISM IN THE ACADEMY AND IN THE HUMANITIES

© 1990
University of South Florida

Publication of this book was made possible by a grant from the Tisch Family Foundation, New York City. The University of South Florida acknowledges with thanks this important support for its scholarly projects.

Library of Congress Cataloging in Publication Data
Neusner, Jacob, 1932-
    Lectures on Judaism in the academy and in the humanities / by
    Jacob Neusner.
    p. cm. -- (South Florida studies in the history of Judaism : 01)
    Lectures delivered 1969-1990.
    ISBN 1-55540-413-8 (alk. paper)
    1. Judaism--Study and teaching (Higher)--United States.
2. Judaism--History--Talmudic period, 10-425. I. Title.
II. Series.
BM75.N4833   1989
296'.071'1--dc20   89-70260
                                                    CIP

Printed in the United States of America
on acid-free paper

FOR

ELIEZER SCHWEID

THE HEBREW UNIVERSITY,
JERUSALEM

IN TRIBUTE TO THE RARE UNION
OF INTELLECT, CONSCIENCE, AND CHARACTER

SO FAR AS THERE CAN BE JUDAIC HUMANITIES IN A JEWISH ACADEMY,
HE SHOWS US HOW — AND THE REASON WHY.

Table of Contents

Preface

The University realizes itself in the formal academic lecture, often endowed and named, when it invites a scholar to speak to the academy as a whole, not to a small group of specialists or senior scholars alone, but to whom it may concern, student or senior professor, specialist, generalist, outsider to learning altogether. That is the moment at which, all together and all at once, the principal parts of the University come together to form a community of shared discourse. That explains why the named lecture presents a splendid opportunity, if also a major challenge, to scholars honored by the invitation to present such a public accounting of their work. It is the University's most distinctive way of expressing in concrete ways the rules of common discourse, the manners required by a decent respect for the opinions and intelligence of others.

A particularly demanding but attractive medium of scholarly expression, the academic lecture, imposes its own discipline. It requires an address to a broad and mixed audience of scholars about one's own specialization. That means the lecturer must speak to the academic world about quite particular results, therefore demanding the work of generalization: what do I have to say to people of intellect who want to know, for their studies, what I have learned in my scholarly undertakings? Not only so, but academic audiences include not only professors but sizable numbers of students, so that the mixture involves not only specialists in different disciplines and fields but also beginners and mature scholars alike. The upshot is that, at the academic lecture, the scholar speaks to the University in its richest sense: a group of engaged minds, working on different subjects, but eager to communicate what they have learned with one another – and with ages to follow.

In the past three decades, and particularly since I came to Brown University in 1968, I have delivered academic lectures on every continent, for every imaginable purpose and audience. I have given more than eighty such addresses, including conference papers and overseas lecture tours, in the average of one every three months for twenty years. Many of these lectures were published in one form or other, as books, as in the case of the Haskell Lecture at Oberlin College, which became *The Idea of Purity in Judaism* (Leiden, 1973: E. J. Brill), and the Richard Lectures at the University of Virginia, which produced *Ancient Israel after Catastrophe* (Charlottesville, 1985: The University Press of Virginia); many of them were issued as articles, or as pamphlets for the local audience. I have used these occasions to present to the University at large what seemed to me consequential and important in my own scholarship and thought. In these pages I have selected the few lectures, out of many dozens, that seem to me to warrant more permanent form than the original oral presentation and (commonly) ad hoc circulation in an offprint for the occasion.

My purpose in collecting and reprinting the lectures that seemed to me to sustain a second reading is twofold. First, I mean to set forth my conception of discourse appropriate for the academy. There are other conceptions that circulate; the concrete results of one choice in preference to some other seem to me worth placing on display. For even now, debate on the character of the academy, on the nature of proper discourse within the academy, and on the calling of the scholar goes forward. That debate is framed both in general terms, in the public press, and also in special language, within the circles of professors of Jewish or Judaic studies and their counterparts in other fields of narrowly ethnic definition and interest. I maintain that every field of the humanities bears the common task of addressing the generality of the University and of doing so in intelligible language and in the framework of shared categories of thought. Since others in word and deed deny that position, I owe it to the academy to show what I mean, as others will show what they mean. Then people can examine the results and decide for themselves what they think is worthwhile.

This collection of essays deals with the place of the study of Judaism in the academy, within the discipline(s) of the academic study of religion. I address in Part One a variety of questions on the definition of the student and the professor who in the academy undertake to study about Judaism. In the same context I explain the role of theology within the religious study of Judaism. In Part Two I turn to questions of literature, philosophy, and the study of religion and society. These yield the final paper of the group, on the nature of category-formation in the academy. I conclude in the epilogue with an account of why I regard the study of religion as a critical task of the academy and a central component of the humanities.

I express my thanks to those whom I consulted in selecting these papers for publication: Professors Ernest S. Frerichs, Wendell S.

Dietrich, and Calvin Goldscheider, Brown University, and William Scott Green, University of Rochester.

Jacob Neusner
The Institute for Advanced Study

Prologue

1

The Liberal Arts and the
Social Order

University of South Florida, Tampa, 1989

In standing up in the classroom, in assigning books to read, in telling people things and asking them questions, on examinations, about what they are learning, I lay down a very extraordinary claim. Along with all professors, I say to students, among the many things you can do with your lives – whether at the age of eighteen or twenty or forty or sixty or eighty – the most important thing you can do with three hours a week is sit in front of me and listen to what I have to tell you; and with another six or seven hours a week is to sit in the library and read the books that I assign to you; and for another few hours a week, off and on, even to think about these things that I am in charge of teaching to you.

Now that is an amazing demand that we professors set forth. And each one of us goes a step further and says, among all the things you can learn in this university, the ones I have to teach you must take priority. When I stand up in front of a hundred students, the moment I walk in the room I bear an implicit message, which is, I have something to tell you of such consequence that, at this particular hour, the best thing you can do, among the many things you can do, is spend your money and your time on listening to the very particular thing that is so urgent, so compelling, so immediate, that you had better sit down and listen!

That formulation of matters raises the stakes of education to that high level that, in my opinion, they should reach. Can I make that claim stick? One case in point – having to do with the liberal arts – will suggest that I can. It has to do with a fundamental problem in our social order, and the way in which, in one component of the liberal arts, the humanities, and in one chapter of the liberal arts, the academic study of religion, and in one paragraph of that chapter, the study of Judaism, we learn in our minds how to confront a problem that society in general today faces but lacks the intellectual tools to solve, I mean, the problem of difference in culture, religion, gender, language, – everything.

Let me start back from the beginning: the liberal arts. As a parent I want my children to get a college degree so that they can get a good job and start a satisfying career. As a professor I want my students to learn how to think clearly, express themselves accurately and to the point, argue and reason intelligently, use their minds thoughtfully and independently. As a professor who is also a parent I wonder how these twin goals can be attained. And that brings me to the problem before us: what is the relationship between the liberal arts and the society that turns to universities to build its future?

Public universities bear a special mission in answering that question because in a direct and immediate way, society, through the political process, directs to public universities a great deal of money – tax money – and expects public universities to use that money in the way in which society, through the political system and its process, requires. I use the word "requires" advisedly, because it has two senses, first, needs, second, directs. Public universities meet needs, carry out requirements of the social order; and public universities also fulfill their mission, carry out the directions of the political process. Accordingly, thinking about the relationship between the liberal arts and the social order in public universities defines a particularly engaging problem: what good is it all, that people in the here and now, citizens and taxpayers, can recognize? And, since my discipline is the academic study of religion, and, within that discipline, my specialty is the academic study of Judaism, can I explain how, in the humanities, in the academic study of religion, in the study of Judaism, I think I do something that contributes to the social order? And if I do, then what, in particular, is that contribution, and how do I suppose that my special knowledge offers a generally intelligible and also important education?

We all know the downside of the liberal arts, the uselessness of learning social science, math and natural science, and humanities subjects and majors: I studied French literature for four years, and now I am working as an administrative assistant in an accounting firm. I studied history for four years, but I couldn't get a job so I had to go to law school. I studied chemistry for four years, and now I'm sweeping the floor of a drug store. So it goes. And if you take a liberal arts major in order to get a particular job, you are going to replicate these same disappointing experiences. For in the liberal arts we prepare people not for a particular job, but for work in general, not to do some one thing in an expert way, but to do many things – anything really – intelligently and thoughtfully. When the liberal arts succeed, what is the result? The chemistry major learns how to analyze the properties of things in a critical, thoughtful way, to form a thesis and test it by experiment. Are there limits to the usefulness of those modes of thought? I cannot think of many. The history major learns how to make connections between one thing and something else, how to think through an event, how to reconstruct a course of events, how to see patterns in small things. Where are there limits to the value of knowing how to put two and two together? The philosophy major learns how to conduct sustained and precise arguments, how to see the main point, how to frame an argument well. The social sciences – economics, sociology, anthropology, political science for example – teach people how to think about human beings in their social lives together: the rules that explain why things happen one way, rather than some other; the ways in which to take up facts of social existence and turn them into patterns that yield insight into what is happening.

Just now I had occasion to wish a person in charge of a program in a federal agency I know had done a better job in college than she did. She was explaining to the governing board of the agency how a major shift in the policy of the agency was going to take place. But the language for the new rule was simply unintelligible, so we could not answer the question, why this, not that? I asked her, is there no rule that will now govern? Do people simply have to call you in Washington to find out whether or not they are eligible, and if they do, how will you know? She answered by telling us the story of the agency. I said to her, "I asked for a principle, but you're telling me a story."

The liberal arts are meant to educate for work, not train for particular jobs. This they do by teaching us how to think, how to use our minds, through skills of analysis, judgment, organization, and abstract conceptualization. In so stating, I quote the language of "a Cornell education," for that language captures the ideal of every liberal arts college and university in this country. Then are there subjects that do something else than educate for work? What happens when people train for a particular job? Then they study not the liberal arts but what in the founding centuries of the University were called "the servile arts." These were vocational subjects, studies that bound a person to a particular function. In those days the liberal arts were arithmetic, music, geometry, and astronomy, also grammar, rhetoric, and logic; the first four serve abstract thinking, the other three, accurate thinking and concrete expression. Then what were the servile arts? Everything else.

Now these observations tell you what we mean to accomplish intellectually, but they do not answer the question with which I promised to deal, which is, what good to society? And, as is clear, if universities cannot answer that question, then society will decide (as the British government appears to have decided) that the answer is, not much good at all! We have in every generation to answer the question, what is the relationship between the liberal arts and the social order because times change and the issues we face do not remain constant. So, looking toward the twenty-first century, do I see value in the liberal arts not only in the formation of well-used minds, but useful minds too?

Let me give a general answer and then draw from my own field of specialization on a very specific one as well.

The twenty-first century demands people ready to deal with change and difference, with a world that is constant only in inconstancy. So what it needs is not people who know how to attach one part of a widget to another (in the language of the Cornell document), because, "by being educated only to perform those specific tasks, the widget-trained person has little that can carry over into another line of work, should the popularity of widgets plummet." What our society needs is people who know how to think through the design of widgets, even to ask, are they any good and are there better ways of accomplishing the same goal that we achieve with our widgets anyhow?

In a changing world knowledge is not static, what I teach my students will be obsolete in five years, because, as a scholar, I intend to make it so. But if my students learn how I think, why I take the initiatives that I do, then they have a model for their own ongoing processes of reflection, inquiry, question-asking and question-answering. If my students see me take positions and defend them, they learn the intellectual equivalent to the lesson of the expert widget-maker. But if they see me, as a scholar, asking me the tough questions about my own findings, if they see me dissatisfied and moving onward, always seeking the point beyond my present position, then they understand not the relativity of knowledge but its open-endedness, not the givenness of the facts but their problematic.

So far I have framed matters in very general and abstract terms. Can I give you a concrete and very specific case of how the liberal arts addresses a very immediate and concrete issue of society today – hence, the liberal arts and the social order of the here and the now? Indeed I can, and I shall try to explain why I think my own field of study, the academic study of religion, and my own specialty within that field, which is the study of Judaism, offer to society at large something of urgent interest. For, as a matter of fact, I lay a fundamental claim upon students, professors, the university, and the society that gives us its children to educate and its money to spend on their education.

As a matter of fact, if you look out at the society we are building for the coming century, you will identify as the single most urgent problem this country faces the problem of social, cultural, and religious difference. The social order is no longer ordered by appeal to the traits of normality: being white, Christian, Protestant, and male; it is now multicolored, it has a vast Roman Catholic population, a vast non-Christian population, part secular, part Judaic, Buddhist, Hindu, Muslim. And it is no longer normal to be male, abnormal to be female. So we have to deal with difference, and we now do not have the intellectual tools or the intellectual experience, to do so. The single most important problem facing this country for the next hundred years, as for the last, is that single intellectual challenge: how to think through difference, how to account, within one's own faith and framework, for the outsider, indeed, for many outsiders.

But we do not know how to deal with difference, intellectually first, in public policy second. All we know is how to tolerate – until we don't know in our minds and in public policy even how to tolerate. Take the case of religion in the confrontation with difference, for example. The commonplace theory of religious systems concerning the other or the outsider, consigning to incomprehensibility the different and the other, finds ample illustration here. What do you do with the outsider? Find the other crazy (as we did Ayatollah Khomeini and Jim Jones of Jonestown), or declare the other the work of the devil (as the Ayatollah did with us), or declare the other subject to such metaphors as unclean, impure, dangerous, to be exterminated, as the Germans – Christians, ex-Christians alike – did with the Jews. To take a very current case, in the case of the tragedy unfolding at Oswiecim/Auschwitz, the theory of the other is difficult to express; I am confident that the Carmelite Sisters have only good will for all persons, and I am equally certain that the Jewish survivors, bearers of the moral heritage of the Jewish people and of Judaism in this setting, bear no ill-will for Christianity. The one side identifies the site in its framework and in its terms, the other in its context, and neither seems to have the capacity to grasp the viewpoint of the other within its own frame of reference. Therein lies a future of not merely intolerance or misunderstanding, but of utter incomprehension. And it is that incomprehension of the other, the inability to explain the other to oneself in one's own terms, that transforms religion from a force for peace and reconciliation into a cause of war and intolerance.

Tolerance does not suffice. A theory of the other that concedes the outsider is right for the other but not for me invokes a meretricious relativism that people cannot really mean. For theories of "the other" that afford at best toleration, at worst humiliation and subordination, may have served in an age of an ordered society, but they do not fit a time in which social change forms the sole constant.

What is the connection to the liberal arts in general, the life of intellect that we nurture in colleges of liberal arts? The connection is direct and immediate. Ours now is an intellectual task, for if we cannot in a rational and rigorous way think about the other, then the good works of politics and the ordering of society will not be done. But tolerance – an attitude not a well-considered principle of intellect – works only in a climate of indifference; when you care, so it seems, you also hate. Toleration works where law prevails, but the limits of the law are set by sovereign power, and the range of difference on the other side of the border stretches to the last horizon. So are we able in wit and imagination, mind and intellect, to form a theory of the other coherent with the entire structure of the world that our religious worldview, way of life, account of the "us" that is the social entity, comprise? The issue of coherence is critical, and that matter of cogency with the whole social order explains why at stake are intellectual problems and propositions. Tolerance is a mere social necessity, but, we all recognize, simply not an intellectual virtue. Anyone who doubts should recall the ridicule that met the position, "It does not matter what you believe, as long as you're a good person," not to mention, "it does not matter what you believe, as long as you believe something."

The liberal arts allow us to address intellectual problems within the framework of the laboratory of our minds. There we have a chance through learning to experiment, to think through, to try things out: what if? and why? and why not? We are not legislators, responsible for what we do. We are thinkers, and we can experiment without paying the price of a failed experiment. We can turn to the experience of others, preserved in the records of civilization to which, through our learning, we gain access. That is the place of the liberal arts in the social order: we are the people, the professors and the students in the classroom, who have the special task of sifting and sorting the inherited knowledge and even wisdom of humanity in addressing a particular problem in the contemporary social order.

And that brings us to the special contribution to be made in the study of the Jews and their cultural and religious traditions and experience that we call, in shorthand, "Judaic" or "Jewish studies." That the subject is intrinsically important hardly requires argument; Western civilization builds upon the Hebrew Scriptures of ancient

Israel, and Christianity and Islam are not to be understood without reference to Judaism. But what do we learn in that area that may prove important in addressing a shared concern, one of public interest? To answer that abstract question in the concrete framework of the problem I have set forth, the problem of difference, let me briefly refer to three important things about coping with difference to be learned in the study of the Jews' history, religion, and culture.

The first is that a single group is richly differentiated. We see sameness where insiders see difference. That is so, for example, in the case of religion. Outsiders see Judaism, insiders see Judaisms. The intellectual experience of differentiating what appears from the outside to be sameness is one that the study of Judaism makes accessible and concrete. And that teaches us to consider the possibilities of differentiating the outsider or the other, seeing the traits that make the other into something much more complex – therefore much more like ourselves.

The second is that what we think we know we often do not really grasp at all. The whole of Western civilization knows, for example, that Judaism is the religion of the Old Testament. But as a matter of fact, Judaism is no more the religion of the Old Testament than Christianity is. Outsiders see the obvious and have to learn that that is not so obvious; students who are not Jews learn when they study about Judaism that much of what they know about the other or the outsider is in fact a fabrication of one's own religion. And once in our intellects we undergo that experience of discovery that what appears familiar is unfamiliar, what we think we know we really do not know at all, then our encounter with difference takes on nuance and richness. The other is not really like ourselves at all. The categories of the other are different from our categories.

And the third is that the other is not "crazy," or "unclean," or beyond all comprehension. When we study about Judaism (among many "others"), we learn about how the distinctive beliefs and practices of that religious tradition address a set of urgent questions and respond with compelling answers. The questions need not be ours and probably are not; the answers by definition are different from our answers (the "our" and the "we" here are people in the twentieth century, whether Jewish or not, studying Jews of the first or the second century – by definition as different from us as can be!). But when we learn how a set of self-evident truths of a given religious system, of a given Judaism in the first or second century for instance, forms a sustained and cogent response to an urgent and overriding question, we can see that sense in things that otherwise appear to be nonsense. That is not an argument for relativism; it is an appeal to the notion that, when we know how a social order takes shape, what it identifies as its most urgent questions, how it responds to those questions with truths it deems self-evident – when we can make sense of difference in its context and terms, hearing its questions and making sense of its answers, then the other seems not so different, not because the other is like us after all or because we are like the other after all. The other seems not so different because we can make sense of the other in the terms of the other, in the context of the other, in the crisis of the other: the other remains different, but becomes part of that same social order that to us makes sense of nonsense.

Let me make these rather general remarks concrete by referring to my own scholarly interests. I work on a literature that is not very accessible because it concerns subjects of which we know nothing, treats as urgent issues that hardly matter in the world we know, speaks in a language of thought that we must find wholly other, and embodies everything alien and unfamiliar in culture. And yet that literature – I refer to the classical and formative documents of Judaism – is important to Jews and interesting to many others as well. How am I supposed to deal with what is different and alien in such a way that I can make sense and find meaning in "the other" that is represented by the classics of Judaism? The answer is in three parts. First, I ask about the context in which these writings took shape. That tells me what problems these writers were trying to cope with. Second, I inquire into the context of these writings, and that tells me the answers that they formed in response to the issues of their day. So far the other remains different and strange. It is at the third stage that I try to overcome difference: I want to know whether the urgent questions that these people address, the (to them) self-evidently valid answers they put forth, in their language and in their terms, correspond to a counterpart in the world that is familiar to me and in my language. The point at which the unfamiliar becomes accessible to me is when I see the stranger struggling with a world I find familiar. True, that does not mean I make the other over into my model; then I learn only about myself, projected onto the other. Rather, it means that, preserving the alienness, the otherness of the other, I am able to find in a common humanity a point of contact.

In two sentences I can say what this has meant in my own research. I work on the Mishnah and related writings, which came to closure in the aftermath of a disaster and crisis, when the society of the Jews of the Land of Israel was cut loose from moorings that had held firm for a thousand years. I read these writings in light of the issues that faced everyone in that time and in that place, and I am justified in doing so because the focus of interest of these writings is on precisely the matters that the crisis – the destruction of the Temple in 70, the end of the inherited political arrangements thereafter – had made urgent. In this way I am able to read the texts, which are alien, in their context, and, further, grasp that context then in the framework of a problem of destruction and renewal that, in the second century as in the twenty-first century, urgently requires solution. They are not we, and we are not they, their life and concerns are not the same as ours. But we and they share a common situation, one that their writings, as a matter of fact, do much to illumine. Only in the setting of the liberal arts, with their interest in history, philosophy, religion, literature, sociology, anthropology, economics – only in the setting of the study of humanity in the humanities and social sciences do we gain access to that other, to the difference, from which, in the end, we can learn what our choices can become.

What do these remarks about thinking about difference have to do with the liberal arts and the social order? My argument has been a very simple one. In the liberal arts we use our minds to allow us to think through problems of an abstract and theoretical character – social problems in the social sciences, problems of the natural world in the natural sciences, problems of abstract thought about human expression and the records of humanity, and accurate expression in the humanities. The social order requires people who can take thought seriously and are experienced at thinking in a rigorous way, not merely repeating what we have done but asking questions about why. In the specific case I have briefly outlined, this country needs people who have thought seriously about difference and have framed theories of how to think about difference and explain it – theories that can help everybody make sense of the nonsense that came to expression in the question, "Why can't a woman be more like a man?" We all know that that is the wrong question to address to the other: why are you not like me? But then what is the right question? How are we to find it and frame it and answer it? In the liberal arts, in the laboratory of our minds, we have the chance of finding out. And so with the whole of the social order: society takes the form it does because of our attitudes, and our attitudes express ideas that are in our minds.

Public policy in the end comes from the shared intellect that in a well-wrought, well-run university forms the thing we make together. What I mean is very simple, and here I close. People wonder if ideas matter, and if intellect is relevant. But everything we do expresses our attitudes and aspirations, and these inchoate matters of sentiment in fact derive from ideas that we hold, and judgments that we make. Before people even think about the practical policy they will follow, they already *know* a great deal that defines for them the goals to be gained through policy. A state university in a great and growing city and region defines and reflects the social order of that city and region because from that state university come not just the technology and know-how but the ideas and values and attitudes that in the end infuse the social order and impart to it the shape and structure that dictate policy and program. America is the creation of – more than any force or power – the power of ideas, shared, public, reasoned, argued-about, labored-over convictions, and everything we have achieved as a nation we owe to our power of shared intellect. It is with good reason that we build great state universities and within them center our attention upon the liberal arts – a uniquely American mode of education, with no counterpart in any foreign university. There we are exploring our present and defining everybody's future in a reasoned and thoughtful way, not by accident but by choice. Studying together, learning together, thinking together, we form a shared community of mind and from our classrooms, libraries, laboratories radiates the community beyond.

Part One

LECTURES ON JUDAISM IN THE ACADEMY

2

Stranger at Home: The Task of Religious Studies

Inaugural Lecture of the Department of Religious Studies
Arizona State University, October 25, 1979

I

We inaugurate a new Department of Religious Studies because many people share the conviction that such a department, working on such a subject, not only belongs in the university curriculum. They hold that the curriculum is impoverished without the academic study of religions – so poor, indeed, that even in these days of poverty for higher education, the administration and faculty of this University have agreed to do what they have done. Since for twenty years I have made my life and my living in the field of religious studies and have known no other life or living, I take this event as a statement of confidence in what my generation of scholars set out to do. But inaugurating a new Department also presents us with an important challenge. We must use this occasion to ask ourselves, once more, what we think we are doing in the study of religions and why we claim it to be so important.

Let me start with the end, the picture of the last graduation day at Brown University. Then our students passed before us, and we before them, in a curious pattern of march and countermarch by which we fill an otherwise empty graduation rite. As the students walked past the faculty, I reflected on how in some past years my colleagues and I had taught so few, but this year so many of these students. I asked myself whether we had made a significant contribution to their education and growth into adulthood, for that is the social task which, quite rightly

15

I think, society assigns to the liberal arts colleges and universities of this country. And as we of the faculty walked past the students, I felt I could look into their eyes with a measure of pride in what my colleagues and I had given them these past four years.

This inauguration lecture, like that graduation ceremony, is a time to reflect on our tasks and the worth of our work to our students and to society. It is a time to think about our responsibility. For we bear a three-part responsibility. We (1) teach (2) a particular subject to (3) students. Here are three elements: that we *teach*, that we teach *students*, that we teach students *some particular thing* in such a way that they learn an accurate and responsible account of a subject worth knowing. If we pay no attention to who sits before us, we do not teach. If we do not tell them anything important, we waste their time. We are educators, scholars. But we also are models of a particular sort of mind, a distinctive kind of response to the world of learning.

If we do not ask ourselves tough questions about the intellectual and social worth of what we teach, we declare ourselves both intellectually bankrupt and socially irresponsible. This we cannot do while asking society for its children to teach and for its resources to support our teaching. I find myself impatient, therefore, when told that any subject, whether religion or biology, is "intrinsically" interesting. I am prepared to concede that all subjects are intrinsically interesting. But I do not know what value there is in such a concession. For we have to make choices, and so does society. It will not do to commend everything and decline nothing. We must exercise taste and judgment. We must also explain the result. That is self-evidently not an argument in favor of a pragmatic or narrowly utilitarian approach to learning. But neither is it going to give comfort to scholars who disdain to teach, teachers who prefer to preach, or faculties which become lazy, unresponsive, and indifferent to their tasks both in education and in scholarship.

No one can hope that there are lasting answers to the question, Why should I know the things which you are telling me? But the generation of teachers and scholars which does not try to answer fails both those who came before and those who are to come.

II

The starting point of any answer should be the educational result we hope to achieve. That result will be in two parts, first, with reference to students in general, whatever their majors, and second, with reference to majors in our field.

The former group is far more important than the latter for the reason I implied at the outset. Our interest is to provide something of cultural and intellectual value to a wide variety of students, to serve the entire community of our university. Given the vocational choices which govern curricular decisions made by the generality of students everywhere, we are not going to see massive numbers of students in our more specialized courses. They will study other things. Most of them will not earn a living from what they learn from us, nor will what we have to teach in concrete ways make them more useful in their chosen business, profession, or calling. My own impression, moreover, is that students who come to us from mathematics and the natural sciences tend to be more engaging because, by the nature of things, in the world about which we speak, they also are both uninformed and rather unformed. Since my own university has impressive numbers of students in pre-medical studies as well as in engineering, mathematics, and the natural sciences, and very large numbers of other students who plan to become lawyers or to go to business school, I must ask myself questions of purpose in a context quite different from that in which colleagues in biology or applied mathematics explain why someone should want to know what they teach.

Our situation in the study of religions is characteristic of the humanities in general. It is our task to shape religious studies within the humanities in such a way that they win the attention of students engaged by other things and cause them to be willing to learn what we have to teach. It is one thing to win attention. It is another to teach something worthy of attention. Ours is the work of doing both. Yet it remains to observe that the generality of our students see us for one or two or three courses, while they pursue their major field for eight or ten or twelve courses. The result is that religious studies, for the main part of their student constituency, take the form of courses which survey a fair amount of material for a sizable number of students, courses which meet a requirement, and from which students themselves demand somewhat more than they do of their majors: to tell them whatever they should know, while, so to speak, we stand on one foot (if not on our heads).

But this demand is an opportunity and a challenge. It requires us to ask, Among the many important and pressing things I wish to share out of what I know, what are the most urgent? Every time we plan a course, we select the few things we can manage in the twelve or fourteen weeks we have. This act of selection, which begins when we claim to do our subject for more than its "intrinsic" interest, continues in the many acts of selection by which we frame our courses, the topics of our lectures, the readings we put into students' hands.

Before proceeding to outline these urgent matters, I call to mind that other, rather select group of students, our majors in religious studies. Since these students only occasionally plan to enter the priesthood, ministry, rabbinate, or other religious vocations and careers, in their vocational character they are not so different from the students whom we serve in a few survey or general courses. Moreover, most of them take so wide a variety of courses within religious studies that nearly every course they elect also turns out to be elementary. If an advanced course is one which demands a prerequisite of some other, prior course, we almost always teach beginners. For an examination of catalogues yields very few second or third courses in our field. Many of these allegedly advanced courses turn out to be just as elementary as the others. There may be an 'introductory' course, required of all students. But, commonly, in no way does such a course pretend to introduce all the other courses students may take. It hardly lays down foundations on which the other courses within the departmental curriculum are going to build. Our field is too specialized, too diverse in its methods. It follows that the bulk of our teaching serves students who ask absolutely fundamental questions, one of which must always be, Why are you telling me these things? Why should I know them? How shall I be changed because I know them?

III

We live in an age of intense faith and of utter indifference about religions. Our work is important both to the faithful and to those for whom religious belief and behavior bear no this-worldly interest whatsoever. Our work is not to reshape the faith of the faithful, nor to kindle interest in the uninterested. It is different. When we say we stand at a distance from the subject, claim to be objective about the "truth-claims" of the religions we study, or solemnly affirm that we do not serve, or violate, the interests of organized religion or of atheism, our protestations are true but they miss the point. What we do in general is simply not suitably described or explained within the frame of reference expressed in terms of faith or unfaith, commitment or doubt, even concern or unconcern about the subject. What we do is to try to interpret the phenomenon of religions as a force in human life.

To answer the question, Why religious studies? we have to ask another: What do people *not* know, if they do not know about and understand religions? What can they *not* explain and of what can they not make sense? Phrased in this way, the question answers itself. For religion is so powerful a force in the contemporary world that without knowledge of religion we scarcely can understand the daily newspapers. A fair example of what happens when people do not know how to make sense of the power of religions in contemporary life is our country's difficulty in understanding the Islamic revolution in Iran, not to mention the Judaic revolution in the State of Israel, the Protestant army of Northern Ireland, the Roman Catholic revolution in Poland and in Latin America, the Christian army of Lebanon, the tragedy at Jonestown, and many continuing evidences of the vitality of religious belief – sometimes healthy, sometimes perverse.

There is of course a bias against religion as a force in culture and psychology. This is surely one possible way of thinking about the character and meaning of society and of life. It holds religion to be dying, a holdover from another age. It therefore claims that religion does not require study. Those of us who find religion an exceptionally interesting phenomenon of society and culture, imagination and the heart, can do little to overcome this bias. But it *is* a bias, for it rests upon the will to wish religion away, not upon the perception that religion has gone away. In fact, much of the world as we know it is shaped by the formation of society and culture around religious beliefs, by the way in which people refer to religions to make their choices about how they will live. These beliefs and choices invoke particular modes of supernaturalism, distinctive expressions of revelation. A country governed by a president who speaks of a personal experience of conversion had better understand the meaning of religious conversion. A nation in which institutions of religion exercise vast influence over citizens' political and cultural decisions is not wise to deny that religion is a formative force in contemporary life. Whether or not people want religions to exercise that power, they do. In fact, religions not only speak about supernatural powers, they, too, constitute powerful forces in this world.

So it is a matter of fact that if people do not understand the character of religions, they cannot make sense of much which happens in the world today. Nor need we dwell upon a still more obvious fact. To understand where humankind has been, to make sense of the heritage of world civilization, the transcendent side of the human imagination and of society and culture constitutes a definitive dimension. There is no understanding of humanity without the confrontation with the religious heritage and hope, whatever may be our judgment of the value of the heritage and the hope. So far as universities propose to teach how to interpret the world in which we live, organizing courses and departments of religious studies is a perfectly natural way of teaching what must be taught.

IV

To this point in the argument I have tried to explain two of the three elements mentioned earlier, spelling out whom we teach and explaining that we teach, that is, transmit, facts, ideas, and insight about important things. We have now to try to speak of the particular things we do in departments of religious studies. It is axiomatic that we do not produce more faithful, or less faithful, Christians, Jews, Moslems, Buddhists, and the like. But it is equally clear that we do claim to attempt to explain these powerful forces in human culture which we call religions.

The task of explanation is accomplished through three distinct approaches to learning – history, philosophy, and social science. Each approach to the study of religions is indispensable. None exhausts the possible approaches to the work. In the area of history, we ask about the role and development of diverse religions within diverse cultures, within the life of various peoples, regions, and territories. Work in this area tends to rely upon literary evidence, for example, holy books, although archaeologists have begun to teach us to take seriously non-literary evidence. In the area of philosophy we analyze the language and claims about truth put forward in various religions; we ask about the ethics laid forth, and speak of the perennial issues of religious truth phrased in terms applicable to any culture. In social scientific approaches we inquire into the social setting and impact of a religion, on the one side, and into religion's psychological meaning, the place of religion in the life of the imagination and emotion, on the other. The enduring classics of theory of religions, for instance, the works of Freud, Weber, and Durkheim, have come from the fields of psychology and sociology of religions. Nor is the study of religions complete without the learning of anthropologists, who, like historians of religion, reach out to alien people, to people who, though living in the present, are foreign to our age, speaking in a strange language, about things we know not what. Anthropologists teach us to understand in common human terms the system, structure, and order of this alien world of our midst.

In this rapid account of the main disciplines of religious studies, we have also to catalogue the sorts of data to be analyzed by scholars of the field. Since human beings express transcendent impulses in every medium of access, scholars of religion have to teach themselves to recognize and hear these expressions wherever they occur. That is why the study of literature of the present and past, of art of today and yesterday, of music, drama, dance, poetry, cinema, as much as of sociology and anthropology, makes formidable contributions to the description and interpretation of religions. Nor may we omit notice of the important lessons to be learned from specialists in fields in which data of religions play only a peripheral part. It is not possible to understand the religions of the West without studying Western civilization, just as one cannot understand the civilization of the West without intimate knowledge of religious institutions and expectations. So we come to our colleagues in history for assistance in our work. Political science, with its insight into how religious convictions and origins play a role in social and political behavior, provides ample data for the examination of religion as a vital and powerful force in contemporary life. Since art, music, and literature give access to what is happening in the soul of a society, there is no way to ignore the sizable work to be done in these departments of learning.

By now the picture is obvious. When we ask what we do in the study of religions, we discover ourselves in the very center of a field of learning which, at its foundations, is interdisciplinary and cross-cultural. It relies so heavily upon so wide a range of disciplines as to be declared the quintessential form of humanistic learning. Religious studies cast a net over land and sea and everywhere find treasure. Whether or not there is a discipline distinctive to the study of religion I do not know. I am certain that there is no discipline of the academic curriculum in humanistic and social studies which religious studies can afford to neglect. This is surely so if we wish to understand this protean force, this ubiquitous thing, religion. For to study religion is to study humanity in its full humanness: integrated and whole, but frail, vulnerable, full of fantasies and fears, and in perpetual quest. It is no wonder that one religion finds its evocative symbol in a criminal in his death throes, and another finds its vindication in the very suffering of its communicants. In these ways and in others Christianity and Judaism, among the religions of humanity, express that vulnerability and frailty which, through religions, humankind has sought to express and to overcome.

V

Thus far I have explained what I believe to be the remarkable power of religious studies: First, their capacity to make their own nearly the entire spectrum of humanistic, and most of the social scientific, disciplines of learning, and, second, their reason for studying virtually every kind of expression of our humaness. But the power of the field is also its problem and its pathos. If we attempt to do so much, shall we not do most of it superficially, and the rest incompetently? That question by no means is to be dismissed. When, years ago, our department searched for a scholar in the social scientific approach to the study of religions, we found it difficult to locate an appropriate social scientist willing to join us. The more intelligent ones preferred to be sociologists of religion in departments of sociology. The sociologists who wanted to join us did not find academic sociology engaging. And the work of both sorts – with its stress on counting and measuring things – seemed to us not very interesting anyhow. But whatever the difficulties, religious studies depend, perhaps more than the study of most other humanistic subjects, upon help from colleagues. Indeed, we constantly refer to colleagues in other disciplines, both to teach us how they do their work, and to guide us in doing our own. The interdependence of religious studies with other disciplines of the humanities and social sciences is a powerful argument for the formation of a distinct department, such as this one. But it is a still stronger argument that, once the department has discovered its identity and purpose, its task is to reach out to colleagues with an interest in the thing we study and to teach us about it and about how to study it.

It is one thing to say that we are interested in everything. But it is quite another to specify the things that, in general, scholars in religious studies do well, and to confess the things which, in general, they tend to do poorly. So any account of the field as it takes up its duties in a new department of religious studies must address this very question. I see four principal sins of religious studies in the past twenty years.

The problems we tend to treat expertly are familiar ones. They derive from Western civilization. The kinds of sources we handle with skill normally are literary. The issues in the study of religions we confront with confidence arise from the Christian and Western philosophical perspectives upon religious experience and thought. In other words we do well what we know, less well what we do not. So while we may rightly claim to be interested in everything, we are disingenuous if we offer that claim at face value. This is the first of four sins of religious studies. The field's diffuse character conceals its cultural sameness, its origins in Protestant divinity schools. To observe that the curriculum of a fair number of departments, particularly in smaller, church-related colleges, replicates too accurately the principal interests of divinity faculties, is to bring no news. To point out that an alternative in both scholarship and teaching has yet to be worked out and made to stick is another matter.

Our vision of the subject remains pretty much what it was. We have the breadth of concern which is the virtue of the Protestant conscience. But we also exhibit the incapacity to attain critical self-consciousness, the conviction of majorities that how we see things is pretty much how they are, which is the vice. The caring for all things is formed into a utensil of one shape only, by limited sympathy. No one has to choose a position of entire relativity of values to notice that, in the study of religions, we tend to bring a rather limited program of interests and concerns. That is why some, who work on religions essentially unlike Protestant Christianity, turn to anthropology for categories of inquiry. We find the narrowly theological, intellectual definition of issues of religious studies to be of limited utility. That is why others turn to approaches borrowed from other data, for instance, structuralism as a mode of interpreting ritual. The inherited, philosophical categories of the field do not present a viable hermeneutic for religions as they are practiced outside of this country's Protestant churches and culture.

A further trait of the field derives, if by somewhat remote connection, from yet another strength of Protestant culture: the power to respond to the events of the moment. It is its capacity to remain relevant to a changing world, to address each hour afresh, which has made Protestant culture so functional to the industrial West. A natural attitude of mind in our field is to respond quickly and relevantly to what happens in ways which some of us, out of more "traditional" cultures, find admirable. At the same time religious studies as a field tend to go from hula-hoop to frisbee, taking as evanescent slogans ideas which the framer means to be handled very seriously indeed. After twenty years in the field of religious studies I have learned to approach with measured enthusiasm the intellectually salvific theories of the moment. When I find at the American Academy of Religion pretty much a single slogan sweeping from one section to the next – whether it is "the social construction of reality," or "phenomenology," or "structuralism," or even something so specific as black, women's, or Jewish perspectives on religious studies – I go back to my room and watch television. For there at least the fads are an honest way to make a living.

What is wrong with the perpetual faddism and sloganeering of the field is not that slogans contains no truth or convey no insight. It is that in our faddism we forget the roots of the academic study of religions. What is new in the marketplace of ideas turns out to be a repackaging of what is old. The second sin of the field thus is academic consumerism. How many steps do we take, after all, from Durkheim to Douglas? And how far a journey do we travel from Weber to Bellah and Geertz? The classicism of the Judaic tradition and of the Roman Catholic form of Christianity – to name accessible modes of belief – has yet to make its contribution to the shaping of attitudes of mind in our nascent discipline. Only in preserving the tension between the claims of the

exciting new and the doubts of the experienced old shall we succeed in
retaining some sort of balance and prudence in our intellectual venture.

The methodological diffuseness of the field, which is its strength,
exacts a price in an absence of critical self-consciousness, on the one side,
and an excess of contemporaneity, on the other. It tends to yield yet
another good thing which also is bad: a general education. In those
universities which lack programs in Western civilization, the study of
two subjects tends to take their place: history, in the form of the general
survey course, and religious studies, in the form of introductory course,
e.g., to Catholicism, Protestantism, and Judaism, or to the religions of
the West, or, still grander, to the religions of the whole world. Surely
it is an act of responsibility and of courage for our faculties to undertake
these kinds of courses. Student response as well as collegial approval
(for others do not wish to tread where we happily proceed) gratifies
and rewards us. If, because of its integrated and wide-ranging
topicality, the study of religions serves as a kind of general education,
it also replicates the dubious intellectual traits of general education.
Our general, introductory courses – often the only ones our students elect
– leave the impression of breadth, when they make a superficial mark;
appear to speak of important things, when they raise issues which are
merely relevant; and evoke the language of eternity, but speak, in the
end, of how we feel today. These are bitter judgments. They judge as
much what I do as anyone else.

The third sin is that in our teaching we are mere generalists, when
we should be specialists speaking in accessible, general terms – a very
different thing. We talk about too many things. This is bad not merely
because about most we come armed only with our impressions. It also is
bad because we lose the power to criticize ourselves, even to distinguish
bad from good in our own thought and understanding. I am unhappy, for
example, at how little effort goes into the careful and sympathetic
reading of the texts of alien religions. It is as if we wish to get the gist
of an ancient tablet without making sense of the glyphs of the alien
alphabet. It cannot be done. Meaning must be expressed in words. Words
come in one language or another, governed by a specific syntax and
intimate grammar of thought and idiomatic expression. Those of us who
teach what is not commonly familiar, because we tend to be
embarrassed at the alienness of our texts, leap over the specificities
into a common language of thought. We chatter in a kind of intellectual
Esperanto which no one really uses at all.

We have not figured out how to teach some one or two texts, in a
given course, which will say things beyond themselves, yet distinctive
and particular to themselves. It is exceedingly difficult to find the
modalities between technical gibberish (which would then place us in

graduate seminars of philology) and insufferable banality (which leaves us right where we are). To put matters more simply: I do not yet know the way which leads from telling my students about King Upupalupu to informing them that "deep down, people really are good, anyhow." In the interstices between knowing how to read and interpret a text or some other datum of religion (a play, a dance, a rite, a prayer), and knowing how to talk to the concerns of the hour and of the particular age through which the students now pass, lies that kind of teaching which, right now, is difficult to define: teaching students something worth knowing.

The fourth and last sin is most serious. No indictment of religious studies as an academic field can fail to charge that we have played our full part in the destruction of the study of foreign languages in America. If I have to point to the single indefensible achievement of our field (it is no defense that we did not do it all by ourselves), it is the propagation of the notion that we can understand what is alien without learning the language of the alien. Our sin is not merely the absence of requirements that our majors learn some language relevant to their studies of religions. It is a failure at the very center of our mission which allows our students to assume that they understand things to which, in fact, they do not even gain access.

Our work is to make what is strange into something human, to teach how to make sense, in *its* alien terms, of what some among us too soon make their own. The study of religions, when not wholly subjective, and therefore not academic to begin with, is the study of the religious life of others. It is not the religious life of a teacher of a given classroom or of every student in that classroom. The other, to be understood, cannot be reduced to ourselves. We have to allow the other to be different – and then to confront and attempt to overcome the difference without dissolving it. It is no news to declare that the work of the humanities is to examine the diversity of human experience and to ask what is human about humankind. But how are we to confront diversity and take difference seriously, when we do not even know that other people talk of things we know not what, in languages which to us are gibberish. The first step in any humanistic venture of learning must be to allow the other to be alien, yet to seek for what is like ourselves in the alien. The final step is to understand more than that the stranger is in ourselves. It is to realize, also, that we are in the stranger.

Now it is one thing to tell people things. It is another for people to experience them. I can think of no more direct, experiential encounter with the specific issues of the humanities than in learning a foreign language. For the beginning of that process of learning is to seek in the language we want to learn analogies and metaphors for the language we already know. But the end of that learning is when the language we want to learn takes on its own reality in our ears, eyes, and mouths, so that we make the alien tongue into our own. When we deprive our students of the opportunity to enter into an alien language, we deprive ourselves of the occasion to teach what we really know, which is more than what our students already know.

In reading finals in my courses I am struck by how many could have been written without taking my courses at all. Students do not hear, because they do not understand that we are not telling them things they already know, even when we may say words they already have heard. I am astonished at how much which to me seems fresh and new enters the students' ears in accord with patterns of thought and definitions of issues established far away and long before they come to me. Many times I try to say, "If you think you already know this, you are not understanding what I am saying." But where can I evoke that consciousness of *not* understanding which must precede the process of seeking understanding among people who have never heard in their lives a foreign word of an alien thought? For students must first learn to be strangers to themselves, before they can see the given as chosen and new, and themselves as free to make choices.

To be sure, this country is not a monolingual society. Each region is rich in its own culture and speech. All parts of the country benefit from the presence of communities which speak some language other than American English. But we tend to ignore what we do not understand to suppose that we all say pretty much the same thing in the same way. In fact we talk past one another, each about something the other could not make sense of, even if it were explained.

We in the humanities vindicate our work because it teaches people how to think. The very absence of a vocational tie between our subject and the students' future justified what we do. Yet if we are training minds, then alongside those skills in clear thinking and accurate expression which we seek to cultivate belongs the direct experience of the alien which comes only in learning a text in its own language. It is not merely because when students never encounter the language other people use they do not do the hard work of cultural interpretation. It is more especially because of something more particular to our own field. When students do not realize, in their own direct experience of the alien, that nearly everything we have reaches us in a labor of translation and mediation, they do not grasp what is at the core of the study of religions. At the center of our intellectual enterprise is this same work – the translation and mediation of alien experience. This is what the study of a foreign language, properly carried out, makes available: the struggle to understand, to make sense in our language, of what is not our own.

VI

What makes the study of religions difficult is also what makes the work important. The principal difficulty is that the students all take for granted they know that about which we are talking. Nearly all of them come from one or another of the religious traditions of the West. Many of them have strong opinions on religions and on questions of theology. So they think they know already what we have to tell them. That is the challenge. But it also is what makes our work important. For, as I shall now argue, the crucial thing we can give, which our students badly need, is the encounter with the unfamiliar in what they take for granted. We can show them that what they think they know contains much yet to be learned. We can demonstrate that the absolute, wholly familiar given of life – that matter of religion – contains within itself a great many choices. Once we persuade them that, within religious expressions, people make important choices about the sort of society and culture they will sustain and the kind of people they will build, we provide them with an insight into their own most urgent task, namely, to learn how to make choices about things which seem settled and decided, to see as strange and new, requiring reflection and thought, what has all the time appeared familiar, routine, and closed. In the experience of discovering the familiar to be strange and to require analysis, our students undergo the experience of intellectual maturing which prepares them for a deeper, inner movement toward adulthood. My claim therefore is not a small one. I argue that the academic study of religions, because of its particular character, presents a splendid opportunity for our students to experience in intellectual terms what in fact is their most profound and pressing personal responsibility: the discovery of self, the engagement with their own individuality. What we do is relevant, in the deepest sense, to the students' task of attaining adulthood.

Let me explain. It is this matter of the encounter with what is not our own which, when our work succeeds, we may declare to be educational success and, when our work does not succeed, we recognize as failure. At the outset I argued that the reason the study of religions belongs in the center of the curriculum is that religions are a powerful and ubiquitous force in humankind. But what it is about religions which we need to master for the sake of useful knowledge remains to be stated. This is to be explained in two aspects. I have, first, to say why we think our students in particular ought to know about the things we

teach. I must explain, second, why the society and community we serve
ought to know them.

Since our students in the main are late adolescents, our work is
defined by the psychological and emotional context of that age group as
much as by its vocational or even cultural aspirations. Indeed, in any
group of university students, however carefully selected, I am inclined
to wonder whether many even *have* vocational and cultural goals. But
all of them are engaged by how they feel, what they think about
themselves, and what their peer group thinks about them.

Now the power of the study of religions is that, in our society, we
speak of kinds of familiar experiences. It is difficult to grow up in
America without knowing that there are churches and synagogues,
religious myths and symbols of various kinds, to which various folk
respond in diverse ways. There are experiences of religious conversion
and rebirth, rites of birth and puberty, teachings about what one may
do and must not do, and institutions for the expression and embodiment
of all of these things. It follows that our students know that about
which we are talking when we speak about religions. That is our
richest asset. But it also is the most formidable obstacle to teaching our
students something worth their knowing.

To explain, I must emphasize that what young people approaching
maturity require is the capacity finally to surpass themselves, leaving
childish things, while retaining the heritage of family, home, and
love. They have to learn how to make their own what others have
made for them, so to enter, finally, into the life of maturity and
responsibility. They come to us as dependents upon their parents. They
leave to take up their own careers. In the four years they spend with us,
we have to guide them from dependence to independence. It is this
supererogatory work of helping in the process of maturing which, in
many instances, is our richest gift to our students.

Now if in intellect we can confront them with an authentic
experience of attaining self-consciousness and of critically,
thoughtfully evaluating what they think they already know in the
encounter with what they do not know – the "alien experience" to
which I referred earlier – then we allow for a controlled experiment of
maturing. That is to say, through their intellectual labor we guide
them in paths which, by analogy and metaphor, lead where life
demands they go.

To state the matter simply: they already know about religions,
more commonly, "their" religion. But they do not know what they
know, or even that they know. For in the main, knowledge about
religions is acquired through inarticulate experience, on the one side, or
through indoctrination, on the other. In both ways it is unreflective;

the learner is dependent. The students think they know and understand things they do not know of their own knowledge. That is why they tend to assume they understand what we are saying. They assume they have already heard what in fact (in our minds) is fresh and unprecedented for them.

When we help students attain the clear capacity to distinguish new from old, the act of understanding from mere assent, the conscious deed of interpretation from the presumption of dumb familiarity, we lead them in mind through the very center of their existential task of growing up. I do not mean we make them less religious or more religious than they were, let alone better or worse Christians or Judaists. I mean we show them that there is more to be learned about what they think they already know, and that they can learn it. It is the experience of that kind of independence of intellect which will both prefigure and replicate the independence of personal existence each student has, in a brief time, to attain.

VII

Explaining why society and our community ought to know what we have to teach comes at the end. Our own country has entered upon a period in its history much like that of the late adolescent, approaching the decisions of maturity. For a long time, like children, we pretended there was no world but our own. Then, in World War II and afterward, we pretended that the whole world was our own. Now is the time to come to terms with a world which is not our own, but in which we have a share. To recognize both what is ours and what is not ours is to understand what is foreign but what we can make our own.

It is this encounter with the alien which requires our community and society to take up the intellectual and cultural tasks of interpretation of what we do not understand out of the resources of what we deeply comprehend. This social and political task of making ourselves at one and whole with an alien world is something we cannot do, if we have not experienced the work in some small place. In the study of religions which are not ours we learn how to enter into worlds which belong to others.

That is why the importance of learning a foreign language and of learning about a religion other than our own is the same: it is to prepare us for the confrontation with difference, to educate our sympathies to welcome diversity, to discover what we can be in what we are not. We must learn to glory in the encounter with difference, not only because we have not got any choice. The reason is also that we should not want it otherwise. In finding out things we did not know, we learn. In encountering and entering into worlds we did not make, we discover. In the learning and discovery, we uncover in ourselves things we did not know were there. We find out we can be more than what we are.

The critical task facing this country in the world and in our life as a nation is to learn to confront difference. Our society now recognizes that there is no single normative culture for all of us to accept. Twenty per cent of the population speaks Spanish. Nearly twelve per cent is black. Three per cent is Jewish. There is a growing minority of Moslems and Buddhists, both native and immigrant. I have the privilege of sitting on the National Council on the Humanities, governing body of the National Endowment for the Humanities, and so I always am studying proposals of many sorts, from many kinds of groups and organizations, in every part of the country. I marvel at the diversity. I am amazed that before us come the ideas of men and women who know how to find the humanist in all of us.

The world in which we live no longer concedes that one way of life or one system is valid for all. The world for which our students now prepare demands, therefore, the capacity to take two steps, first, to discover oneself in the other, so that the alien seems less strange, and second, to discover the other in oneself, so that the self seems more strange. When our students study a religion other than the one in which they were brought up, they discover themselves in what is different. They undertake the exercise of empathetically interpreting the alien in terms which allow for their act of understanding. When they study the religion in which they were brought up and for the first time undertake the task of sympathetic, academic analysis and interpretation, they discover the alien in what they thought belonged to them. Questions which seem settled long ago turn out to be unsettling. The alien is within. Where we are most at home, there we are mostly strangers.

If our notion is that we study with profit only someone elses' religion, we deprive ourselves of what we most require. To take on example, if contemporary Jews take for granted that they also know all about and define Judaism, they transform themselves from isolated and not necessarily representative or consequential facts about a given religion, Judaism, into the measure of all things Judaic. So they reduce a complex tradition, going back for nearly three millenia, into only its most current, and not demonstrably its most representative form. The same is so for Christians. It is when our students realize that even what they think they know best, themselves and their own culture, contains mysteries yet to be uncovered that our work begins. It is when we understand that, in the work of learning, we remain perpetually outsiders in our own richly complex traditions, strangers when we feel most at home, that our work begins. So my friends of Arizona State University, let the work of the study of religions begin.

3

Understanding Seeking Faith: Studying About Religion and Doing Religion with Special Attention to the Case of Judaism

*Address, University of California
Santa Barbara, 1986*[1]

I. What Does It Mean to "Do Religion"?

When philosophers move from the descriptive to the normative task, they do not abandon philosophy but in a fresh way define their work within philosophy. For they always are philosophers, but shift to philosophy in a different mode. The historian of theologian who, through the criticism of the thought of important figures out of the past, undertakes to give expression to an autonomous and fresh theological position, remains in the same continuum of theological study, but at a different point on that continuum. That historian of theology expresses an educated judgment not about but within theology. The same perspective, the same informed, experienced intellect prevails. And so too, when a scholar in the academic study of religion moves from the descriptive to the interpretive task, and when, further,

---

[1]University of California at Santa Barbara address, Wednesday, June 4, 1986, for the series, *Revising Graduate Education in Religious Studies*. The basic question addressed to this paper is as follows: What role does creative reflection play in religious studies? Is it possible to "do" religious studies in the manner in which one "does" theology or "does" philosophy? Or is the urge for creative reflection little more than a nostalgia for what used to be possible within a believing community or a specific cultural heritage?

that scholar presents interpretation as a legitimate position within the religion under discussion, that "doing of religion" remains a dimension of the study of religion. The reason, as in the case of philosophy and theology, is that the method and the intellect remain constant, while the purpose and frame of discourse shift. The method of the study of religion yields descriptive results, but it also produces ideas relevant to the life of the faith or tradition that is studied. When, therefore, a scholar who studies about religion takes the step beyond the study, that scholar remains a person of learning, critical judgment, and substantial intellectual experience and attainment: a scholar. So we may invert the received program, faith seeking understanding, to a contemporary plan: understanding seeking faith. The understanding of religion attained within the academic study of religion for some scholars of religion provides the beginning of engagement with religion in one of its innumerable concrete forms.

Religion is a generalizing science, and the "doing of religion" beyond the work of the description, analysis, and interpretation of religion, will carry forward that labor of generalization. The study of religion, furthermore, attempts to define the subject under study in two ways. First of all, when we study the several religions, we wish to report what they are, one by one, and that in the end imposes a task of definition. Second, our ultimate goal leads us to want to know not merely how to define religions, but also how to define – that is, describe, analyze, and interpret – religion. Accordingly a scholar's creative reflection within a particular religious tradition will address that same subject, again, in two parts. First, the scholar will want to define that religion, now for the purposes not of the academy but of the faithful. Second, the scholar will further intend to explain what we learn, from that religion, about religion, and this too for the purposes not of the academy but of the faithful. Both definitions – the religion in question, religion in general – will bear valence for the one who is "doing religion" that differs from the weight assigned to the labor of definition for the one who is studying about religion. But the work of definition is the same. And it is in the academy that we learn how to define, carrying what we have learned to our labors beyond the walls of the academy.

On the basis of these rather general remarks let me offer an answer to the two questions assigned to me:

1.   What role does creative reflection play in religious studies? Creative reflection within the intellectual discipline of the academic study of religion leads us to ask the descriptive question in a different way, one in which members of a religious group will wish to answer also. Do I think creative reflection appropriate to the academic study

of religion? With a few obvious stipulations, yes. First, the classroom is a pluralistic setting. Nothing we teach should ignore the interests of all students, omitting reference to any one of them. If creative reflection, for example, on the definition and classification of Judaism, leads us to positions pertinent to believers, the non-Jew may find the discussion exemplary, a datum for the study of Judaism, but the non-Jew has the right to be invited to see the discussion as exemplary, to be taught what points, about Judaism, find exemplification in discourse on normative definition. Second, the work of creative reflection must come at the end of a sustained and cogent process of description, and the labor of description, analysis, and interpretation within an entirely neutral framework has to reach its conclusions. Then, on the basis of those conclusions, publicly accessible, universally intelligible, exemplary of something beyond themselves, that other, more distant step in what is still the study of religion may be taken. What renders that other step pertinent to the academy is that it does constitute a further mode of the study of religion, remaining within the intellectual framework established in the original and principal mode. That is why I emphasized the labor of definition as appropriate in a distinctive way to the scholar of religion embarked on creative reflection.

2. Is it possible to "do" religious studies in the manner in which one "does" theology or "does" philosophy? For reasons now amply clear, my answer is entirely affirmative. I do not mean to pretend to know what theologians or philosophers do when they do theology or philosophy. But so far as "doing" the subject involves taking positions on controverted questions produced by that subject, then yes, I believe scholars in the field of religious studies will find it entirely possible to do religious studies in a manner entirely consistent with their work of scholarship. Indeed, for reasons I have explained, I see scholars of religious studies as particularly well equipped to conduct unusually interesting exercises in the "doing" of religion because they learn, in the academic sector of their study of religion, things that only they know: ways of thought, modes of analysis. And, if that is the case, then a further conclusion presents itself: for those scholars of religion who belong to a particular religious community, it is not only possible to "do" religion for and within the community. Because of the particular gifts of intellect bestowed through the academic study of religion, it becomes their duty to "do religion." And doing religion as a step outward from studying about religion carries out one's intellectual responsibility. It bears nothing in common with mere "nostalgia for what used to be possible within a believing community or a specific cultural heritage." Indeed, I see in the creative reflection of the scholar of religion the opposite of nostalgia: it looks for tomorrow, not yesterday, and proposes

not merely to affirm but to criticize. In the terms of the received explanation of philosophy as faith seeking understanding, I should frame matters in the opposite terms. When the scholar of religion proposes in appropriate and intellectually responsible ways to do religion, that scholar brings understanding in the search for faith.

II. Theorizing on the Definition of Judaism

The ideal way to study is to start with a text – then digress. Starting with a text gives us a clear point of entry, structure, and cogency to our work. Digressing, by which I mean, moving beyond the limits of the text, leads us to generalize, compare our text and its (proposed) generalization to other texts of the same classification, contrast that corpus of texts and their generalization to a quite different corpus of texts and what they yield. Digression then leads us to propositions of general intelligibility. The course of my own work, only now becoming clear to a broader universe of readers, has always led me to start with a detailed picture of a single text, read in acute concern for the smallest traits, then to a picture of that text as a whole, read as an autonomous statement, further to a reading of the text in its relationships to other texts of its kind or classification, and, finally, to a perspective on that same text as part of the entire continuum of the canon of Judaism. My further program, then, is to develop an analysis of that text in accord with a program of questions deriving from, useful for, a variety of texts, and, finally, to draw together the results into a systematic account of the world yielded by the text with which I started and those to which I brought it into relationship. This work of description, analysis, and interpretation requires me to describe a single text, analyze that text through the work of comparison and contrast, and then interpret the results in the setting that greatly transcends my own area of initial work. In this way I propose to offer out of Judaism cases for comparison and contrast, that is to say, propositions of general intelligibility for which Judaism supplies interesting examples.

In line with that general program, let me draw upon what I have regarded as the principal task of the scholar of religion who concentrates on Judaism for his or her source of examples for the study of propositions of general intelligibility. It is to define Judaism as part of the work of defining religion.[2] That means to explain what we do when

---

[2]I began that work in 1964, when I came to Dartmouth College, in response to questions presented to me by colleagues there, particularly Hans H. Penner, Jonathan Z. Smith, Wayne A. Meeks, David Kelsey, Robin Scroggs, and Fred Berthold. I continued the work from 1968 onward, in my years at Brown, though outside of my colleagues in the religious study of Judaism, Ernest S. Frerichs

we define any religion, what sort of definition will serve, and a long list of further explanations to questions familiar to us all. After a quarter of a century of systematic study, I have come up with two exercises of generalization that fall within the classification of definition. I claim to be able to offer definitions of Judaism that yield propositions of interest to the study not of religions (Judaism, Islam, Christianity, their similarities and differences for example) but of religion – that alone. My propositions complement one another, and I believe that in offering them, I move across the boundary that separates the study of religion from the doing of religion within the context of the study of religion.

To revert to the questions assigned to me, in this way, through example, I explain the role creative reflection plays in religious studies. My answer is that, for the case of Judaism, creative reflection moves us from the work of description to the work of normative definition as the natural next step beyond description. For defining Judaism in a set of descriptive initiatives, I do offer comment on the definition of what Judaism should, or should not, be and become, and that constitutes a judgment resting on creative reflection. Is it possible to "do" religious studies in the manner in which one "does" theology or "does" philosophy? In the case of Judaism, taken up as it is with its divisions and distinctions, the disciplines of the religious study of religion invite that further step, and Judaic religious life can only benefit from the discoveries of those who take it. The urge for creative reflection, which I freely confess leads me on, constitutes an act of intellectual adventure, bearing nothing in common with nostalgia for what used to be possible within a believing community or a specific cultural heritage. I wish to do an old work – the study of Torah, in Judaic theological categories – in a way made possible, rendered plausible, only within the academic study of religion. That is the opposite of nostalgia.[3]

---

and Wendell S. Dietrich, I have never enjoyed the advantage of scholars of religion with whom to engage in ongoing discourse, since Brown has a Department of Religious Studies that in general does not study religion.

[3]The uniformly hostile reception to my work, both religious-historical and theological, within the Judaic world, whether Orthodox or Reform or Conservative, whether in the Diaspora or in the State of Israel, secures me from the charge of mere nostalgia. Those whose rich capacities for nostalgia would find sustenance in a nostalgic essay accept nothing from me.

III. Defining Judaism (I) "Judaism" and the
Question of a Linear and Incremental History of Judaism

One familiar and entirely natural claim concerning Judaism is that there is such a thing as Judaism. That Judaism began "in the beginning," whenever the person who frames the claim identifies the beginning as having taken place. Then that Judaism continued a single, linear history, and all future developments stand in an incremental relationship to that Judaism. The inner logic of Judaism ("the Torah") and not the adventitious events of historical time accounts for the linear and incremental history of Judaism that scholarship is supposed to record. A corollary to that theory of a single, linear Judaism is that no religion outside of Judaism and after Judaism made an impact upon Judaism. For were we to admit the contrary proposition, we should implicitly deny the theory of linearity and incrementalism. But two problems, entirely familiar to historians of religion, form obstacles in the path to a single, unitary and uniform "Judaism," a single Orthodoxy resting on a merely descriptive basis. First, Jews in various times and places have produced as their statement of their worldview and way of life for their version of "Israel" quite incompatible theories of definition of Judaism. Second, harmonizing these diverse Judaisms into a single Judaism represents an act of theological judgment formed within the framework of an a priori Judgment of what is Judaism. Leaving out what is not Judaism and including what is Judaism (or "Torah") therefore sorts out on a theological basis, after the fact, what through historical description, analysis, and interpretation constitutes a collage of diverse and divergent systems.

I see no such thing as Judaism but only Judaisms. Surely that allegation contradicts the common sense view that "Judaism" differs from "Christianity." The search for a useful metaphor draws us back to human life. The several Judaic (or Christian, or Buddhist, or Islamic) systems form a family, with certain traits in common. But the family is made up of individuals, each with her or his biography. And, when it comes to families, we live and die pretty much alone, one by one. So it has been, and so it is, with Judaisms (Christianities, Buddhisms, Islams). Each forms both part of a family, with clear filiation, but, as it is born, lives, and dies, also and essentially a singular system to itself. That singular system possesses its own identity, each one with its distinctive definition, its way of life, its worldview, its address to (in the case of a Judaism) an Israel of its own designation (even the whole of Israel, the Jewish people, though that is ordinarily a matter of disbelieved rhetoric). Each demands study not in categories defined by its own claims of continuity, but in those defined by its own distinctive and characteristic choices. For a system takes shape and then makes choices – in that order. The choices, the selections out of the received materials of Judaisms – these come after the fact. The fact is formed by the (prior, fully formed) system: its points of stress, its values, above all, the problems that system has chosen for itself and has determined to solve (and has very commonly solved).

What forms the fact is what the earliest generations of the new Judaism find self-evident, the truths that demand no articulation, no defense, no argument. What is self-evident forms the system and defines its generative exegetical principles. And if I want to know what people find self-evident, I have to uncover the questions they confront and cannot evade. These questions will dictate the program of inquiry, the answers to which then follow after the fact. If I know what issues of social existence predominate, I can also uncover the point – the circumstance – of origin of a Judaism. To be sure, no one claims to know the source of urgent questions: whether political, whether cultural, whether formed within the received condition of the faith, whether framed by forces outside. Debates on such issues of beginnings rarely yield consensus. The reason is simple. In the end no one is present at the beginning, so we have no information to settle any important questions. We work our way back from the known to the unknown. But all we wish to know is whether what we trace is old and continuous, as its apologists invariably claim, or essentially new and creative, a testimony to human will and human power and human intellect, as I maintain it is: a new Judaism, for a new circumstance.

In work of mine I have argued a set of theses in opposition to that theory of a single Judaism, to be described on a merely phenomenological basis.[4] These three theses, one on the history of

---

[4]I summarize the results of a trilogy, in which I present a general theory of the history of Judaism, beginning, middle, and, in its received form for most of Jews of the West, end. The work begins with [1] *Judaism in the Matrix of Christianity* (Philadelphia, 1986: Fortress), continues with [2] *Judaism and Christianity in the Age of Constantine. Issues of the Initial Confrontation* (Chicago, 1987: University of Chicago Press), , and concludes with *The Death and Birth of Judaism. From Self-Evidence to Self-Consciousness in Modern Times* (New York, 1987: Basic). In the first work, *Judaism in the Matrix of Christianity*, I set forth the thesis that Judaism in its received and classical form took shape in the fourth century. That thesis, further, is argued on the strength of the results of my *Foundations of Judaism. Method, Teleology, Doctrine.* (Philadelphia, 1983-1985). I. *Midrash in Context. Exegesis in Formative Judaism.* II. *Messiah in Context. Israel's History and Destiny in Formative Judaism.* III. *Torah. From Scroll to Symbol in Formative Judaism.* In those exercises I repeatedly came to a single result, which is that, when we come

Judaism, the other two on the nature of religion as exemplified by the history of Judaism, derive from a labor of description, analysis, and interpretation, and do not draw upon a priori judgments of a theological character. They therefore fall within the framework of the academic and religious study of religion.[5] But they yield, as we shall see, important implications for the theological study of Judaism, and so form a bridge from studying about, to doing, religion, in the present instance, from studying about Judaism to studying Torah. The theses follow.

    1. The dogma that Judaism never took account of the challenge of Christianity is false and is the opposite of the truth. Judaism as it flourished in the West was born in the encounter with Christianity in

---

upon the first expression, or, at least, adumbration, of what becomes the definitive statement of a matter, we repeatedly find ourselves time and again in the pages of the Talmud of the Land of Israel. That led me to the thesis that it was in the fourth or early fifth century that Judaism took shape in the form that became normative. (I further had the pleasure of finding the same thesis, on the basis of other evidence, announced by Rosemary Radford Reuther in *Sciences Religieuses/Studies in Religion* 1972, 2:1-10.) To extend and test that thesis, in *Judaism and Christianity in the Age of Constantine,* I compare the treatment of three important topics confronting the two fourth-century heirs of ancient Israel's heritage, asking how each dealt with an issue that both had to consider. In this way I wish to compare and contrast the one with the other and so to place into a larger context the initial results of *Foundations of Judaism* and *Judaism in the Matrix of Christianity.* That book lays the foundations for this, because its thesis on the centrality of a political crisis in the shaping of the theology of the Judaism of the Dual Torah extends to this book. In *The Death and Birth of Judaism* my view is that, when Christianity lost its status as self-evident truth to Christians, the Judaism framed in the encounter with that claim, which in Christian Europe for fifteen centuries provided an alternative and compelling truth for Israel, the Jewish people likewise lost its self-evidence to Jews. And after the end of self-evidence – looking back, we call it innocence – came self-consciousness. For Jews the modern age in the history of Judaism then began. In the three works I therefore propose a general theory on why Judaism worked – that is, enjoyed the self-evidence for Israel, the Jewish people – when it worked, and therefore, also, why it did not work when it did not work.

[5]I refer to *Judaism and Christianity in the Age of Constantine. Issues in the Initial Confrontation* (Chicago, 1987: University of Chicago Press), for the first of the theses and *The Death and Birth of Judaism: From Self-Evidence to Self-Consciousness in Modern Times* (New York, 1987: Basic Books) for the second and the third. In the next part of this paper, I work on the complementary problem. Once we recognize the diversity of Judaisms and understand that each system began on its own and only after the fact connected itself to (some of) its antecedents, choosing its canon from its own, and also from inherited, writings, I ask whether there is a paradigm that joins all Judaisms into one Judaism.

the definition in which it defined the civilization of the West, and that same Judaism lost its power to persuade Jews of its self-evident truth when Christianity did. Judaism as it attained definition in late antiquity reached its initial formulation in the fourth century and appeared for the first time in documents redacted in the fifth, in the aftermath of the Christianization of the Roman empire, and principal components of that Judaism responded to the issue framed by the political triumph of Christianity.

2.   The dogma that Judaism "unfolded" in a linear and incremental history is false and the opposite of the truth. The study of a sequence of Judaic systems in modern times shows the contrary. No Judaism (hence, as a matter of hypothesis, no religious system) recapitulates any other of its species let alone of the genus, religion. Each begins on its own and then – only then – goes back to the received documents in search of texts and prooftexts. Every Judaism therefore commences in the definition (to believers: the discovery) of its canon. All Judaisms therefore testify to humanity's power of creative genius: making something out of nothing. That something, that system, serves to suit a purpose, to solve a problem, in our context, to answer in a self-evidently right doctrine a question that none can escape or ignore.

3.   The dogma of an ahistorical Judaism, exempt from the laws of historical change, contradicts the facts of the formation of Judaisms in modern times. The modern age has witnessed the death of Judaism as a set of self-evident answers to urgent questions and the birth of Judaisms that ask quite different sets of urgent questions and propose – in the nature of things – their own self-evidently true answers to those questions, answers entirely out of relationship to the received system of the Dual Torah framed in response to the challenge of Christianity. To account for the ongoing formation of new religious systems, new Judaisms which take up inescapable questions and produce ineluctable answers, I offer a simple thesis.

The thesis is as follows: religion recapitulates resentment. A generation that reaches the decision to change expresses resentment of its immediate setting and therefore its past, its parents, as much as it proposes to commit itself to something better, the future it proposes to manufacture. So when, in the second of the three theses, I say that the urgent question yields its self-evidently true answer, my meaning is this: resentment produces resolution. The two, when joined, form a religious system, in this context, a Judaism.

Let me spell out the thesis of definition outlined in these three generalizations. In modern times a long-established system of Judaism formed in ancient days – a worldview, way of life, addressed to a distinctive Israel, framed in response to urgent and perennial questions –

lost its paramount position. That received Judaic system gave way to a number of new Judaisms – that is, Judaic systems, each with its own set of self-evidently true answers to ineluctable questions. Each of these systems in its way claimed to take the natural next step in "Jewish History," or in "the Tradition" or to constitute the increment of Judaism ("the Tradition") in its unfolding, linear history.

The step outward from studying about religion to doing religion follows along the path of the simple judgment that all Judaisms, each with its theory of its own linear and incremental relationship to "the Torah," err. And that error produces remarkable illumination. Because they all err gloriously in perfect self-delusion, each one testifies to the powerful imagination of humanity, the courage of people to face urgent questions and to compose, in solving them, systems of belief and behavior capable of creating whole worlds of meaning: sensibility and sense alike. So in the gallant courage of Jewry to create and call new creation old, in its capacity to renew hope in the face of despair, I find what it means to be in God's image, after God's likeness. And when we speculate about what the Torah means when it says, "In our image, after our likeness," we no longer study about Judaism. We study Torah.

So I begin with the claim that, in calling itself reform or historical or authentic, or Torah-true and traditional, in amassing prooftexts for its propositions, the new always errs in linking itself to the old. In fact there is no such thing as "the Tradition" to which to reconnect in a fresh beginning. There are only Judaic systems, each a response in a new way to a new day. The proof lies in the demonstration that people, knowing in advance something that in the received Judaism they did not find out and could not have found out, invariably proceed to pick and choose – after they have completed their (unself-conscious) work of invention. Of special interest in this connection is the most contemporary Judaism, the one that yields what is called "a return to Tradition." True, those who "return to Judaism" or "repent" call what they invent discovery, but what they find in the received materials of former Judaisms is what they have gone to seek. And the picking and the choosing, whether among colors on a pallet or sounds on a scale or those gifts of grace we call religious faith and religious works, testify to humanity's power of rebirth, renewal in response to radical revision in the human condition.

IV. Defining Judaism (II)
The Systemic Paradigm of Judaisms

The work of definition begins in the recognition that each Judaism works outs its own definition. But when we understand that there have been a multiplicity of Judaisms, we quite naturally wonder whether we can identify anything that permits us to speak of Judaism at all. In a quite distinct exercise I have explored that complementary and necessary question.[6] Again, we ask a question to be answered through description. And yet, self-evidently, the answer bears profound and far-reaching theological consequences. Let me spell out the results of an inquiry into the recurrent systemic pattern, the deep structure of a paradigm that so universally recurs in diverse guises as to require us to speak not only of Judaisms but (in a curious way) of Judaism. And, as we shall rapidly recognize, once we discover that systemic paradigm, we learn about religion as exemplified by Judaism a proposition of considerable weight. It is that religion constitutes (in the language of statistics) an independent variable, a force that is not contingent on any other force but that operates on its own. Again, if I can demonstrate that proposition, I offer for creative reflection a consideration of more than routine consequence. Let me begin in a way appropriate for a study of doing religion in the case of Judaism. Reverting to the text that for the present purpose serves as my canonical appeal and authority, I cite a verse of Scripture and then a comment of a rabbinical commentator on that verse. In an attenuated way indeed, that episode constitutes an act of study of the Torah.

> But the serpent said to the woman, "You will not die, for God knows that when you eat of it your eyes will be opened and you will be like God."
>
> Genesis 3:5
>
> "...like God" [means] creators of worlds
>
> Rashi (R. Solomon Isaac,
> 1040-1105)

The theory of religion, exemplified by Judaism, offered here is the one first stated in the fall of humanity, the notion that to be "like God" is to "create worlds." I refer to the statement made by the serpent at the fall of Adam and Eve. Explaining why the couple in the state of grace should not eat of the fruit of the tree of the knowledge of good and evil, the snake says, It is because God knows that, when you do, you will become like God. The greatest exegete of Scripture in Judaism, Rashi, then explains the matter, and his statement I take to be definitive. My thesis is this:

Judaisms create Jews' worlds. And there is a very specific and paradigmatic Judaism that from the beginning imparted its shape and structure on all Judaisms.

---

[6]It is *Judaism: Past, Present, Future* (Boston, 1987: Beacon).

I offer a particular, sustained exposition of, and argument for, that thesis. I move beyond my field theory of modern Judaisms to a single, encompassing field theory to explain the entire history of Judaism, past, present, and (by way of making possible others' testing of the thesis long after its enunciation) future. I account for the shape and character of all Judaisms that have ever flourished and predict the structure of any Judaism that will ever come into existence. I may state that theory in a single paragraph.

Because the Mosaic Torah's interpretation of the diverse experiences of the Israelites after the destruction of the Temple in 586 invoked – whether pertinent or not – the categories of exile and return, so constructing as paradigmatic the experience of only a minority of the families of the Jews (most in Babylonia stayed there, many in the Land of Israel never left), through the formation of the Pentateuch, the Five Books of Moses, the events from 586 to 450 B.C., became for all time to come the generative and definitive pattern of meaning. Consequently, whether or not the paradigm precipitated dissonance with their actual circumstances, Jews in diverse settings have constructed their worlds, that is, shaped their identification, in accord with that one, generative model. They therefore have perpetually rehearsed that human experience imagined by the original authorship of the Torah in the time of Ezra. That pattern accordingly was not merely preserved and perpetuated. It itself precipitated and provoked its own replication in age succeeding age.

A Judaism therefore would for time to come represent a reworking of the theme of exile and return, alienation and reconciliation, by an Israel, a group troubled by the resentment of that uncertain past and of that future subject to stipulation. A Judaism therefore recapitulates the original experience.

To state matters in more general terms, religions recapitulate resentment. All Judaisms that have come into being have conformed to that paradigm, and, so long as framers of Judaic systems – ways of life, worldviews, addressed to an Israel subject to particular definition – refer to that same holy scripture, the Five Books of Moses in particular, all Judaisms that will emerge will focus, in one way or another, upon that same generative resentment.

In so framing my general theory of the history of Judaism, I enter a dissent to a prevailing view of the origin and character of religion as contingent, and not as an independent variable. For many maintain that religion originates in or expresses considerations of an extrinsic character, for example, motives of a psychological or economic or political character. That theory of the matter overstates the impact, upon religion, of the society and politics that sustain religion. I argue that in the case of Judaism, for reasons I shall spell out, religion exercises the power to impart its pattern upon its social world, the polity of Jews. As is clear, my general theory of the history of Judaism – which may or may not serve as a model for a general theory of the history of other systems that form distinct species of the genus, religion – is that a particular experience, transformed by a religious system into a paradigm of the life of the social group, became normative – and therefore generative. Under other circumstances, in other times and places, that experience preserved in authoritative Scripture consequently imparted its form and substance upon Jewish polities that, in point of fact, faced the task of explaining a social world quite different from the one that, to begin with, had generated that original and paradigmatic experience.

That is why I maintain that the social world recapitulates religion, not that religion recapitulates that social and political datum, the given of society, economy, politics, let alone of an imaginative or emotional reality. The study of Judaism provides a source of interesting cases for the proposition that religion shapes the world, not the world, religion. In our setting and language, religion creates social worlds of meaning and explanation, a society, a polity, – in the case of this general theory of the history of Judaism, an Israel, a Judaism. Specifically, it is the Jews' religion, Judaism, that has formed their world and framed their realities, and not the world of politics, culture, society, that has made their religion.

This single field theory of the history of Judaism is meant to account for the character of every Judaism that has emerged through time and that will take shape in the future. It points to a particular identification and interpretation of events, the character of which imposes its singular shape upon all Judaisms that followed it, then to now. That event treats as typical and paradigmatic an experience of the ongoing group so that, in one form or another, group after group finds the logic of its social existence in the original moment, that is, in the first imaginative labor of identifying happenings as events and of interpreting their meaning. Not only so, but that logic, inescapable for reasons of imagined social fact and invented political reality, stands for a situation to escape, overcome, survive. That is to say, the generative paradigm perpetuates profound resentment: why here? why us? why now? And, to the contrary (and this is the resentment) why not always, everywhere, and forever? So we may say that a Judaic religious system recapitulates a particular resentment, relating to other religious systems that address and go over that same matter, each in its own way, each on its own, all addressing the same original experience. That paradigmatic event, then, is recapitulated in age succeeding age, whether by one Judaism in competition with another or by one Judaism after another. But, as a matter of systemic fact, no Judaism recapitulates any other, though each goes over the same paradigmatic experience.[7]

The essential theory that denies there is now, or ever was, a single Judaism bears the affirmative claim is that there is no linear and incremental history of one continuous Judaism, beginning, middle, end. But there is a single paradigmatic and definitive human experience, which each Judaism reworks in its own circumstance and context. In a broader sense, therefore, the present field theory of the history of a particular religious tradition that comprises a variety of expressions may be summarized in these propositions:

1. No religious system (within a given set of related religions) recapitulates any other.

2. But all religious systems (within a given set) recapitulates resentment, that is, a single persistent experience that for generation after generation captures what, for a particular group, stands for the whole of the human condition: everything all at once, all together, the misery, the magnificence of life.

What I have said requires the immediate specification of that single paradigmatic experience to which all Judaisms, everywhere and under all conditions, refer. As a matter of simple fact, we may identify that generative and definitive moment precisely as all Judaisms have done, that is, by looking into that same Scripture. All Judaisms identify the Torah or the Five Books of Moses as the written-down statement of God's will for Israel, the Jewish people (which, as a matter of fact, every Judaism also identifies as its own social group). I suppose that on the surface, we should specify that formative and definitive moment, recapitulated by all Judaisms, with the story of Creation down to Abraham and the beginning of his family, the children of Abraham, Isaac, and Jacob. Or perhaps we are advised to make our way to Sinai and hold that that original point of definition descends from heaven. But allowing ourselves merely to retell the story deprives us of the required insight. Recapitulating the story of the religion does not help

---

[7]That is the argument of my *Death and Birth of Judaism. From Self-Evidence to Self-Consciousness in Modern Times* (New York, 1987: Basic). There I argue at some length that no Judaism stands in a linear relationship with any other, none forms an increment on a predecessor, and all constitute systems that, once in being, select for themselves an appropriate and useful past – that is, a canon of useful and authoritative texts. And that is the order: the system creates its canon. These issues play no role in the present book, although in chapter seven I review, with much revision, some of the results of the other work.

us understand the religion. Identifying the point of origin of the story, by contrast, does. For the story tells not what happened on the occasion to which the story refers (the creation of the world, for instance) but how (long afterward and for their own reasons) people want to portray themselves. The tale therefore recapitulates that resentment, that obsessive and troubling point of origin, that the group wishes to explain, transcend, transform.

For all Judaisms, for all Israels, Scripture forms the first statement of the normative paradigm, the human condition of Israel. The context of the formation of Scripture preserves that definitive moment, restating as always authoritative that original, now-paradigmatic experience. Since the Five Books of Moses were composed in the aftermath of the destruction of the Temple in 586 B.C. and in response to the exile to Babylonia, the experience selected and addressed by the authorship of the document is that of exile and restoration.

The critical step in the argument now has been reached with a single word: selected. I say "selected" because no Jews after 586 actually experienced what in the aggregate Scripture says happened. That is proven by simple facts.

1. No Jew both went into exile and then came back to Jerusalem. So, to begin with, Scripture does not record a particular person's experience.

2. More to the point, if it is not autobiographical, writing for society at large the personal insight of a singular figure, it also is not an account of a whole nation's story.

The reason is that the original exile encompassed mainly the political classes of Jerusalem and some useful populations alongside. Many Jews in the Judea of 586 never left. And, as is well known, a great many of those who ended up in Babylonia stayed there. Only a minority went back to Jerusalem. Consequently, the story of exile and return to Zion encompasses what happened to only a few families, who identified themselves as the family of Abraham, Isaac, and Jacob, and their genealogy as the history of Israel. Had those families that stayed and those that never came back written the Torah, they would have told as normative and paradigmatic a different tale altogether.

That experience of the few that formed the paradigm for Israel beyond the restoration taught as normative lessons of alienation: the life of the group is uncertain, subject to conditions and stipulations. Nothing is set and given, all things a gift: land and life itself. But what actually did happen in that uncertain world – exile but then restoration – marked the group as special, different, select. That experience of the uncertainty of the life of the group in the century or so from the destruction of the First Temple of Jerusalem by the Babylonians in 586 to the building of the Second Temple of Jerusalem by the Jews, with Persian permission and sponsorship returned from exile, formed the paradigm. With the promulgation of the "Torah of Moses" under the sponsorship of Ezra, the Persians' viceroy, at ca. 450 B.C., all future Israels would then refer to that formative experience as it had been set down and preserved as the norm for Israel in the mythic terms of that "original" Israel, the Israel not of Genesis and Sinai and the end at the moment of entry into the promised land, but the "Israel" of the families that recorded as the rule and the norm the story of both the exile and the return. In that minority genealogy, that story of exile and return, alienation and remission, imposed on the received stories of pre-exilic Israel and adumbrated time and again in the Five Books of Moses and addressed by the framers of that document in their work over all, we find that paradigmatic statement in which every Judaism, from then to now, found its structure and deep syntax of social existence, the grammar of its intelligible message. To generalize:

1.   No Judaism recapitulates any other, and none stands in a linear and incremental relationship with any prior one.

2.   But all Judaisms recapitulate that single paradigmatic experience of the Torah of "Moses," the authorship that reflected on the meaning of the events of 586-450 selected for the composition of history and therefore interpretation.

That experience (in theological terms) rehearsed the conditional moral existence of sin and punishment, suffering and atonement and reconciliation, and (in social terms) the uncertain and always conditional national destiny of disintegration and renewal of the group. That moment captured within the Five Books of Moses, that is to say, the judgment of the generation of the return to Zion, led by Ezra, about its extraordinary experience of exile and return would inform the attitude and viewpoint of all the Israels beyond. What has been said now requires that we review the opening propositions of the preface. My thesis bears for the study of religion the theory as to the character and origin of religion that in the case of Judaism, religion imparts its pattern upon the social world and polity.

My generalizations on the history of Judaism (now, not Judaisms) bear a simple implication for the character and definition of religion. I maintain that the social world recapitulates religion, not that religion recapitulates that datum, the given of society, economy, politics, let alone of an imaginative or emotional reality. Because of the generative, social power of a single paradigmatic experience, which defines and constitutes the exegetical fulcrum for the present theory of religion in the case of Judaism (and, I should postulate, other religions of its classification) religion shapes the world, not the world, religion. Specifically, it is the Jews' religion, Judaism, that has formed their world and framed their realities, and not the world of politics, culture, society, that has made their religion.

4

The New Setting for Jewish Learning: Towards a Theory of University Studies in Judaism

Bernstein Lecture, University of Rochester, 1976
With responses by William Scott Green and Arthur S. Goldberg

The great movements in Judaism in modern times are the work of intellectuals. Two dominant movements changed the face of the community and reshaped Jewish history: the development of non-Orthodox modes of Judaism, Reform in particular, and Zionism, the creation of Jewish nationality and the State of Israel. Both are the work, to begin with, of thinkers, not of doers, of scholars and intellectuals, rabbis and journalists, and above all, of university students. Reform is the work of scholars and students. Zionism is the creation of journalist, Herzl, a novelist, Nordau, and Jewish students of that time, represented by Weizmann. For a long time thereafter Zionism was led by lawyers, judges, and other intellectuals. This fact is important because our present perspective is that Reform Judaism and Zionism depend upon the support of middle-class businessmen and of millionaire politicians. We must not forget that the businessmen and politicians came aboard only much later. Zionism was already a safe investment. Reform Judaism was not created to serve as a vehicle for the bourgeoisie to legitimate their imitation of their neighbors' ways. Zionism was bitterly opposed by all of the Jewish millionaires whom Herzl approached. By the time the monied classes joined these movements, the movements themselves had ceased to serve as the generative force in the formation of values and ideals within the

51

Jewish community. Indeed, they had passed from their creative stages
entirely. They no longer found much that was new and interesting to
contribute in the formation of the consciousness and imagination of
Jewry at large. The two value-forming – mythopoeic – and vital,
interesting movements in modern Judaism have passed into the hands of
the middle-class and rich businessmen. They exist chiefly to raise
money so they may continue to exist.

If the creative forces in modern Jewry take shape on the campus, we
must ask, what is the meaning of the newest university development,
the academic study of the Jews and Judaism, broadly defined? The
university is a quite new setting for Jewish learning. Its imperatives are
only now becoming clear. To begin with, we have to define the sort of
university to which the field of Jewish learning responds. After all,
many institutions of learning, not all of them of "higher learning," are
called colleges or universities. There are colleges of hair dressing and
plumbing as well as of liberal arts learning. In as yet unpublished
research, Paul Ritterband has shown that Judaic studies find their
original place in the research-oriented universities, only later on
moving into the more serious liberal arts colleges, state and city
universities and colleges, and the like. Accordingly, the university of
which we speak is a place in which knowledge, its discovery, criticism,
and transmission, takes the first place. Jewish learning is located
within faculties devoted to serious study and serious teaching. It is not
a subject much pursued at other sorts of colleges and universities.

With the increment of experience, the new generation of professors
of Jewish studies learn about their new situation and its potentialities.
The most important discovery is that the university is an essentially
assimilatory agency. Differences of origin and culture are obscured. A
single standard of thought, reason, and logic applies to all analysis and
all data. There is no ethnic physics. Courses taught only by Jews,
specifically for Jewish students, on the subject of Judaism are equally
incongruous with the university setting. And above all, all statements
of truth are subject to verification, therefore to the test of evidence and
falsification.

The inestimable sociologist, Marshall Sklare, has already stated
the assimilationist traits of universities so far as they affect the
personal and social commitments of Jewish professors in general
[America's Jews (New York, 1971), p. 68]:

> The problem of maintaining a Jewish identity among academicians
> comes not so much from the possibility of a sudden rejection of that
> identity but rather from a diminished involvement in and
> commitment to the Jewish community. Gradually such commitment
> becomes less meaningful than commitment to one's profession and to

the academic community. In the end commitment to the Jewish community may come to be replaced by commitment to the academic community, and to the value that the academic community places on universalism over particularism...

Sklare illustrates his fine insight by reference to intermarriage among college students and professors. But there is another point of relevance, the intellect. Let me now rephrase his observation: "The problem of maintaining Jewish studies as an ethnic field, validated entirely in terms of the prior ethnic affirmations of professors and students, comes not so much from the possibility of a sudden rejection of that approach but rather from a diminished involvement in and commitment to the social sources of its self-validation. Gradually Jewish studies as an ethnic field intended to strengthen the Jewish loyalty of the students and help them find meaning in being Jewish becomes less meaningful than commitment to the disciplines of the university's approaches to learning and to the values of the academic community. In the end, commitment to the values of the Jewish community may come to be replaced by commitment to the values of the academic community, in particular to the value that the academic community places on universalism over particularism." I think the matter is clear and requires little elaboration.

To recapitulate the argument: The most vigorous and interesting things happening in Jewish life today are things which happen on the campus and in peoples' minds. The center of the Jewish learned world is now at least as much in secular universities as it is in Jewish institutions of Jewish learning. Considerably more scholars – that is, people working full-time at teaching and learning – are employed by universities than by Jewish seminaries, teachers' colleges, and the like. And the university is essentially an assimilatory agency, as Sklare says. Its values stress universalism over particularism. And the Jews are particular and inward-turning. The action in Jewish intellectual life – from which must come whatever vitality and vigor the Jews will have – has moved to the secular campus, and the secular campus lives by values which, on the face of it, are hostile to the conduct of Jewish intellectual life in its old ways.

To phrase the central question in simple terms: what are the models for university learning which are relevant to the Jews' situation as a particular people in a universal and open society? Having stated the question in these terms, I have of course phrased the central dilemma which has faced American Jews from the beginning. Just as we in universities are Jews in an undifferentiated and attractive world, so Jews in the open society of America have to find the measure of their lives in an undifferentiated and attractive society. What place for difference, with what justification, and above all, what is the meaning and what the end? Whatever theory we may develop to make sense of our situation in universities is apt to provide a theory for the situation of Jewry as a whole.

Let me now state the two contradictory theories of the place and shape of Judaic learning in universities.

The first holds that we do in the new home what we did in the old, but pretend to be doing something fresh. The second maintains that the task is integration and assimilation. The separationists seek to organize the field in autonomous departments of Jewish studies; the integrationists, primarily in disciplinary departments, perhaps joined through interdisciplinary committees or programs. The separationists identify themselves with ethnic studies, the integrationists do not. The theory of the separationists begins in the conviction that an entity, the "Jewish people," exists, not in faith but in fact, and that one therefore studies as a unity, and without regard to discipline, method, or inner, yet common, logic, the literature, history, and sociology of people in widely separated places and epochs. Jewish studies in an autonomous framework – whether yeshiva, seminary, or department of Jewish studies – measure their worth by their success in molding the values of the living generation. Jewish learning defined as Jewish studies is pursued not simply because it may illuminate some aspect of the humanities or social sciences, but because it will help the Jewish student to form beliefs by reference to the tradition of which he is part and should be part.

The contrary theory of the subject begins in the reassessment of assimilation, as phased by Gerson D. Cohen ("The Blessing of Assimilation in Jewish History," in J. Neusner, ed., *Understanding Jewish Theology* [New York, 1973] pp. 251-258), "The first shibboleth which all of us have been raised on is that Jewish survival and above all Jewish vitality in the past derived in large measure from a tenacious adherence on the part of our ancestors to all basic external traditional forms." But this view is false, Cohen argues, and the facts in particular show it to be false. Cohen says, "There are two ways of meeting the problem of assimilation. The first is withdrawal and fossilization....There is and always was an alternative approach of...utilizing...assimilation as channel to new sources of vitality...the healthy appropriation of new forms and ideas for the sake of our own growth and enrichment....The great ages of Jewish creativity have always been products of the challenge of assimilation and of the response of leaders who were to a certain extent assimilated themselves." The theory of integration, further, holds that the Jewish data are to be subjected to the same methods and interpreted in accord with the same principles as pertain to all other data in the humanities and social sciences. There are no values and methods specific to the study of Jewry, distinctive to the analysis of Judaism in all its forms. The integrationist seeks to discern and understand structures, the separationist, to inhibit them. In the integrationists' view, commitment is to scholarly method and result and therefore to disciplinary department; in the separationists' view, commitment is to the content of what is studied. The former deems advocacy to relate to scholarly alternatives, not to the spiritual condition of students, let alone professors.

These conflicting theories of the field produce important curricular debates as well. Two major and contradictory theories presently guide the formation of programs in the field of Jewish learning in North America, Europe, and the State of Israel. The one denies the possibility of investigating matters of Jewish concern outside of specific disciplines. According to this theory, "Jewish studies" constitute a body of data subject to investigation in accord with various disciplines. Jewish studies are properly organized, within the curriculum, along disciplinary lines. They belong within departments defined by common methods. For example, one legitimate discipline, or rather, composite of methods, is that shaped within the academic study of religions. Accordingly, the disciplinary thinking emergent in the academic study of religions imposes its questions and its larger theoretical interests upon the formation of specific courses on Judaism as upon other religious traditions. There are, self-evidently, other valid and important disciplines pertinent to the study of the Jews, including Judaism. The work, however, is shaped within the conceptual framework of a departmental setting. It is to be guided by problems shaped by, and shared with, colleagues studying other data and from other perspectives.

The second theory, corresponding to the position of the separationists, is that Jewish studies should be organized where possible in a single department, without primary or fundamental regard to matters of method and discipline. The conceptions of method and discipline characteristic of this second position have not been spelled out. Rather, they are taken as self-evident, because the Jewish community outside the university and many Jewish scholars within it make the same assumptions about the Jews and their culture. And they also take the same position toward the university. The university is to be exploited for "Jewish survival." It enjoys no autonomy. It bears no legitimate character of its own. Yet the power of the separationist theory of Jewish learning is not to be dismissed because of the absence of intellectual articulation. On the contrary, much evidence of its compelling cogency is to be found in its present predominance. Large and powerful departments and institutes of Jewish studies exist. Seminaries, teachers' colleges, national associations of scholars, majors in Jewish studies, journals centering upon Jewish subjects with no interest whatever in disciplinary cogency – all of these testify to the weight and power of the nondisciplinary and essentially extra-university and even anti-university approach to Jewish learning, the approach which, as I said, stresses the self-validating, mythopoeic character of the data.

My hope is that I have presented the alternatives with a measure of respect for each. But now I must make explicit my implicit position on the Issue. I believe that the goal of learning is to comprehend structures of knowledge, to apprehend how facts fit together and illuminate still larger sets of facts. I do not consider that knowing this and that about the Jews – or about anything else – constitutes the acquisition of significant knowledge. I find it self-evident that knowing about the Jews significantly and materially enhances our understanding of the humanities and humanity.

We have now to ask about the issue of objectivity, which is generally held to differentiate seminary from university studies in Judaism. It is widely supposed by separationists that the primary difference between universities and seminaries is that professors in universities are objective. But that is naive. They hold that university teachers do not advocate; they merely teach. In fact, professors in both settings perceive that facts bear meaning, constitute a whole which transcends the sum of the parts. They enter into ultimate engagement in what, to the world, is merely interesting. The commitment on both sides is the same. But the advocacy in form and objective is different on the campus. A university professor of Judaic studies does not advocate Judaism but ultimate seriousness about the problematic of Judaism, about the interpretation of Judaism as an aspect of the humanities, a very different thing. We are not agents of the Jewish community or rabbis. Our students have rights, after all, and one of these is the right to be let alone, to grow and mature in their own distinctive ways. They have the right to seek their own way, as we find ours, without being pestered. We are not missionaries, but professors. The professor leads, says, "Follow me," without looking backward to see whether anyone is there. The missionary pushes, imposes self upon other, autonomous selves. That is the opposite of teaching and bears no relevance to university scholarship. Our task indeed is to teach, which means, not to indoctrinate; to educate, never to train. There is a fine line to be found, an unmarked, but dangerously mined frontier, between great teaching and aggrandizing indoctrination. So there are risks to be endured in the search for the center and the whole. There are courtesies to be observed. The virtues of the professor are self-restraint and forbearance, tolerance, and objectivity.

From one perspective, these virtues appear to begin in the conviction, held by the university professor and rejected by advocates of ethnic identification, that knowledge and understanding do not bring salvation. That is why, at a preliminary glance, they do not have to be imposed upon the other person. After all, if what I know will not cure what ails the other, why force it down his throat? Knowledge is not gnosis. It saves nothing. It cures nothing. It solves no problems, except by indirection. Knowledge is interesting and engaging, but serves itself. Separationists see the processes of learning as important because they serve a purpose beyond themselves, specifically, because they produce ethnic identification. They stem the tide of assimilation. They thus contribute to the solution of the contemporary "Jewish problem."

If knowledge – Jewish learning – is not asked to serve some other, extrinsic purpose, no one can seek salvation through learning. None can come to Jewish studies as a gnostic system and seek a gnostic experience of salvation. What salvation do we offer, who deem scholarship to be the recognition of ignorance, who seek consciousness not so much of what we know but of how we know and of what we do not know? Scholarship is drawn by self-criticism, compelled by doubt and curiosity. The professor knows the limits of knowing, exactly the opposite of the gnostic. Soteric gnosis is not ours to offer. What advocacy is there for skepticism and ignorance? How shall we advocate humility before the unknown, but arrogance to think we can know?

Yet that is not entirely fair to separationists and not wholly candid about the inner conviction of assimilationists. If we give our lives to what we do, then for ourselves we do find salvation. If what we give our lives to is learning, then learning for us bears soteric and salvific meaning. We cannot accuse the other side of caring and claim we do not care. That is not honest and does injustice to ourselves. We devote ourselves to the things we study, to our data. These data in their way take over and shape our consciousness. The things we study become part of ourselves. Whether or not this is a deemed gnostic salvation is not quite to the point.

Let me propose a different distinction, a different set of alternatives for a theory of the university study of Judaism and the Jewish people. To begin with, let us call to mind the classic trilogy of Judaic theology, God, Torah, and Israel, meaning, the Jewish people. There was a time in which Jewish learning was undertaken in the service of God. The Jews today are secular. Whether in universities or in seminaries (excluding Orthodox yeshivot), they do not study for religious reasons. But in the contemporary Judaic consciousness, the element of Israel, the Jewish people, now stands at the fore. In what I have said, I hope with accuracy and fairness, about the professors who see themselves as contributing to the solution of the "Jewish problem," I find the focus upon that element. Accordingly, within the primary mythic structure by which Jews understand themselves, exactly that element – Jewish peoplehood – which predominates in the consciousness of the community at large also is central in the theory of advocates of survival through Jewish learning.

Yet there is a third element in the trilogy. It is that element which I think pertinent to the situation of university professors of Judaic studies: Torah, broadly understood as Jewish learning for its own sake. That element is remarkably congruent to the central value of university professors at large. Humility before the unknown and arrogance to undertake the task of learning, knowledge for its own sake – these are the shared and common values of our colleagues and ourselves. In physics or philosophy or engineering or religious studies or Judaic learning, we give ourselves to our data and are shaped by what we study. This, as I said, bears for us soteric and salvific meaning. I propose that element in the Judaic myth which, in its unfolding, best explains who we are and what we do, is Torah. *The seal of the Holy One, blessed be he, is truth.* In the nature of things to do our work in the university, we must assimilate, set aside parochial concerns and private realms of meaning in favor of the shared world of common discourse. the world of the university defines our lives together, and this accords, happily, with the definition imposed by Judaism upon those same lives.

The university is, as Sklare tells us, a place in which our commitment to the Jewish community is diminished, commitment to our profession and to the academic community and its values heightened. I argue exactly that: commitment to the Jewish community as we now know it *should* be replaced by commitment to the values of the academic community, so that in time, the Jewish community will be reshaped by the values of learning, gain renewed access to its own intellect. Jewish studies in universities which do not lead to a shift in commitment and focus are unlikely to serve either the Jewish community or the university. But the value of the academic community is not principally emphasis upon universalism over particularism, though from Sklare's perspective as a sociologist, that is certainly the case. There are academic values which bear no relationship to the sociology of the academic community. I think the primary and dominant one is complete devotion to one's subject and the critical examination of the disciplines through which one investigates that subject. What subject do we study? To what data do we make that ultimate commitment of self and of mind? Self-evidently, we give our lives to learning in and about Judaism and Jews. We deem the act of knowing the Jewish sources to be its own validation. We deny it is to be justified by reference to anything beyond itself. We do not measure our success by whether our students go off and join Jewish organizations, refrain from eating pork, seek a Jewish mate, or do any of the other things which the Jewish community deems important. We do not even think that the rich student's mind is more important than the poor student's mind, and, in the context of the organized community, there can be no greater heresy than to deny the self-evident superiority of having and giving money.

Such power as is ours is the power of our sources. What we have to offer is their beauty and the poetry of their logic. We are overcome by the ineluctable and ineffable force of this alien world, the reality constructed by our data. My own work for many years has been in the historical interpretation of the Judaic law, particularly the law dealing with purity. Now that law has not been kept, in the main, for nearly two millennia, and much of it is in any event imaginary and mythic. Yet as I plunge into its depths, I become intoxicated by its filigreed subtleties, its interplay of conception and formulation. The data, the facts of the law, take hold and begin to shape a new canopy, an arcane framework of compelling meaning. I take as my task, therefore, to help others perceive the poetry of the law, framed as it is in its little, perfect units, spun out from generation to generation like a rope without end. If the law is seen to be mysterious and beautiful, in its form and in its substance, then, it is my conviction, it will capture others as it has taken my mind and my heart, and as it has engaged the intellects of so many, much greater learners, for a lifetime of centuries, eighteen hundred years, from the second to the twentieth.

At the beginning I pointed out that great events in the life of the Jewish people in modern times begin on the campus, among students and professors. They have been carried forward by university graduates, journalists, lawyers, doctors, and other practicing intellectuals. Clearly, something very new and interesting begins to take shape in universities, an event, in Judaism, rich with potential force and complex meaning. Our theory of what happens on the campus, therefore, bears implications for what happens in the community. And that is so not solely for historical and sociological reasons, but also for practical ones. Today hundreds of full-time professors of Judaic studies, both of Jewish and of gentile origin, spend their lives in the humanistic study of Jewish texts, broadly construed. If, as I have argued, these texts bear their own weight and power, they are bound to begin to reshape the imagination and even the character of the people who study them. These people, our students, go out into the community and help define it.

What then is the meaning of Jewry, therefore, of the renaissance of Jewish learning in universities? Within the tripartite structure of Judaism, God, Torah, and Israel, the second element once more comes to prominence, drawn to the fore in its remarkably just new context. For a century, the condition of the Jewish people, Israel, has occupied our minds. There has been no alternative. I need not rehearse our tragic history as a people. But in centering our attention upon our condition in the world, we have neglected our inner life, the rational construction of our minds and the revision of reality to respond to what is in our minds. We Jews do not perceive the world as Judaic tradition interprets it; nor do we see the world through other myth. Our tasks have scarcely allowed us to ask Judaic questions and seek Judaic answers, to interpret what happens in the context of the enduring perspectives of Torah. Indeed, the persistent tasks to be done for Israel, the Jewish people, have demanded otherwise. To survive in this world we have had to learn its ways and accept its disciplines. The world, alas, is our school. It imparts its meanings upon being Jewish, imposes upon us acute consciousness of 'being Jewish' with little pity and no sympathy. Education in the Judaic imperatives takes place in the arenas of world opinion and in the headlines of newspapers. We have not enjoyed a moment of benign neglect, but an epoch of malignant attention.

But that has meant we could go on 'being Jewish' by devoting our public selves to that aspect of our being. Our private lives, our inner reflections, our search and sense for individual meanings – these are unattended to. We are a generation of public commitment to Jewish affairs, and private neglect of the Jewish life. Devotion to Jewish activities and indifference to their inner meaning and direction share the same national soul. People who lavish their best energies, their money, and their time upon Jewish activities also live lives remote from distinctive and particular Judaic meanings. That is the result of the century we have endured, the unspeakable disaster, for Israel and Torah alike, of modern Jewish history. For the Jewish people in America and Canada, the opportunity has come to gain renewed access to the fundament of wisdom, the inner experience of the Jewish people, even to transform the life of Israel through transcendent Torah.

For Torah too this unprecedented opportunity bears the potential of renewal. For if Jewry has found itself too busy for Torah, Torah also has been neglected, unable to speak and to be heard. Those who had access to its parts could say nothing of the whole. Even the parts they knew appeared to them distinct and separate, isolated both from one another and from the world of human affairs. They had no language, there were no words, neither could they make their voice heard. Torah existed, but not in, not for, this world. In anguished search for a place in the world, Israel joined the world, changed itself, its language, its clothing, its way of making a living, its conduct of life. Israel became part of the modern world not only in form, but in inner perspective. Torah, the most distinctive and particular aspect of the Judaic heritage, could do little but fall silent. Ours is the opportunity to speak out of the silence, for we do have some of the words, we do master the rudiments of the language, and our voice is heard. So far as we are taken up and reshaped by the power of the texts, ours is an authentic message, an insight of integrity.

But our voice is modulated by the shape of the hall in which it is heard. The words bounce against indifferent walls. We find ourselves in the lecture halls of universities, severe, undecorated places. Whether it derives from the austere heritage of our beloved New England, mother of the American mind, I do not know. But university classrooms and lecture halls, like New England churches, are strangely barren places, without art, without design, without color. Their light is unmodulated and pitiless. They are used for many subjects, so are meant to be neutral, hospitable to all but according special welcome to none. And, it goes without saying, their visual neutrality bears a deeper meaning. The world before us in universities is open, willing to listen, but only to one language for all. It is, as I have stressed, a world in which, in deep ways, people assimilate to common value and adopt a single culture, the discipline of mind. If there is diversity in the classroom, it is in clothing and cosmetics. It is not in special pleading. Accordingly, the world before us is curious, but merely that. Our subject is no more and no less welcome than any other subject. We speak to issues common to all humanities and to humanity.

But, as I have argued, that is profoundly appropriate to the intellectual condition of contemporary Israel, the Jewish people. It too is neutral, open to, but unmarked by, Torah. Our existential circumstance within the university corresponds to that outside. The world flows through and beyond. Our students come from some place and go on to some other, and so do we, professors and Jews. What forms the Jewish problematic also is the issue of the common culture: the place of the particular in the undifferentiated world. Such theory as shapes the study of the Jews and Judaism in universities has at the end to interpret and respond to the condition of Jews and Judaism in the world outside universities. Within the disciplines and tasks of Judaic learning, we seek words that speak to all, but to none in particular, language to convey a distinctive perspective upon, and to, undifferentiated humanity. These words have then to address common concerns with uncommon truth.

Within Torah are such words, I think, because Jews who make Torah are human beings and part of a common humanity. Through the exceptionally particular language of Torah, they give distinctive form to insight and truth deriving from experiences and perplexities common to the human condition. The Jews are a peculiar people, in their pilgrimage through nearly the whole of recorded history and across all the continents. But in their intense engagement with one another, with their peoplehood as Israel, they endure and record in Torah what happens to everyone and, at one time or another, everywhere. Their questions – the perplexities of life's course, the terror of holocaust and memory, the quest for redemption and for a house to have but not to come home to – these questions face the generality of humanity. Torah marks the human being as different, as Israel. But it does so by making Israel into humanity; Torah shapes the condition of Israel into a paradigm of the human condition. Torah is what makes the Jew into a *mensch*, "in our image, after our likeness." *So God, created man in his own image, in the image of God he created him; male and female he created them.*[1]

Response
William Scott Green
University of Rochester

Professor Neusner here offers a penetrating and suggestive analysis of the central issues that inform the present debate about the place of Jewish learning in a university setting. Among scholars of the Jews and of Judaism in American universities, he, almost alone, has devoted a consistent and sustained effort to this matter, and the theory he propounds in his essay culminates more than fifteen years of serious and careful deliberation. Since my own introduction to Jewish learning and whatever competence in it I subsequently have achieved are the results of educational experiences in universities, I self-evidently can have no

---

[1] I have benefitted from the critical comments of my dear colleagues, Horst R. Moehring, Wendell S. Dietrich, Ernest S. Frerichs, John P. Reeder, David R. Blumenthal, John Giles Milhaven, and Sumner B. Twiss; of Mrs. Lois Atwood, administrator of the Department of Religious Studies at Brown; and of Professors Paul Ritterband, City University of New York, William Scott Green, University of Rochester, and Baruch A. Levine, New York University. While I invariably owe much to those named, my debt in the present regard is uncommonly great.

complaint with either the arguments he makes or the conclusions he reaches. I therefore would like to gloss what he has said with some elaborations and refinements.

Let me begin by restating in terms somewhat different from Professor Neusner's the issues of the debate between the separationists and assimilationists. It seems to me that what distinguishes the separationists' posture is not only the conviction that the "Jewish People" constitutes an historical and factual entity, but a fundamentally romantic vision of all things defined by them as Jewish. Within the separationist framework, Jewish learning, indeed, all Jewish life and history are perceived and presented as a grand romance, "a drama of self-identification symbolized by the hero's transcendence of the world of experience, his victory over it, and his final liberation from it."[2] With this perspective as a foundation, each act of learning can become a ritual of attachment to the heroic people, and each classroom session a rite of participation in the romance itself. The separationists' position virtually assumes a Jewish epistemology, allegedly derived from the historical and religious experience of the Jewish people, which should govern all Jewish learning regardless of its location. The separationists will argue that university disciplines, which originate in a non-Jewish intellectual setting, are not sacrosanct, and that any attempt to force Jewish learning into these established modes of investigation can fragment the unified and coherent life experience of an entire people into artificial and vacant compartments and thus deny the uniqueness and meaning of Judaism, the Jews, or both. Behind the separationist stance, I think, lies a nagging anxiety about misrepresentation, a persistent concern that university studies in Judaism will remake the romance of Jewish learning, of "being Jewish," into a satire, or worse, a tragedy.[3]

In principle there can be no quarrel with this position; it has firm warrant in both biblical and classical Jewish literature. The validation and support it provides are essential to the survival of the Jews as a group and to the continued vitality of their communal life. But there is little in the environment of universities to sustain or encourage this position.

---

[2]Hayden White, *Metahistory* (Baltimore, 1973: Johns Hopkins), p. 8.

[3]White (*ibid.*, pp. 7-11) uses these terms to represent different modes of writing history. My use of them here is somewhat less technical. On the question of "disciplines," see the instructive remarks of Lou H. Silberman, "The University and Jewish Studies," in Leon A. Jick, ed., *The Teaching of Judaica in American Universities* (New York, 1970: KTAV), pp. 9-19.

At the basis of university learning is the demand that people not only know what they are talking about, but also be able to communicate what they know to others in agreed upon ways. The uniform, technical language of academic disciplines, disparagingly labelled as "jargon," is designed to make such communication possible. The university's insistence on the accessibility of knowledge, however, presupposes an explicit rejection of private, self-enclosed worlds of experience and meaning that only can be transmitted to initiates. This universalistic posture of university studies in the social sciences and humanities results in a relativism that denies the possibility of extraordinary differences among groups or individuals and affirms that human beings everywhere and at all times are subject to similar pressures and vices. Consequently, all legitimately may be examined and understood according to standardized categories of inquiry. As Professor Neusner observes, the university obscures cultural differences. It should be underscored, however, that it primarily does so not with respect to what is to be studied, but rather with respect to how things are to be known and how that knowledge is to be expressed.

In one sense, therefore, the separationists' apprehension about Jewish learning in a university setting is justified. University learning will claim that the Jews differ in particular as a cultural and religious group from other such groups, but that they resemble the others in general. The Jews, their culture and religion therefore may be explored using the same universalistic criteria that are applied to other peoples, cultures, and religions. There can be no role here for arcane modes of knowing, no possibility of romance. But while university learning denies Jewish distinctiveness at one level, it exposes and affirms it at another. By subjecting disparate phenomena to a single standard of inquiry we discover that although peoples, cultures, and religions are comparable, they are not identical. More important, we are able to specify with accuracy and moderation the ways in which they differ from one another.

Let me illustrate what I mean with an example drawn from Professor Neusner's scholarly work. In his *A History of the Jews in Babylonia*, Professor Neusner offered a critical assessment of the figure of the Talmudic rabbi and the ways he exercised power and influence in Babylonian Jewish society of late antiquity. His depiction of the rabbi, unlike those of his predecessors, used not the circumscribed and self-validating standards set by the Talmud itself, but the universalistic criteria and analytical techniques supplied by the history of religions. He constructed his inquiry in terms of broad questions about the nature of religious leadership and enriched his investigation by comparing and contrasting the rabbi with types of religious leaders in other contemporary Babylonian religious groups. The result was a fascinating description of the rabbi as a "holy man." This first phenomenology of Jewish religious leadership sharply differentiated the rabbi from both monk and magus, and this analysis in turn helped determine those characteristics distinctive to rabbinism. It also opened the inner world of rabbinic Judaism to other scholars of religion who previously had regarded rabbinism as esoteric, uninteresting, or irrelevant.

This illustration suggests that we may further discriminate the separationist and assimilationist approaches to Jewish learning in terms of the dissimilar curiosities nurtured by each. From the perspective of ethnic studies, materials are deemed to be interesting because they are Jewish. Within an autonomous Jewish educational framework, whether departmental or institutional, curiosity tends to be parochial, and the questions brought to Judaic materials often focus on details and on the acquisition of specific, but not necessarily related, pieces of Jewish information. In disciplinary departments in universities the investigation of discrete Jewish phenomena is more likely to be pursued within a context of larger, more general questions about human imagination and behavior, questions extrinsic to particular Jewish concerns. There is, after all, an important difference between learning Jewish prayers and using Jewish liturgy to help explain and comprehend the phenomenon of human worship.

The dichotomy described above means that the imagination of assimilationist professors of Jewish subjects, regardless of where they teach, is shaped not only by the materials they study, but also by the problems they seek to solve. As Professor Neusner points out, we do not want to know just anything about the Jews, nor do we want to know everything about them. We want, rather, to understand something, some aspect of their history, culture, or religion. Our decisions as to which aspects are most interesting and engaging are conditioned by the disciplines we practice and the hermeneutics we employ to understand and explain what we think we know. As university professors, we claim not only that the study of Jewish texts is its own reward, but also that solving our own problems is its own reward, indeed, the only reward. It would be unfortunate to construe us as the new servants of Torah, for we ask Torah to answer our questions, and we do not worry if those questions are meaningful to any but ourselves. Our Torah, finally, is neither the Torah of tradition nor the Torah of the Jewish community. Indeed, to some who live outside the university, our words of Torah, modulated as they are by barren and alien walls, must ring with artifice.

The issues raised in Professor Neusner's essay, however, transcend the question of Jewish learning in the university setting. They go to the heart of the definition of the university itself. Professor Neusner argues that universities must be places in which people can learn for the sake of knowing, places where people can conjure and then try to solve their own intellectual problems. His essay serves as a warning against reshaping the exercise of learning to serve some external purpose, whether that purpose be identity with a people, sexual self-understanding, or the preparation for a career. The university exists to nurture the life of the mind, and its distinctive contribution is rooted in its refusal to follow any other agendum except that generated by its disciplines and its subjects. When universities begin to reshape themselves and their curricula according to a utilitarian model, their special responsibility is defaulted, and uniformity, mediocrity, and boredom cannot be far behind.

Response
Arthur S. Goldberg
University of Rochester

Professor Neusner's paper poses a serious problem for me. That is because I am so wholeheartedly in accord with his position that I find it difficult to obtain a critical purchase on his argument. The University is indeed a unique institution, and it is, indeed, assimilationist. It is unique in that truth is sought there and alleged truth is assessed there against "the test of evidence and falsification." While the epistemologies of the sciences and the humanities are not identical, they share an aspiration to common "standards for thought, reason, and logic." The University is assimilationist in that its members are more strongly committed to "the test of evidence and falsification" than they are committed to any particular idea system. With this assimilationist characteristic, I find myself wholly at ease, for the commitment to the criteria of reason and evidence is our only hope of pushing back the frontiers of ignorance.

A word or two of clarification may be in order about this assimilationist characteristic as a process. As new ideas are introduced, they are not diluted and absorbed into a homogeneous mass. Rather, as their truth value is judged against the criteria of reason and evidence, these ideas may displace some older ideas, modify some others, cause a rearrangement of the existing mix of ideas, raise new questions, and even become modified themselves. To the extent that a system of ideas is pressed against these criteria it goes through a refinement, in the process of which its truth value rises and the dross is squeezed out. Jewish studies have nothing to fear from such a process.

Indeed, no set of ideas with an initially substantial truth value need fear this process.

Having established that I am in, of, and for the assimilationist position with regard to the place of Jewish studies in a university setting, let me speak for a bit to the contribution which I believe Jewish studies can make to the intellectual life of the University.

There are many aspects to Jewish studies. There is the history of the Jews to be studied, the languages of the Jews, their migrations, their interactions with other cultures – to name a few. This particular sample fits very nicely with the disciplines of history, linguistics, demography, and sociology. There is not much question but that the study of the Jewish experience of life from these several perspectives will enrich the content of these disciplines – as wold the study of any other ethnic group's experiences of life. I would like to focus on a rather more distinctive and perhaps more controversial aspect of Jewish studies, namely Talmud. It is the study of Talmud in a university setting which makes the separationists uneasy. They are loath to have Talmud tested against any external standards. They prefer the risk of ossification to the risk of falsification. The secular scholars too are, at least in some instances, discomfited by the notion of the study of Talmud in a university setting. They fear that the criteria for judging truth value will be jeopardized by proselytizers. I believe that all of these fears are ill founded, as, in my view Talmud and the University are eminently suited for one another.

I am much indebted to Professor William Green for my perspective on this, for it is he who first offered me the following question as the central issue in Talmud, namely, "How shall a man know how to live his life so that God would be willing to live in his home?" When I heard Professor Green say that, it resonated profoundly with what I take to be a central theme in the intellectual life of a university. How does one live the good life? Of what does virtue consist? How shall one know? These issues have preoccupied even the progenitors of universities – Socrates wandering through Athens arguing with his students, Aristotle writing his lecture son ethics. Consider, for example, this assertion by Aristotle:

> Inasmuch as happiness is an activity of soul in accordance with perfect virtue, we must now consider virtue, as this will perhaps be the best way of studying happiness. [*Nichomachean Ethics*, Book I, Chapter 13]

To what does such an assertion speak, if not to the issues raised in Talmud? I believe that universities and Talmud intrinsically speak to very much the same issues, and that Talmud, as a living system of ideas, could hardly find a better setting than the University within which to address its central concerns. It has a great deal to contribute to that setting and much to derive from it.

From the perspective of the Jewish community, Professor Neusner's paper carries a profound message. He addresses the phenomenon of stultification of intellect within the Jewish community. It has been my own impression that within the contemporary Jewish community, slogans have come to replace ideas and customs have come to replace values. Therefore, I believe that we should take very seriously Professor Neusner's argument that

> commitment to the Jewish community as we now know it should be replaced by commitment to the values of the academic community so that in time, the Jewish community will be reshaped by the values of learning, gain renewed access to its own intellect.

For what is the Jewish community without a commitment to the values of learning and without a vibrant intellect?

From the perspective of the University, this is a most propitious time for the scholarly pursuit of Jewish studies – particularly as those studies speak to ethical questions. Indeed, there is a great need for the revitalization of religious and ethical studies in general. Our young people have too readily and for too long come to view the University as a place where one studies in order to learn how to make a living, rather than as a place to study in order to learn how to live a life. These same young people have come to hunger for ethical guidance. In their search for such guidance, they have turned to regions far from their own cultures – indeed, they have even generated instant religions and instant messiahs. Yet there are a growing number who are turning to the scholarly study of religion and ethics, and for them the University is a most appropriate place. For while, as Professor Neusner points out, it is not the proper role of faculty to teach students how to live a life, it is their proper role to help students identify central questions in such an inquiry, to exemplify for them care and integrity in the articulation and examination of ideas, and to teach them to recognize sophistry when they encounter it.

In his book *World of Our Fathers*, Irving Howe uses a beautiful phrase which well defines a central concern of the University, namely, "a life worthy of the idea of man." The search for such a life has been at the cultural and ethical core of Judaism from time immemorial. To the extent that Jewish studies are well articulated against the internal criteria of the University, we cannot but draw closer to that goal – "a life worthy of the idea of man."

5

"Being Jewish" and Studying About Judaism

*Inaugural Lecture of the Jay and Leslie Cohen Chair of Judaic Studies
Emory University, 1977*

I formulate in terms of Judaism the issue of descriptive and normative dimensions in the study of religions not because I am a Jew or because I must talk about things I know. The reason is that, in general, discussions of the relationship between religion and religiosity and the academic study of religion, or between piety and the academic analysis of piety, exhibit flaws of abstraction. Supposedly addressed to the generality of religions and conceived within the notion that piety is piety wherever it is found, these discussions actually homogenize all religions within the conceptual norms of Christian – and post-Christian – experience. They generalize on the basis of one very particular, if widespread, formulation of the question, never recognizing that the issue has been stated in a way distinctive to that one group alone. Many sorts of religions come under study, and diverse sorts of believers, sometime-believers, and nonbelievers engaged in study. I therefore shall state matters in the context of a single, small, and unrepresentative religious group, those Jews who also are Judaists, people of Jewish origin who also believe in and practice Judaism. In doing so, the theological norms of a concrete and carefully delimited religious tradition may be permitted to illuminate the discussion, something they simply cannot do when under discussion is piety or religiosity in general.

My argument is in two parts. First I propose to take up an important criticism of the academic study of religion, the view that by insisting upon detachment and disengagement, we place an obstacle in the way of

69

the understanding of religion. Students seeking religious knowledge for their own use do not find it in our classroom. The defense of the position that religions are to be described, not advocated, rests upon a theory of the limitations of the classroom. In the second part, I turn this theory into a critique of the descriptive study of religions. My point is that exactly the same limitations of the former position set the bounds for the latter. In point of fact both approaches to the study of religion – descriptive and normative – replicate a profound flaw in the humanities in general, a flaw which, I shall suggest, derives from the modes by which our minds grasp and respond to reality.

I

The academic study of religions in America and Canada and, more recently, in Britain, has developed a set of norms and convictions on the place of religiosity and individual belief in the classroom. We do not pray in classrooms. We do not advocate that students adopt belief in God, let alone specific theological positions. Our lectern is not confused with a pulpit. We do not preach. We teach. We do not teach religion, moreover, but we teach *about* religion, a distinction absolutely fundamental to our work. It goes without saying that we take as our principal responsibility the task of preserving objectivity about our subject, neutrality on its truth claims. Scholarly standards of careful inquiry and dispassionate examination of facts are the norm. These convictions form the theory in virtually all departments of religious studies in universities and colleges, whether public or private, Church-related or secular. If they are subject to serious challenge, it is not in the paramount journals and scholarly societies devoted to the academic study of religions. To be sure, these principles set up a norm by which all, when measured, may for one infraction or another be found wanting. Their practical applications and their implications, moreover, remain subject to much deep thought. Honorable people disagree on the requirements for the academic approach to religion-study. But if there is disagreement on the principle that religion in the academic setting is to be studied with detachment and objectivity (however these words be interpreted), it is not public. It enjoys no powerful advocacy known to me.

Yet one commonplace criticism of the position just now outlined, stated crudely and often advanced by sectarian advocates *pro domo*, is this: If Moses, Jesus, or Muhammed, let alone Confucius, Zoroaster, or Buddha, were to apply to your department, and if (in this truly eschatological moment), you actually had an opening, under no circumstances would you take seriously his application for a position. It is all right to teach about Jesus. But Jesus may not teach. On that basis you exclude believers an practitioners of faith. Twenty-five years ago the notion was widespread that believing Jews should teach what they believe as Jews, and so too with the varieties of Christians, with Moslems, Buddhists, and the like. Now, by contrast, you give preference to an attitude not merely of secularity and distance from the subject but of militant secularism. You do not give place to courses within religious belief, only courses about religious belief.

It is an evasion to reply that the classroom is not composed of members of a single church, so that advocacy and commitment leave no room for students who do not believe what is advocated (except that they convert). The pluralistic character of most universities is a fact, not a norm. It defines the context, but it cannot be asked to govern, or even to explain, what is done in context. It would, after all, be quite feasible to teach courses in Judaism for Jews, and courses in Judaism for non-Jews, and so with the other religions. It is not merely an evasion but deliberate fraud to claim that only people outside of a tradition, who cannot be suspected of advocacy thereof, are capable of scholarship and therefore of truly academic teaching about said tradition. The fact is that scholarship depends for its agendum, its definition of its task, upon social and cultural conditions. Scholars, moreover, study what interests them. A natural and perfectly legitimate criterion of interest is personal engagement.

If one is engaged by a subject, how is the subject not given the benefit of advocacy by its mere location at the top of the agendum of a course or department? Professors of Free Enterprise need not advocate free enterprise. By merely giving their courses, they cannot avoid placing into prominence, and therefore, exposing the claims of, free enterprise. Advocacy is beside the point. In this regard the Soviets provide us with a fine model. They have institutes of religion *and atheism,* surely a fairer and more objective way of phrasing the agendum, if truth claims of religion be at its top. I regard as false in fact and bigoted in spirit the claim that believers simply cannot engage in scholarship. If, therefore, we are not prepared to appoint Jesus or Moses, or people today who lay claim to do their work and embody their spirit and speak their message, the reason has to be made clear.

I wish now to restate the question as it is phrased by a colleague. After reading my published lecture, *The New Setting for Jewish Learning: Towards a Theory of University Studies in Judaism* (Rochester, 1976: The University of Rochester), Professor Arthur Green, University of Pennsylvania, replied as follows:

What I find disturbing about the university as a setting for most of Jewish studies in America is not so much its assimilatory character or its preference for the general over the particular, as its deep secularity. The conviction expressed in our curriculum seems to be that the sacred was an important part of human existence in primitive society, and perhaps survived right down to the eighteenth century, but it surely has nothing to do with contemporary existence. Given the uncomfortable relationship so many of our colleagues have with their own confessional backgrounds, departments of religious studies are the last places a truly searching student should go to learn about the religious life in any sort of personal way. I do not advocate missionizing. But I do wonder whether our highly self-conscious commitments to critical distance and objectivity do not do a disservice both to our students and to the subject we teach.

What I find pertinent in Green's observation is his question of whether we truly analyze and interpret the data of religion within the hemeneutical framework I outlined earlier. In the same letter, Green states an alternative worthy of serious thought: "A real commitment to the humanities must involve a search for wisdom and entails a kind of learning pertinent to personal growth and openness of mind. Our work suffers from the bifurcation of the search for wisdom from the quest for knowledge."

II

Our education and inclination prepare us to teach about these worldly phenomena, the effects, of religion. We bring to the classroom the facts produced in this world. We then try to analyze those data in accord with the worldly hemeneutic: the inner logic, the social meaning, the world-constructing power of myth, for example. The materials we study and teach bear other meanings. They claim to speak of another realm of reality, to know not only about this world, but also about the supernatural world and sacred things. We should need far more direct knowledge and experience of the world of the sacred to go in our teaching beyond the sole imminent facts of religion in this world. To analyze "sacred perspectives on the sacred," to view religion religiously, we should need a more complete grasp of how that other, transcendent world of the sacred is to be expressed in the utensils of language and concept, expressible (if not verifiable) experience. For so far as the classroom is not meant to be a place of religious experience and activity, it makes no room for such experience, but only the (admittedly antiseptic) analysis of such experience and its effects. The academic world is made of words, not supernatural experience. We do not sing, we do not pray, we do not meditate, we do not repeat sacred formulas, we do not fast, burn incense, dance, or otherwise move or control our bodies and attain visions. All we do is talk and think.

Having completed the descriptive task which words permit, we simply are not able to replicate the experience of the religious life. Even if all the students were Jewish, not all of them have the capacity or will to enter into the religious life of Judaism. But even if they all perceived themselves as religiously Judaic, what academic purpose, for example, would be served by having them first analyze the formal and conceptual structure of the Jewish Prayerbook, then pray it? No one can claim that having done the analysis, we have said all there is to be said. We have, however, said all that we can and should say upon the basis of our own knowledge and experience.

But there is a second, still more powerful limitation to the possibilities of bringing into the study of religion the experience or practice thereof. The religious life, complex and subtle, does not begin here and now, but in a rich range of experiences of birth and upbringing. Religious experience rests upon prior experience of home and family, church, nation, and society. It cannot be realized, let alone replicated, in the classroom solely upon the basis of analysis of a book and its ideas. For example, prayer itself depends upon altogether too subtle a context: light, sound, gesture, the organization of space, the presence of sancta, adepts, and virtuosi. Jewish prayer depends upon dancing, music, and silence; it is physical, expressed through the body; it is intensely personal, yet collective. The prayers which are said evoke worlds not present. When we *daven,* we move through many ages and situations. Yet in the person of the individual and in the reconstitution of the sacred community, they are very much at hand. How dare we pray except in the congregation of Israel, before the Torah of Israel? Analysis of the ideas and structure of the Prayerbook does not facilitate prayer. It may not even be pertinent to praying. It is simply a small movement toward interpretation and understanding.

To recapitulate this part of the argument: In the classroom all we have is language of a particular kind to deal with an aspect of an experience of a distinctive sort. Language cannot wholly replicate and encompass, but can only diminish, the totality of the religious world of Judaism. We indeed use language suitable for description and analysis. That language cannot recreate the inner meanings and rich dimensions of the Judaic religious life. We distort and destroy those inner meanings if we pretend that they are to be replicated outside of life's disciplines, the everyday experience of history's meanings. The classroom, which is to say, the act of study by itself, is inadequate. Even if all students were Jewish and wish to become Judaic, in the university we cannot promise them what we cannot give: the authentic growing-into-Torah and reaching toward, responding to God through Torah, which form the center of the Judaic life. This takes place in the setting of the this-worldly life and supernatural context of the Jewish people. One enters the Judaic situation solely by being raised a Jew or deliberately and in full consciousness turning toward Judaism. Nurture, whether from birth or from conversion, takes place in the encounter with life through the prism of Torah. It is in the streets and in the home. The intellectual side is subservient, even within the Judaic system, to the experience and construction of the world through the knowledge of Torah. Religiosity attained through nurture is not gained by academic inquiry.

The reason that we address the issue in terms particular to a single religious tradition should now be clear. The question takes its departure from a false conception of the theology and piety of Judaism, an inappropriate notion of what "expressing Judaism" or "personal engagement with Judaism" requires. Classroom advocacy of the truth claims of Judaism, of acceptance of Judaism as one's religion, is irrelevant to Judaism because mere confession of the truth of the tradition is insufficient. Only by a whole and complete definition of one's way of life in terms of the discipline of Torah, entering into the common life of the sacred community of Israel, devoting one's life to the demands of Torah upon all modes and aspects of life and thereby submitting to God's will, does one enter into the Judaic framework. Too small a part of life takes place in the classroom. Too modest a portion of the intellect is engaged by the claims to truth subject, to begin with, to advocacy in class. Advocacy is irrelevant to what is advocated. To state matters simply: Judaism does not happen in a classroom, and to begin with, it is not learned principally in books.

The issue in fact is phrased in terms of a religion which deems propositional advocacy to form the center of the religious life. Solely within such a notion of what being religious means does one confront the challenge of the "truly searching student who wishes to learn about the religious life in some sort of personal way." But I cannot think of any religion to which such a search pertains, other than a religion consisting wholly of philosophy. A philosophical religion expressing its worldview, constructing reality, and defining and shaping experience, entirely in terms of statements claimed to be of fact, does not exist. Religions exist in nominalist reality: churches, not religious institutions, Torah, not revelation, the God of Abraham, Isaac, and Jacob, or God the Father, the Son, and the Holy Spirit, not the divinity, Talmud Torah, not the study of facts about the Jews. True, we *talk about* religion, as though there were such a thing. But we *study* religions, concrete, specific things.

To conclude: Talmud Torah, the Hebrew words which signify study of the holy books, does not take place in a university classroom because Talmud Torah happens only in the community of Israel. It follows that what we do in the classroom is something quite different, even though the form – the act of study of books deemed by Judaism to be sacred and the processes of learning in them – is on the surface the same. What we do when we study religions is to be defined in its own terms. The classroom is incongruous to the religious quest. The holy community is the appropriate locus. The Judaic religious life in all details takes place within the setting of Israel, the holy community upon whom is set the mountain of Sinai. God without Israel is not the Lord (*hashshem*). Torah without God is not Torah. In religious context, Israel without Torah and God is nothing, a no-people. All elements of the triad define and delimit all others. To the tensions and inner stresses of the Judaic religious life, therefore of the quest for a point of entry into that religious life, the classroom is, in an exact sense of the word, *cosmically* irrelevant.

III

What do we legitimately undertake in the academic study of religion? We have now especially to confront the challenge of whether, and in what ways, what we do distorts the thing to which we do it, religions.

We do not distort something by describing some of its external traits. If I am able to explain to students some of the central symbolic and mythic structures of Judaism, to account for and clarify lines of their development through the ages, to demonstrate the complexity and subtlety of the tradition, so to call into question the possibility of defining as an *-ism* so diverse a corpus of phenomena, and yet to insist that definition is possible – if I can do these things, I have not taught the students something untrue to the subject. I have only not taught them everything true about the subject. The great methodologists of the academic study of religions have given us a dense agendum of questions to be brought to the data of the various religious traditions. In asking those questions, we do not inquire into all aspects of the diverse traditions. We interpret only those which impinge upon society and intellect, the shared imagination of the community of the faith, its capacity to shape the reality in which that community makes its life.

The whole truth of necessity eludes us. There are things we cannot know. Much which we do know we perceive only dimly and through a dirty mirror. But the delineation of the realm of knowledge marks out the frontier of ignorance: conceptual incapacity. The process of interpretation of things transcendent and the search for understanding of other, inner worlds begin and end in humility before the unknown. But the process and search do affirm that some things are to be understood in the immanent context of society and intellect.

In my view, the claim that only the insider, the participant, is able to study and fully understand a religious tradition constitutes a polite statement of obscurantism. For who is the insider, and who is further inside the tradition than some other, to tell us when we have reached the inner precincts of the temple of belief? I know no keepers of the grail, no guardians of the sanctum of the faith, possessed of the ultimate authority over us all to say, "Yes, this indeed is Torah and what it truly means." The corpus of diverse opinions on all important questions within Judaism testifies against the certainty claimed in behalf of the insider. The insider furthermore is apt to lose all perspective on the whole. The participant is unlikely to perceive the interrelationships between one religious tradition and all others, to understand that most basic fact about religions, which is their context within humanity. Accordingly, what interpretation is possible, what understanding is to be promised, without perspective on the whole of a massive historical religious tradition, on the one side, and on its still larger context as religious phenomenon, on the other?

The academic description and interpretation of religions nonetheless do distort the data of religions. But this is in a different way. The distortion is in the very act of academic perception. For the classroom is a place of talk. Its capacity to replicate the reality to be subjected to interpretation depends upon words. Through the processes of the intellect we recreate the thing we wish to examine. We lay forth its traits, define its terms, describe its modes of functioning, then ask about its meaning within the hermeneutic disciplines at hand.

The obverse side of the critique of the criticism of the academic study of religion is at hand. Since we do not dance, or sing, or pray, burn incense, fast, or mumble sacred formulas, it follows that all we do is try through words to lay forth what happens to those who do dance, pray, form transcendent community, interpret history, and thereby know god. The academic classroom by its nature and by definition effects a kind of subtle reductionism. Without intellectual articulation of their convictions intellectuals carry forward the belief that, through the intellect, reality is recreated and thereby subjected to interpretation. Our strength also is our weakness: our minds cannot but mislead us. In the study of religions in particular the act of learning begins in the reduction of religions to words. The misstep of learning is reductionism through intellectual reification.

What makes learning possible is the capacity to set into words things which are observed or experienced. What facilitates learning is the vast corpus of intellect produced within religions. For what we study is written texts, ideas, the language to which religions are committed. Yet the problem of correctly interpreting the holy books is exceedingly complex. For words are written down by someone, in some context. True, we may describe the person and the context. Yet words also continue to endure, take up a life of their own. The context changes, therefore meanings imputed to words change also. If, as I said, intellectuals maintain that through the intellect, they recreate and therefore interpret reality, then what is the reality laid forth by the words – the propositions of faith, the prayers, the stories – subjected to study? Is it that of the writer, or of a person who read and appropriated for his or her own life that which was written? Is it then a century, or two centuries, or a millennium after the text embarked on its journey through history? A central obstacle to the academic study of religions is the fact that religions change, and even though we accurately describe and interpret the world of a given religion at some one point in its history, that which we describe is not the totality of the religion under study. As intellectuals we construct systems. But the task of construction and interpretation is made rather complex by the fact that systems scarcely endure for a generation, while religions go on and on through time. This second aspect of the problematic of studying religions is now to be given appropriate emphasis. For my claim is not only that the intellect is insufficient to the replication of that which is studied. It also is that what the intellect is best able to do in this context, which is description and interpretation, is itself not congruent to that which is studied.

In the case of Judaism, for example, we have an exceptionally dense corpus of writings of intellectuals (intellectuals by definition) on the things which, through words, seem to them susceptible of inscription for transmission and study in the coming generations. It was their conviction that the study of the holy books they produced and handed on for transmission would succeed in evoking for the coming generations the truths set down in those holy books. They could come to such a conviction that writing things down is all right, specifically because they took for granted the words would be read in their very own context. Context is defined by both community and conviction. How could someone in fifty or a hundred years, living as I do and experiencing the world as I experience it, *not* precisely grasp the meaning of my words? But when those who do not stand within the context of the writers-down of words come to see those same words, how difficult it is to do so? In the study of religion, accordingly, deep calleth unto deep, the religious intellectuals, laying down the norms and meanings of their worlds in words, speak to the intellectuals who describe religions. By definition, the one is deprived of the power of speech, the other of the power of hearing. In the academic study of religions, the dumb address the deaf. The dumb, to be sure, in general are dead. But the living deaf pretend to hear. There is no remedy to this grotesque dilemma, because the classroom simply cannot serve for the replication of life's full and rich context. Even if we danced, sang, burned incense, or spent our fifty minutes with our students reciting Psalms, even if all our students were Jews and we all were rabbis, we still should not have entered into the realities both interpreted and created by these merely intellectual processes.

What impeded the authentically *religious* study of religions in the classroom also presents an obstacle before the authentically *academic* study of religions in the classroom. The changing reality we seek to describe and interpret is outside. We are inside. The reason is clear when we define that "we" who are inside. We are intellectuals, people who suppose that words will serve to create a context for the analysis and interpretation of reality. We take for granted the capacity of language and thought to correspond to reality. But the very statement of a thing obscures its character.

I offer for one evocative example what happened to me when I tried to define and describe cult in the setting of Israelite and Judaic religion of antiquity. I asked, "What is cult?" The answer, "Sacrifice." I: "True, but where is cult?" The answer: "Temple." "Fine," I said, "And what is Temple?" "A place of cult." "Splendid. And what happens in the cult?" "Sacrifice." This little colloquy left me with the uneasy sense that we had gotten nowhere, yet had used all the right words for the right things; there had been a true rectification of names. Then it occurred to me that the students had no visual perspective of sacrifice. I began again. "A priest gets up in the morning. He comes to the Temple. What does he do first to 'engage in the cult'?" Silence. Finally the wheels begin to turn. "He washes up." "Why does he wash up?" Silence. "Well, all right, he washes up. We'll talk about the reason later on. Then what does he do?" "He *sacrifices*." I (tearing my hair): "He does *what?*" "He sacrifices." "O.K.: *What* does he sacrifice? And what does he 'sacrifice' *with?*" "He 'sacrifices' an animal, a sheep." "Great. With what?" There followed along silence. finally, I: "How about a knife?" After general agreement that you 'sacrifice' a sheep with a knife, I asked, "Then, in this context, *what* is sacrifice?" "Taking a knife, taking a sheep, cutting the sheep's throat." This step forward yielded the next question: "What happens then?" It would be hopeless to list the answers – "the priest prays" "God is pleased" "everyone says psalms." No one proposed: "The sheep bleeds to death." After I contributed that stunning fact, I asked, "What happens to the blood?" And so it went.

In point of fact, the language I had used to approach this most central aspect of the Israelite and Judaic religious life, this "mode of serving God," had in fact obscured the exact reality of what is done, what really happens. *Temple* bears no relevance to the known experience of the students. Does *butcher-shop?* "Sacrifice" in our setting is so elegant and elevated a word, so full of noble and "spiritual" nuance, as to have been deprived of its concrete and ordinary meaning. It hardly needs saying that, when I returned to the matter of "purification" from "uncleanness" – that is, "the priest washes up" – another very long process of freeing ourselves from the burden of the meanings associated with our everyday language had to begin. Words had to lead us to reality both contained within and obscured by words. The lack of learning can be done in some measure. It is a long and painful process, to which we have to subject ourselves to begin with, our students only afterward.

If it is generally agreed, therefore, that the study of religions appropriate to the classroom is the description and interpretation of religions, then I think the requirements of description have more fully to be realized and spelled out. For I do not conceive that the work cannot be done. I argue only that it presently is not much attained.

The reason is, first, our stress, in the generality of courses in religious studies, upon the intellectual analysis of the work of intellectuals. We pay disproportionate attention to issues of faith in theological and other intellectually accessible form. That of course is to succumb to the temptation of the classroom, to the one thing it is easy to do there.

Second, description through words, as I have tried to illustrate, is incomplete when we have not made certain we have fully analyzed the words we use against the evolving thing the words are supposed to contain, recreate, or evoke. The large words of religious studies speak of things done by people who are not professors, and who would not grasp the words which *we* apply to the things *they* do. That of course is of no consequence. But the students to whom we speak also take up our language without understanding that to which it refers, imitate us without understanding, just as we may well imitate our teachers, the books we read, without taking that additional step of imagining the thing at hand. Using "sacrifice" instead of "take a knife and cut a sheep's throat and collect the blood," to return to my example, facilitates intellectual reflection upon vast and lofty things. It does not tell us in a concrete way exactly what happens, the thing about which we think.

If our being intellectuals stands in the way of our mind's work of description as much as it makes that work possible, the philosophical frame of mind within which our work is done limits our capacities at interpretation. For proper interpretation of religions requires the description of context, of the things which come before the thing we seek to interpret, the things which, round about it, form its setting, and those that come thereafter. Suitable description of religions requires us to set all things into relationship with all other things, sacrifice to Temple, priesthood, social caste, doctrine of atonement and sin, for example. If we capture these things all at once, as they balance with one another and form a whole house of meaning, we may begin to interpret and understand what holds the whole together, that ultimate point at which all things make sense. But the house of meaning is a house of cards. The cards themselves are cut-outs. When they form a house, it collapses, to be reconstructed in age succeeding age.

The movement and dynamism of religions require description over a long continuum, just as much as the static construct of religions is to be laid forth for some one moment. The histories of religions, not merely the phenomenon, the condition, of religions at some one moment in those histories, remain to be described. These histories, in my judgment, form the exegetical fulcrum for the interpretation of religions. Intellectuals' modes of thought are notoriously unable to cope with change. Endings and beginnings are disorderly. Systems are susceptible to philosophical description and analysis only when in their middle, stable stages. But the modes of thought of historians commit exactly the sort of reductionism for which, I have tried to suggest, philosophers bear guilt. For to them there are no systems, no worlds of meaning, but only sequences of ways in which for a moment things happen to fall together. The philosopher in the guise of anthropologist seeks to define and describe taxonomies of systems. The philosopher in the guise of historian asks for hemeneutic guidance on how these sorts of systems interrelate, how one dialectically arises from the last and generates the next. It follows that the work of description and interpretation is deeply flawed, both because the thing described and interpreted comes to us from intellectuals, and because we ourselves are intellectuals.

IV

The dilemma of religious studies is authentic to the character of its subject: religions. The nature of religions is to be traditional. As Jonathan Z. Smith states, "Regardless of whether we are studying texts from literate or nonliterate cultures, we are dealing with historical processes of reinterpretation, with tradition....For a given group at a given time to choose this or that mode of interpreting their tradition is to opt for a particular way of relating themselves to their historical past and social present." All religions which last for more than a moment have therefore to confront the dilemma of continuity, to find a way either to legitimate change or to obviate its meanings. *The way is through interpretation, in a synchronic framework, of the diachronic facts of faith.* And whether the expression of interpretation be through philosophy, theology, history, or myth, the task is invariably one and the same.

The dilemma of our work is elegantly captured in a myth of Talmudic Judaism, which for its part must find a way of bringing into relationship with the Written Scriptures the rich and divers developments of the Judaic religious life over the many centuries since Scripture. I quote the story at some length because it states, in its own way, the problem of continuity in religion, therefore giving concrete expression to the dilemma of students of religion: What is it that is subjected to description and interpretation? (Happily, the story also permits us to account for our unwillingness to appoint Moses to the faculty of religious studies in the area of Judaism.) It is found in Babylonian Talmud, Menahot 29B:

> Rab Judah said in the name of Rab:
>
> When Moses ascended on high, he found the Holy One, blessed be He, engaged in affixing coronets to the letters [of the Torah, that is, putting three small strokes on the top of various Hebrew letters in the form of a crown].
>
> Moses said, "Lord of the universe, who stays thy hand? [That is, is there anything lacking in the Torah, that these additions to the letters in which the Torah is written have to be added?]" He answered, "There will arise a man, at the end of many generations, by the name of Aqiva b. Joseph. He will expound upon each tittle heaps and heaps of laws."
>
> "Lord of the universe," Moses said, "Let me go and see him."
>
> He replied, "Turn around."
>
> [Moses then is transported to the academy of Aqiva.] Moses went and sat down behind eight rows [of Aqiva's disciples, and he listened to the discourses upon the law.] He was not able to follow the arguments or to understand what was said. He became ill at ease. But when they came to a certain subject, the disciples said to the master, "How do you know it?"
>
> Aqiva replied, "It is a law given to Moses at Sinai."
>
> Moses then was comforted.

Moses then returned to the Holy One, blessed be He, and said, "Lord of the universe. You have such a man – and yet you give the Torah through me!" He replied, "Be silent, for much is My decree."

Then Moses said, "Lord of the universe. You have shown me his Torah. Now show me his reward."

"Turn around," said God. Moses turned around and saw people weighing out the flesh of Aqiva at the butcher shops [for Aqiva is believed to have died as a martyr in the time of the Bar Kokhba war, and his skin was flayed from his body].

"Lord of the universe," cried Moses, "Is such Torah and such the reward for Torah?!"

"Be silent," God replied, "for such is My decree."

The second part of the story introduces a highly dissonant element, since, to begin with, the issue of the reward of Aqiva is hardly required by the issue of the story at the outset. Had the tale ended with the comforting of Moses, it would have been complete and wholly satisfactory.

The issue, it is clear, is the accommodation of change to the condition of a continuous religion which claims to be perfect, therefore unchanging. The central claim of Judaism is to be continuous with Sinai, just as a principal concern of Christianity has been to establish its continuity with the Old Testament. The problem to be solved by the Judaic thinkers is not so easily solved as that facing the Christian ones. The latter claim that Torah is fulfilled at the end, in Christ. The former for obvious reasons can lay no equivalent claim in behalf of Moses, and therefore turn the matter on its head. The continuity is projected at the outset, not at the end. The Oral Torah is present at the beginning of the Written one. Everything which the greatest master of the Oral Torah would say already had been said by the great authority of the Written one.

In historical context, the story assigned to Rab, an authority of the third century, deals with and expresses an opinion on the claim, laid forth in behalf of Mishnah, to be Torah. Mishnah, a vast code put together toward the end of the second century, is set before the people of Israel as God's will, as Torah to be kept by the Jews. Yet Mishnah's laws are assigned to first and second century authorities, who rarely purport to base their views upon Scripture, to reach their opinions through exegesis of the Written Torah. The Oral Torah therefore is subject to criticism of two kinds. First, its claim to give law upon the foundation of reason, rather than scriptural exegesis, is challenged (in Sifra, for instance). Second, its claim to be Torah is made to depend, as in the present story, upon its relationship to Mosaic revelation, which is to say, if Moses had not already said it, then Aqiva could not be believed.

But of course the critique also contains within itself a formidable defense. Mishnah indeed does depend upon exegesis. Moses truly did say what the latter day authority, Aqiva, without citing Mosaic revelation, also says. The tradition is continuous. The continuity consists – so it is claimed – in the unfolding of the inner logic of the law, the discovery, by later generations, of meanings logically implicit in the words of earlier ones. The whole, of course, testifies to the deeply intellectual character of the people who to begin with ask the question and find the answer. For it is they who perceive the discontinuity to begin with. The intellectuals find themselves constrained to ask the historical question of data which, to begin with, are meant to construct an enduring reality, not subject to history. Had the story ended with Moses' being comforted, we should have concluded with this observation: The inner dynamic of Judaism, its capacity both to respond to the changing circumstances of history and to accommodate the effects of change within its enduring, unchanging world of meaning, corresponds to, is replicated by, the dilemma of the academic study of religion.

For the limited capacities of intellectuals, studying religion begins in the use of language for the purpose of study, both to contain and to create reality. And reality cannot, in the nature of things, find whole and permanent place within language. Language best serves to give unchanging names to things which are supposed to remain always the same. It is suited to the one-time rectification of names. But the names it gives obscure the changing things which are named, place over them a veil by which the intellect both grasps and misunderstands that which is subject to thought, the thing beyond. The naming of things generates the forming of systems and structures of names. These, in the nature of things, must be static and unchanging, for structures or systems serve only so long as they stand still and remain in balance. A system which changes in even one of its constituents changes in them all. the system then described is no longer the system which has been described.

A taxonomy of systems will not serve, unless the processes by which one system yields the next and derives from the last, accommodates new elements and sloughs off old ones, are both documented and then themselves systemically described. If all that endures, in the work of studying religions, is an account of the dynamics of change, then religion is described as it never has been experienced, solely as a process of becoming, but not as a state of being, understanding, and enduring. And yet, we should have concluded, the central dilemmas of our work accurately correspond to and replicate the character of the data which are subject to our descriptive and interpretive labor. In that wry and ironic fact is to be located the apologia for the infirmities and incapacities of our intellect: in mind we indeed do construct flawed reality corresponding to flawed reality outside.

Yet the story does not end with Moses' being comforted. It raises two dissonant notes, neither of them within the original melody. We cannot expect the question, Why is more Torah needed? to be followed by, Why is *Moses* needed? And had the story ended there, it still would have been complete. Why then ask, "You have shown me his Torah, now show me his reward?" The first of the two notes strikes a dissident chord, and so does the second. Still more disconcerting is the story's twin-response: "Be silent." "That is how I want things." Why ask a question, if you have no answer to it?

We surely cannot deem the story apologetic or place it into the category of didactic tales either. "Why Moses and not Aqiva? Because God wants it that way" – *cui bono?* For whom is such a question deeply relevant. "Why a reward of martyrdom? Because God wants it that way" – *cui bono?* To whom is the question of reward compelling? Why the way of martyrdom at the end? In the context of what I think is the shallow apologetic for Judaism constructed by nineteenth and twentieth century philosophers of Judaism, the one thing we should not have anticipated is invocation of silence before the unreasonable divine decree. We should find that Moses is preferable to Aqiva because – with diverse, rationalist answers given to complete the thought. Martyrdom will be set into the context of Israel's suffering; we shall hear about Job; and the story will be inserted whole into a homogenized mixture of homilies.

But that is not what happens in Rab Judah's report of Rab's story. In all its specificity and concreteness, the story speaks for, and to, someone. To whom is the question important: Why Moses and not Aqiva? To whom, if not the person who identifies with Aqiva and wants to find justification for his participation in the creation and relevation of the Torah of Moses. Why Moses and not *me* – since I self-evidently discover truth not stated by Moses (if, to be sure, to be located within the words Moses did say)? The answer, I think, is self-evident once the question is asked as I have asked it. The question troubles the intellectual who sees his own contribution to be one of worth, yet who also is constrained to locate that contribution within the processes of tradition. It is a question for the schools. Moses, not you, because God wants it that way. And if you ask, why me, and not Moses, the answer is the same. The processes of mind are subject to God's will. God made the mind, you use it. And the matter of reward need hardly detain us. For who can deem self-evident a tie between the achievement of the intellect and the reward of this world? Who if not the intellectual? In a time of martyrdom, why should Aqiva *not* be martyred? Why is it not obvious that Torah invokes no privilege within the community of Israel? Learning does not invest the learner in a cloak of immunity from the condition of Israel as a whole. Such is the divine decree: Be silent.

V

It is difficult to imagine a more just punishment of intellectuals than the penalty of silence. To be told that, at some points, in response to some questions, the answer is found in silence is to invoke the notion that truth is found in what is whole, in the completion and complementarity of opposites. The work of intellectuals is conducted in words. Their thought, which is their being, is to give form through speech not only to thought itself but to the thing to which thought is devoted. We remind ourselves, therefore, that, just as the whole consists of both speech and silence, just as speech is only one side of the unity of which the other side is silence, so our whole work consists of opposites.

The one side is the *hubris* of thinking that we may know and grasp things. The other is the *humility* of admitting the limitations of thought itself. The one side is the exclusion of Moses from our faculty because we do not need him. The other is the devotion of the faculty to the study of the one we do not need, even to the exclusion of the Torah of the one who engages in that study. We argue that the classroom is not a suitable place for the expression and practice of religion. For the same good and substantive reasons it also is not a wholly satisfactory locus for study *about* religion.

Critical distance and objectivity do not do disservice to religions about which we teach. It is our own frailty: the incapacity of mind, the distortion effected by learning, therefore teaching. This, I believe, captures the paradox in which we make our being, the ineffable tragedy of mind's incapacity to do its work, to grasp the human condition. For the mind too is mortal. In thought about itself, mind cannot transcend its own participation within the human condition. We cannot be more than what we are. That is why God tells us, through death, to be silent: Ask no more, risk no more, think no more.

6

Professors or Curators?
Universities or Museums?
The Case of Jewish Studies

On the occasion of receiving the Distinguished Humanitarian Award for 1983 of the Melton Center of Jewish Studies at the Ohio State University, 1983

I

When the study of the Jews and Judaism entered universities, the subject came as part of what we now realize formed a new wave of humanistic learning. The new humanities comprised subjects never before studied – histories, literatures, philosophies, religions, human experiences and insights formerly neglected. What happened in the 1960s and early 1970s turned out to be a considerable expansion in the established curriculum of humanistic learning in American and Canadian universities. Departments of history, formerly centered upon American and Western European history, made a place for regions and groups formerly ignored, such as Asia, on the one side, and blacks and Jews on the other. Programs and departments of literature, formerly interested in English, American, French, German, and Russian literature, began to ask students to read Afro-American and Latin American writings. The single most dramatic development of the 1960s proved to be the opening of the study of religion to encompass traditions and religious communities beyond Christianity, first and foremost, Judaism. In these and other ways, therefore, the humanistic disciplines paid attention to history, literature, and religion of groups formerly assumed to have none worth studying.

If we ask ourselves why at just that time, university humanists discovered importance in subjects formerly not recognized at all, we may point to three factors.

First, in the 1950s, America had assumed a considerable position in world affairs, with the result that Americans took an interest in parts of the world formerly beyond the horizon. Accordingly, Russian studies were born, and alongside, the conception of area studies took shape. An area or region such as the Soviet Union, or the Near and Middle East, or North Africa, might provide the focus for diverse disciplines and their practitioners: historians, literary specialists, not to mention anthropologists, geographers, sociologists, political scientists, scholars of religions. Once the iron-hold of the established areas and regions – Western Europe mainly, America secondarily – gave way, area studies would encompass the whole of human civilization. Indeed, the first important break with convention lay in the establishment of American studies as a recognized field of not only literature and history, but everything else. Now once the universities had made a place for regional studies, it would be difficult to include one region and yet exclude some other.

The reason for the difficulty, second, lay in the entry, into the classes of those whose opinions counted, of formerly submerged or ignored groups. Whether constituted as a group by race, ethnic origin, religion, or gender, these groups wished to make their presence felt in higher education. Most could not state exactly what that ought to mean. But they knew they did not wish any longer to be ignored, treated as invisible. Who were they? Jews and Catholics, then blacks, Puerto Ricans and "other Hispanics," Asian-Americans, American Indians, not to mention Scandinavians, Italians, and Poles, and women – the list is long and varied. The components of the list do not compare to one another, except in the shared aspiration to enter the academic curriculum. As I said, no one could say for sure what that entry ought to mean. But with the enormous diversification of the constituency of universities, with Jews no longer carefully counted one by one and instructed not to count at all, with blacks no longer completely isolated, with other groups no longer forgotten, with women no longer merely tolerated so long as they acted as men wanted them to, universities clearly had to change. They had to come abreast of fundamental changes already taking place in the character of American society and culture. Social change produces symbol change. The curriculum of a university, whatever else it does, serves as an enormously effective symbolic statement about what matters and what does not.

So with the emergence of America as a world power with global interests and with the glacial shifting of the structure of American society to provide a final accommodation for the new immigrants' children of two and three generations earlier (including the black immigrants from farm to city and South to North), the demand for the end to exclusion in society carried echoes even into the campus of the university. These two factors – a change in the nation's politics, a shift in the nation's catalogue of recognized groups – joined with yet a third to produce the changes I have characterized as the birth of the new humanities.

That third change affected the universities alone. It consisted in the effects of the tidal wave of growth, as the generation of the post-war baby boom reached university age, on the one side, and as the proportion of college-age young people choosing to go on for higher education vastly increased, on the other. These two facts joined to impose an enormous increase in size upon old universities and to force the creation of new universities, colleges, community colleges, and the like. What followed in the age of unprecedented expansion, including inclusion, in the college population, of groups formerly excluded from it, could have surprised no one. New teachers had to be hired. These teachers could no longer come only from the protected castes – "Anglo-Saxons" and those who acted like them. So just as women demanded a place and attention in the curriculum, so some women found a place, also, in faculties, as did Jews in numbers unthinkable a generation earlier, Catholics, once no more welcome than Jews, and pretty much anybody who could present appropriate credentials. The homogeneity of old American universities, with their old American faculties and their old American names and genealogies, gave way. A small indicator of the shift derives from the development of professing Jewish communities in college towns in which, formerly, Jews served as a curiosity at best. As one of the first Jews to reach tenure at Dartmouth College, I remember what things were like, how much change I brought in my very conviction that, at sundown on Friday, something changed in Hanover, so far as I was concerned.

II

Once universities had opened their doors to the much larger and more diverse social and ethnic constituencies than they had ever known, the question confronted faculties and students alike: what do we do now? The answer lay in the decision to do more than had been done before. That meant that students would seek to study what was familiar in their own background. But this was quite natural and just as students had always done. The old Americans had always known what was theirs – Classics, after all, was a gentleman's hobby, English literature belonged to the descendants of English immigrants, and American history was the history written by the old Americans' great-grandfathers. A certain snobbery, of course protected these scheduled subjects; people absorbed the prejudice that, quite naturally and predictably, these were things *any* educated person should know. Knowing these things, this list of selected books (the one hundred books for the one hundred families that count) – that knowledge defined education. Hence a core curriculum and general education seemed possible. No one needed to ask about the excluded hundreds of thousands of books, classic to the excluded groups, and the millions of excluded families, out of which students now came. Everybody knew what was what: what was of worth and represented taste, what shaped thoughts worth thinking, what defined values worth adopting. And, it should be added, people who knew these worthwhile things also could look forward to careers of worth and standing: in banks, law firms, corporate offices, hospitals, and universities, and the other protected professions reserved for those who knew the scheduled subjects and came from the right castes.

All that had to change, and it has changed. But no one has yet reckoned with how to take hold of the change and make sense of it. For the change proved not entirely for the good. True, the old humanities may have insisted upon Classics and biblical Hebrew, but not Italian and never modern Hebrew; American and Western European history, but not Latin American, Canadian, or Eastern European history, let alone Asia, let alone Africa, let alone Polynesia, which have no histories (an opinion I myself took for granted as a youth); American and British literature, but not Afro-American literature and not Polish or French-Canadian. But the old humanities preserved not only privilege but also a center, a sense of purpose. Their imperial view did encompass everybody. That is the main point. The old humanists indeed imagined that they had something to say to the whole of humanity and that what they had to say demanded a universal audience. The established humanities could indeed point to books they believed everyone should read. And they could say why. The same reasons pointed to traits of intellectual excellence and relevance. They therefore could imagine such a thing as a general education. So, they held, people could determine why one book did matter more than another, and why one philosophical tradition deserved close and careful scrutiny, while another preserved mere gibberish. The power of the conventional and established humanities lay in the exercise of educated taste and reasoned judgment. The promise of the old humanities to impose order upon the chaos of information, to sort things out and to select some few that truly changed persons and nurtured character and culture – that promise has never met competition from the motley crowd of new humanities now demanding entry to the campus, giving only politics as the reason.

For what did the new humanities offer to justify their entry into the realm of the disciplined intellect? The mere presence of a new sort of human being, formerly excluded, hardly constituted a persuasive argument. After all, that new person, whether black, Catholic, woman, or Jew, could readily enter the classics of the established curriculum and adopt its values. Generations of "minorities" had done so. But what universally accessible human experience did the new constituencies bring to the campus, to measure up to the classics of human intellect that, all together, had constituted the old humanities? Where was the Jewish Aquinas or Plato, the black Shakespeare, the Catholic equivalent to the Reformation that everyone studies with such admiration? And, when the new humanities pointed to their heritage of art, music, fiction, and poetry, few were prepared to take a look. So people took for granted, both old and new alike, that the blacks would come, to be sure. But then blacks would study what blacks had done. Jews would study Jewish studies. Women would study women's studies. But everyone, anyhow, would still study the familiar philosophy, the Shakespeare, the Reformation that everyone had always studied, in the ways in which everyone had always studied them.

So was formed the benign consensus of the 1970s: insiders teaching private things to insiders, and everyone learning public things as they had always been taught. Everyone for a time accepted the compromise. The newcomers felt quite at home, as well they should, having never left their ghettoes. The established humanities retained their ultimate governance. Making room for newcomers, they found themselves essentially unchanged. The old privileges endured and did not even have to be shared. What emerged, then, through the 1970s, was curricular tokenism, a kind of intellectual affirmative action: the black women receptionists, the clever Jews in the research department, to be sure – but the board of directors would come from the same good folk that had supplied members for generations past. Everyone would be contented.

Unhappily, the easy compromise of the 1970s has fallen away. The new humanities cannot sustain themselves within its terms. The established humanities turn out unable to explain themselves any longer. The newcomers prove inadequate to the labor, and the old timers have fallen into bankruptcy. How so?

The new humanities, in their dominant form, lay no important claim upon the university. They consist of Jews teaching Jewish things to Jews, and blacks to blacks, and women to women, as I said. But universities understand themselves as places where everybody speaks to whom it may concern. Scholars speak about truth and matters of scholarship and interpretation. None sustains private truth and speaks of inaccessible experience and demands assent to unreasoned interpretation. Accordingly, the established distinction between insider and outsider, upon which the new humanities have built, finds no solid ground in the foundations of universities.

The new humanities, moreover, lay no claim to have much to say to the community at large. So they offer no reasoned counter to the argument that some things do matter more than others, white things more than black, Aquinas more than Maimonides, the Old Testament as Protestants read it more than Scripture and tradition as Catholics know them or as "the whole Torah of Moses, our rabbi," as Jews revere it. Once the new humanities conceded that theirs was an essentially private and particular heritage, to be promoted for parochial purposes (to give blacks self-confidence, to persuade Jews to remain Jewish), they also turned themselves into mere pressure groups on the campus, extensions of political forces deriving from outside the campus.

The result for black studies has proved disastrous. The *Washington Post* reports, in an article by James Lardner (December 3, 1982), that in the late '60s and early '70s, there were more than 500 formal programs in black or Afro-American studies. Today only 275 programs survive, of these, only 65 or 70 departments. Scholars of black studies concede that their field has entered "a state of near-crisis." Why? Because the black students themselves avoid black studies. The scholars excuse themselves by explaining that the students are "more job-conscious and more interested in courses that will make them employable." This is pure self-indulgence. In this same period Classics has enjoyed a renaissance, although few jobs these days demand knowledge of Attic Greek or the ability to read Plato in the original. Lest the *Washington Post* report be regarded as exceptional, I point also to Edward B. Fiske's article in the *New York Times*, January 13, 1983. He too reports that, in black studies, enrollments decline, and while people once estimated there were as many as 800 black studies programs, today estimates fall in the range of about 500. Enrollments exhibit a decline of approximately 25 percent from the highs of a decade ago. Anyone who doubts that the same story may be told of Jewish studies and other ethnic studies needs only to attend a meeting of the learned societies of those fields. The atmosphere in times past provided more evidence of hope and energy.

Not only the newer subjects in the humanities, but also newer disciplinary foci give evidence of regression. The new field of the academic study of religion, which was born in the later 1940s and fully realized in the 1960s as part of the larger development under discussion here, grows old and feeble. At its national meeting just now the scholars held a caucus of "endangered departments." One participant guessed, "Every religion department from Springfield, Missouri, to the tip of Maine is endangered, whether the department chairmen know it or not." The simple fact is that people take for granted you can have a university without black, Jewish, women's, or religious studies, but you cannot have a university without history, English, philosophy, or sociology.

What went wrong? The new humanities have not yet taken the measure of universities. Universities have not yet imparted their distinctive character to the new humanities. That is one fact, with two complementary effects. The new humanities have a future in universities only if they will join the sort of discourse that universities nurture. The university, for its part, must build its future upon the broadest social foundations and draw upon the deepest cultural resources of human experience and culture. And that can happen only when the university demonstrates, as it has not yet shown, the universal power of its program of inquiry to illuminate the analysis of human experience across the globe, to make interesting and public what is presently self-serving and private. So each side, whether new or the old, the outsider or the one at home, bears part of the responsibility for the reform of the new humanities, and, with that reform, the renaissance of the academic humanities as we now know them.

III

At issue in universities always and everywhere is only one thing: scholarship. By scholarship I mean systematic learning of important things, the conduct of experiments to test theories, the pursuit of possibilities of knowledge – in all, the game and play of unending learning, purposeful curiosity, pointed and skeptical argument about what we think we know. What matters in the end, and decides what universities make a difference and what do not, is solely scholarship.

In universities, to be sure, frail humanity works on lesser things. Wars are fought for trivialities such as this one's good name and that one's right to work or self-respect. But however things appear to the ones who invest their energies in politics, in the end truth, meaning scholarship, settles all substantial questions. The difference between universities and other large institutions is that in universities in the end you do not build a career on the blood of someone else. You cannot achieve lasting importance through politics, even through popularity, but only through intellectual achievement. That is the stern fact of life, the unyielding law of institutions of learning.

Scholarship by its nature pays no attention to claims or privacy. A proposition that one cannot understand unless qualified by gifts of genealogy or other-than-intellectual standing gains no hearing at all. A course on a subject only Jews can understand will not endure and in the end will attract no Jews. A book that speaks to people only if to begin with they believe the book to be true or self-evidently important will enjoy a long life on the library shelf. The binding will never suffer endless openings and closings. Such a book is a mere curiosity, something for anthropology to interpret, not for the humanities to confront. Such a course serves no relevant purpose. In the end, even those amenable to special pleading will turn away. For, as I said, at issue in universities is scholarship alone. Scholarship, as we know it, comes to us from the age of reason and speaks to us of what is subject to public scrutiny and reasonable judgment.

That is not to argue that a book for a handful of believers will never find its readers beyond those believers, or that a course directed to a preselected audience will never reach outsiders. It is rather my view that such books, such courses, in the end go the way of all claims at reaching judgments through other than critical and reasonable modes of thought. They enjoy the fate of all allegations of a truth we know a priori, and not through inductive inquiry and testing, all convictions about a knowledge of reality exempt from processes of verification and falsification – the oblivion of all deductive propositions. Scholarship as we practice it is inductive, aims at falsifying or verifying all claims to truth, subjects all propositions to the same critical and reasonable modes of thought, and so, in all, as I said, comes to us from the age of reason.

We organize culture and preserve learning in more than a single way, that is, through more kinds of institutions than one. Universities constitute only one sort of institution of learning. In addition, for Judaism, to *yeshivas,* there are, after all, museums. They are staffed by expert curators. Museums also preserve knowledge. Curators also know a great deal. The difference between a university and a museum, between a professor and a curator, may emerge from one fact: the trait of how facts are displayed. In a museum people lay things out, they show the artifacts of culture, the glyphs and tablets that preserve it. The curator proves expert on the details of a given culture. the highest form of learning is ethnography, the accurate description on a well-preserved culture, the reliable portrayal of what a social group has made to express and preserve its viewpoint. A museum may accommodate what a group deems private and serves to preserve what people claim to be

Professors or Curators? Universities or Museums?

unable to communicate. That is the power of a museum, the gift of the curator, the contribution of ethnography.

When professors serve as curators, scholarship falls into one of two inappropriate categories. Scholars either return to that level of culture we know as hunting and gathering. Or they engage in the game of show-and-tell. Or they do both. They may achieve stunningly expert knowledge of details, lovingly and expertly hunted down and gathered. They then present what they have collected in the secure knowledge that others implicitly concede the self-evident importance of the collection. So scholarship becomes no more than one of its essential components: ethnography alone. Then the professor serves as a curator, the university as a museum, and all the different subjects of the humanities come to place, each one in its room, all of them in their carefully arranged showcases.

What is right with all this is simple: without ethnography, there can be no anthropology. So too without the work of hunting and gathering, showing and telling, there can be no substance to the humanities. What is wrong is equally self-evident to me: the work in the end proves mindless because no one wants to make any points. No one argues any propositions relevant to anyone outside the room, the showcase, the tray, the artifact itself. When universities treated ethnic studies as special, when practitioners of those studies claimed to speak only to their own kind, then scholarship fell away. So far as the new humanities were to flourish, it would be through stupefying learning about what no one much cared to know. Playing an endless game of show and tell, justified by self-indulgent special pleading, the professors of the new humanities hunted and gathered everything but a reason for their profession. For their part, the universities accommodated what in fact most people despised and would dismiss as soon as they decently could. For universities are not museums, and professors mean to add to knowledge, not only preserve and display it.

IV

Since universities draw nurture from the societies that sponsor them and the politics that give effect to social policy, universities will hardly benefit from reversion to the old world of institutionalized prejudice and cultural snobbery. American society will never tolerate the reintroduction of quotas to exclude Jews, let alone the implementation of the bigotry that blacks cannot learn and women should not. For their part, the new humanities fail the universities and the society that depends upon them, if they continue the exclusionary theory of themselves. The task of the new humanities is to gain legitimate entry into the intellectual life of the universities. The task of the universities is to insist upon the same principles of reasoned discourse and public accounting of all propositions that have framed scholarship and defined learning we deem worthwhile. Both parties have to move from the initial stage of an uneasy accommodation of the old to the new, the reticence of the new to gain true entry into the old.

How shall we move to the next stage in the labor of bringing the new humanities into universities? I mean, how shall we frame matters so that universities may gain the strength of the great creative forces of our day, represented as they are by new groups coming of age, new bodies of learning demanding analysis, new sorts of human experience requiring interpretation.

Let me frame the answer in terms of the curriculum. How shall we achieve the integration of the new humanities within the university's conception of its own work? To begin with, let me state my own philosophy: *I teach students.* By the way, what I teach to students is about Judaism – in that order. To generalize, we teach two things: (1) a subject to (2) a student. What we teach students, through any subject, is about thinking, about using their minds for specific tasks. The curriculum then consists of two components: first, information we offer, which students learn, and, second, our example of how we compose that information into intelligible propositions, arguments about possibilities, which students may choose to imitate and improve. Whether we teach undergraduates or graduate students, the issue is the same. Students should be concerned with modes of analysis and means of interpretation, through which they learn the particulars of information. When we impart information without articulating how we have formulated matters and worked them out in one way rather than some other, we do only part of our work, the part, alas, most rapidly forgotten or rendered obsolete. In the phrasing of my co-worker, William Scott Green, University of Rochester, "Teaching means to teach students how to do something, how to know something, how to understand something."

By this criterion, one subject serves as well as any other, the history of the Jews as much as the history of the ancient Romans or the medieval French or the modern Americans, the literature of the American blacks as much as the literature of the English, the religious world of Islam as much as that of Christianity, the Roman Catholic experience of Christianity as much as the Protestant – not to exclude the woman's view of things as much as the man's. For whatever we teach stands or falls by the same criterion: does the subject at hand present the possibility of analyzing generally intelligible propositions? Does the area of learning generate theses worth sustained testing, ideas capable of providing insight beyond themselves and transcending the limits of the world that gave them first light? To accord to white male experience the status of the norm and black or female experience the status of the abnormal then no longer proves a proposition worth attention. For human experience properly described, analyzed, and interpreted speaks to us all. But without analysis and argument, no experience *self-evidently* establishes the norm (or diverges from it).

Accordingly, universities engaged in scholarship not only accommodate the new humanities. They no longer can imagine scholarship in ignorance of the corpus of human experience and achievement taken up in those new humanities. Rigorous thought about what matters by definition focuses then upon black as much as white, as much as biology or anthropology, respectively, inquires into the blood of anyone or the social culture of any group. The very nature of the disciplines and discourse of university scholarship requires the full recognition of the new humanities alongside the established ones. Why? Because we cannot do our work without them all.

What must come to an end, however, has also to be specified. Let me express the matter in terms of Jewish studies. Jewish studies locate themselves in universities. But they have yet to become part of universities. They remain an area of learning in which the bulk of the practitioners see themselves as part of a world outside of universities: intruders. In that other world, the familiar realm of Jewish learning practiced by Jews for Jews, Jewish learning regards itself as self-evidently important and valid. The questions it raises – questions of fact, questions of interpretation – emerge from the Jewish experience treated in isolation from the experience of the rest of humanity. Those questions are urgent because Jews need the answers. The way in which one finds the answers gains definition from established modes and procedures of Jewish learning in particular. These turn out to be conducted essentially beyond the accounting to a broader range of learning and in behalf of an essentially private constituency.

So Jews write books for Jews about Jews and imagine no broader public. Scholarship deemed in this context to be great proves erudite and technical, self-absorbed and narrow, limited and parochial. We admire the erudition; we must master the technicalities. We in universities, however, remove ourselves from our life when we accept the limitation, the parochiality, above all the self-absorption. The principal problem derives from the failure to treat problems or answer questions. Jewish learning in Jewish auspices provides information. It rarely makes the effort to relate that information to something beyond itself.

When scholarship is at issue, then textbooks emerge that espouse a viewpoint, find organization within a theory, propose to answer a question or solve a problem. But textbooks for Jewish studies in general disgorge information. Scholarship yields a curriculum, a systematic program of orderly learning, through which students learn how to do first one thing, then the next. Just as the field of religious studies has yet to develop a curriculum, because it lacks a program of study, so the field of Jewish studies yields nothing one might call systematic organization of the subject (except for instruction in elementary Hebrew). A field with no agenda, (in William Green's phrase) no cognitive purpose, no disciplined curiosity also nurtures no curriculum. Without a limited program of inquiry, without generally understood (if not universally accepted) standards by which we can tell a bad piece of work from a good one, without a reasoned problematic and a curiosity subject to explanation and transmission, Jewish studies also generate no energy. So we find the source of the lethargy. That is why arguments about why Jewish students are duty-bound to take courses in Jewish studies today circulate as a rationale for the field. It is the usual appeal to guilt. And that explains also the intellectual lethargy and academic bankruptcy of the Association for Jewish Studies, the American Academy of Jewish Research, and the other academic learned societies that claim to embody Jewish studies in meetings from year to year and in journals lacking all cogency.

When scholarship is at issue, then we can point to how a field is to be introduced. When people trained in Jewish studies for the doctorate, enter disciplinary departments or disciplinary fields, as they commonly do, they discover an interesting problem. If they join history departments, they find themselves unable to participate in the introduction to Western Civilization. When they join philosophy departments, they find it difficult to teach the introduction to philosophy. When they enter departments of religious studies, a fair number of them will face the task of offering the introduction to religion, whether formulated as "methods in the study of religions" or "theories of religion" or the principal religious traditions of the West. This they cannot do. Few of the more influential and admired figures in Jewish studies, for example, the heroes of the young people who make up the bulk of the participants at such ethnocentric celebrations as Association for Jewish Studies meetings, could give the introductory course in the departments of which they are members, excluding only Hebrew. If, further, they find employment in departments of Jewish studies, few of these same widely appreciated heroic figures could even define what such an introductory course in such a department ought to teach.

V

How shall we proceed? In my view the task falls upon the shoulders of the new humanities. If we claim right of entry, ours is the burden of presenting a valid ticket of admission. No one doubts that we belong. The books people wrote in the submerged and ignored sectors of humanity, those of the wrong religion, race, sex, part of the world, have won our place for us. Ours is the task to ask what is general and accessible, suggestive beyond itself, in that range of particularity and parochial, private experience about which we have informed ourselves.

The answer to that question will emerge in the definition of those issues of general intelligibility to which, each in its own way, the new humanities also contribute. The key lies in asking one simple question: What does the private exemplify about what is shared and public? To what does the specific fact give testimony in what is shared? And how do we all exemplify a common experience of humanity? When we see the ways in which we are alike, and the ways in which we are not alike, the other or the rest, then we may speak intelligibly and claim a full and solemn hearing for ourselves. Then we serve scholarship as universities practice scholarship – that alone.

7

Contexts and Constituencies: The Diverse Responsibilities of Higher Jewish Learning

Inaugural Address, Guest Lecture Series
Dropsie University, 1980

The development and rapid expansion of Jewish studies in undergraduate college and universities over the past two decades have created a new context and a fresh constituency for Jewish learning. The context is the liberal arts B.A., mainly in the humanities, in which knowing something about many things is deemed the goal. The constituency is the American undergraduate, both Jewish and gentile, drawn by (mere) curiosity, rewarded by insight, and alas, more often than not, sustained by professors' instant wisdom. At the same time, these new developments have called for a reconsideration of existing contexts and constituencies. What is now needed is a fresh asking of the question about (1) who teaches (2) what (3) to whom. For at the center of higher learning is the simple exercise of learning, in which one person teaches a given subject to some other: subject and predicate of accusative and dative. The context determines who teaches what. The constituency decides to whom. These are critical issues of Jewish learning.

Thirty or forty years ago, it was hardly necessary to raise them because the answers were rightly deemed to be obvious. The constituency of Jewish learning was Jews, or some of them. The sole context was schools for training rabbis or teachers for the Jewish community. So the field was made up of Jews teaching Jewish subjects to Jews. There was no appreciable constituency for scholarship except for a few rabbis and unusual teachers. There were no important undergraduate or graduate programs in the major graduate centers of learning. That is not to say there were no important scholars at these centers, since everyone knows the record of Baron at Columbia and Wolfson at Harvard. But they did not systematically produce and place young scholars; and since, nowadays, a number of us do systematically produce and play young scholars, the difference is clear.

Once we recognize that an important change has taken place, we confront a rather broad, if ignorant, range of assessments of that change, ranging from those who maintain that nothing of importance for Jewish learning has taken place, to others who hold that a revolution has happened. In my judgment, the question to be analyzed is not properly phrased when we ask whether everything or nothing has changed. We have on our hands a new context, which has taken its place (so to speak) alongside existing ones. We further have seen the development of a new constituency, again, alongside existing ones. Clearly much has changed. But to understand what has happened, and is happening, we must reflect upon the entire context, the whole of the constituency of Jewish studies, paying attention to the old as well as to the new. Our question is how things now fit together, how they now work. In this setting, I may point out that some hold there is no need for Jewish institutions for Jewish learning, now that universities provide so ample and compendious a place for the subject. In the present context: Why do we need Dropsie University if there are programs and departments of Jewish studies in universities? I shall deal with that question. To be sure, the same question is addressed to Jewish seminaries, teachers colleges, and various other types of contexts of higher Jewish studies, and in due course others will answer.

I

We may take up the matter precisely because we stand at the end of a period of rapid change and enter an age of stability in higher Jewish learning. Twenty years have passed since a fairly substantial number of appointments in Jewish studies took place. The rate of growth is not what it was. Important institutions for Jewish studies, new journals, fresh monograph series, a broad program of conferences, annual meetings, exchanges of ideas, book reviewing, a variety of substantial graduate programs – the whole repertoire of a field of academic study at the height of its vigor and in the full bloom of its vitality now flourishes. Journals are read. Monographs are widely reviewed. The constituency for learning is sizable and solid. In the USA and Canada it soon will be time to assess how and whether the age of growth has produced significant learning, substantial in content, important and lasting in form.

The first principle and single most important criterion in my view is simple: each context – each type of program in higher Jewish learning – has its distinctive and important task. All of them together, the old and the new, must come under analysis. No setting for Jewish studies has yet proved to be superfluous. None is without its task. No constituency is to be ignored.

Whatever we have must be enhanced. Nothing must be lost, or there can be no gain at all. If the expansion of Jewish learning into universities leads some to suppose that there now should be a contraction outside of universities, then those people profoundly misunderstand the meaning of the new, and misconstrue the value and the achievements of the established and enduring old. The various programs and institutions serve important constituencies, form significant and promising contexts for learning. We cannot concede any one of them to be superfluous or superannuated. What we must do is discover the strengths of each and to discern how all fit together into a single and whole context, serving a diverse but essentially consistent (if not uniform) constituency.

II

There are four contexts for higher Jewish learning in the USA and Canada: (1) seminaries, (2) teachers colleges, and university programs of two distinct sorts, (3) the former, small programs, (4) the latter, large and sizable ones. There are many examples of small university programs. Brown University, for example, has three regular appointments (one in Tanakh, two in post-biblical Judaism), as well as a number of teaching assistantships for Hebrew and Talmud. Brown also has a fair number of courses offered by specialists in other areas with expert knowledge in some area of Jewish learning, such as American Jewish literature, Jewish demography, political scientific work on the Jews, Zionism, and the like. The quantitative difference between small and large becomes qualitative (a new context) when we compare Brown's solid but modest program with the one at Brandeis, with sixteen full-time appointments in Judaic studies, numerous teaching assistantships, and the like. Brown represents one context, Brandeis a quite separate one, each with weaknesses and strengths.

In this typology, Dropsie belongs in the context of a large and free-standing program in Jewish studies. Since, moreover, Dropsie not only calls itself a university but also is entirely independent of theological or political commitments, it is to be located within the context of university-founded Jewish studies. If an important task is to be defined, Dropsie should be able to find it in the context of universities and serving the neutral constituency of college professors and students. In order to define such a context, we have to turn to the description and evaluation of that context and constituency framed by US and Canadian academic life.

In the neutral academic context of colleges and universities, anyone who wants to teaches anything at all to whom it may concern. There is no focus, no center, no clear-cut purpose, except as may be articulated within the local circumstance of a given department or university. I mean that we have no way of predicting what will be taught, or assessing the preparation and qualifications of the teacher, of explaining the place and importance of the subject in the education of the students, or of answering those other questions about curriculum and learning which, in general, make sense of learning. In so describing matters, I refer to not only the state of higher Jewish learning in universities, but also the state of university studies in general. The diversity and uneven character of higher education in America are replicated in the small and unimportant field of Jewish studies. We call many different things by a single name. There is no predicting what a college or a university will be – for surely, the university which is Dropsie and the university which is Pennsylvania exhibit noteworthy differences and contrasts.

At the same time, because of the amplitude of positions, a further fact has to be noted. Most, though not all, Jewish scholarship in this country emerges from colleges and universities. This is a simple fact demonstrated by such factors as: Who writes the articles and books? Who reviews them? Who gives papers at meetings of learned societies, of a regional or national character? Who attends those meetings and participates in the discussion of them? These are simple measures, requiring neither judgment nor approval. The bulk of Jewish learning in this country is the work of professors in colleges and universities. It is not the work of professors in Hebrew teachers colleges, who, except for a few individuals, produce very little. It is not the work of professors of Jewish seminaries, who, with exceptions, tend to see as their colleagues and students rabbis in the pulpits, rather than other professors in colleges and universities.

The paramount reference group and professional society for Jewish Theological Seminary of America professors is the Rabbinical Assembly for it is the agendum before the RA which occupies their time and attention, as the conflict over the ordination of women indicates. The same is true of professors at Hebrew Union College-Jewish Institute of Religion who look to the Central Conference of American Rabbis, rather than academic societies, to make their academic presentations, and in the journal of the rabbis that they print a fair number of their articles. Other articles find their way, mainly but not exclusively, into HUC's house journal – a very good one to be sure – the Hebrew Union College Annual, refereed by themselves. The result is that they tend to talk mainly to one another about a common agendum and within agreed-upon limits of discourse.

In general, with some noteworthy exceptions (some at HUC, fewer at JTSA), the bulk of Jewish scholarly activity – measured solely by concrete achievement – in the USA and Canada takes place in the context of universities. I suppose that should not be surprising, since for the humanities, nearly all serious learning in this country emerges from universities. If we take the narrower, but more appropriate, measure of scholarship in religious studies, it appears that the bulk of scholarly achievement, but by no means all of it, is located in university departments of religious studies or in university divinity schools.

To determine why this is so, we may use the example of American economists who dominate the field of economics and receive the larger proportion of Nobel prizes awarded in that field. The reason given by Gardner Ackly is that:

> America's total population of trained economists is so much larger than any other that here there can be and are a great many trained and competent scholars, interested in every aspect of the subject. *They interact, criticize, evaluate, and stimulate each other and their graduate students, within and among campuses and research institutes, through journals, seminars, the exchange of working papers, and incessant shop talk.* [Italics supplied.]

What is characteristic of economics applies also to the humanities in general, and the Jewish sector of the humanities in particular.

In universities we enjoy the stimulation of constant challenge. We are challenged to explain what we do by people outside our field. This is stimulating, because it forces us to ask ourselves fundamental questions all the time. We are challenged to take up questions of common interest, and to answer those questions out of the data of Jewish experience and insight, which none concedes to be parochial. We are challenged to address ourselves to a sizable and complex agendum of learning coming to us from not only other specific fields of humanistic learning but also from theorists of humanistic learning in general. The humanities in America for the past thirty years have enjoyed a renaissance. Important ideas, stimulating questions, stunning problems for inquiry, new modes of analysis and interpretation come out of our own universities, as well as European center. To be sure, American scholars are the persistent brides of Western learning, always in search of something new, something old, something borrowed – if not something blue. The new is always with us. We are experts *a la mode.* The old to us seems fresh. In our naivete, we invent the wheel every day. We borrow like magpies, ideas from everywhere. And, if the truth be told, surrounded as we are by people of vitality and insight, we cannot become bored, self-absorbed, uninterested, or, therefore, the academic equivalent of blue.

So in universities there is a large critical mass of academic workers in Jewish studies. Their education in secular graduate programs and their professional context are broad and stimulating. They are not narrow in their interests. They constantly are with one another, by phone, at meetings, by letter, and in journals. They also are with people in other areas of learning adjacent, and by no means merely tangential, to theirs. There is constant shop talk. We teach one another. We criticize one another. We provoke each other. And the measurable results stand for all to see: in the journals in our field, and the disciplinary journals in other fields to which we contribute; in programs of the learned societies in our own field, and the learned societies in other fields and disciplines in which we take an active part; through the monographs and books we address to colleagues in our own field, and those we write for colleagues in a variety of fields; in the books we read and review. Truly, it is an age of remarkable vitality. And the age, so far as higher Jewish learning is concerned, presently belongs mainly to universities.

That the faculties of Hebrew teachers colleges and seminaries tend to prove bored and boring, and less productive than those in universities, may be due to the inbred character of their faculties. It is a fact that most of the professors at the Jewish theological institutions are rabbinical and even doctoral graduates of those same institutions. Only a few of them have taught elsewhere. As I said, it is commonplace for those professors to attend and speak at the rabbinical meetings of the graduates of those schools. It is much less commonplace for them to speak at, or even attend, meetings of university professors in their fields. Anyone who has attended the public sessions of the American Academy for Jewish Research must wonder at the absence of the collectivity of Jewish scholars employed by Jewish seminaries and teachers colleges. The Association for Jewish Studies' annual meeting attracts negligible numbers of professors of rabbinical schools and fewer still from teachers colleges. The program features their participation in disproportionately small numbers. So, in all, when these people stay home and see only one another, I suppose, they find so much about which to agree that the stimulus is lacking for any fresh work. Why take risks at all? Perhaps the absence of a grain of sand in the impenetrably hard and tightly closed shells of the Jewish schools accounts for the difficulty we have in finding pearls. But it is a fact that not many rabbinical oysters yield pearls of great price, at least relative to the size of the oyster bed.

III

Now if we wish to discover where we are weak, we had best look closely at where we are strong. The strength of the university setting lies in its diversity and rich sources of intellectual stimulation. The weakness is in that same place: the diffusion of Jewish studies across the curriculum – just as it should be: the negligible number of professors of Jewish studies in any one place, just as in the case in other small fields, the absence of a generally accepted standard of learning, so that professors of anything who happen to be born Jewish speak as equals to professors who have devoted their lives to the study of Judaica. The result is that courses take shape around a totally unpredictable program. As I said earlier, in universities anyone teaches anything to whom it may concern, and calls it "Jewish studies."

We not only find a diversity of standards. We also discover no consensus that there are standards at all. People in general do not wish to submit their educational work, their curricula, their programs, and course syllabi to the criticism and review of colleagues. Nor do they wish to learn from colleagues' ideas about teaching. In this regard, I believe that we at Brown, patiently publishing our syllabi and not only sharing them but soliciting (and sometimes getting) the comments and judgments of colleagues, are alone. In general what is taught is a closely guarded secret.

Now it may be an open secret. For one instance, nearly every college has a "Holocaust" course, and everyone is supposed to know what to "do" in such a course. The fact that the study of the extermination of European Jewry has reached a high level of solid learning and professional scholarship does not deter colleagues who specialize in anything but that tragic era to embark on the teaching of "the Holocaust," mainly fiction and theology. This too can mean anything from what really happened to what people feel about what happened, and, it goes without saying, among the hobbyists the appeal of novels and cheap theology is irresistible.

To take another example, for the generality of teachers in language and literature courses, a course consists of the title of a book or a tractate. What one "teaches" is that book or tractate – chapter by chapter, line by line, by the so-called "exegetical method." So the framer of the syllabus of the course is the one who wrote the book or redacted the tractate. Now that framer may be hardly qualified as an educator. The redactor of a tractate is not one who has thought through what someone is supposed to learn in his tractate, why one should study it in a particular way and order and not in some other way and order, and what the student will derive as benefit from the tractate. These are not the relevant issues. Books are not written by people who ask such educational questions.

But if teachers of language and literature abdicate the labor of thinking through the purpose and structure of their courses, teachers of history assume that their work is to say what came first and what happened then. Consequently, the syllabus of a course of history, in general, will be provided by someone's conception of the sequence and order of events. It is as if the principal point requiring explanation were why things happened in some given order, and it is as if the answer to the question is that they happened in that order, and so that is what they mean. I do not intend a charicature. But it is difficult to find an other-than-chronological principle of organization in the teaching of Jewish history. (Still, chronology is a step beyond the apologetics of "blood and peoplehood" which students get as "history" before they reach university studies, Jewish theological categories are supplied by the commonality of theology and filled with the detritus of rabbinical quotations out of context, wise sayings lacking all social relevance. So, overall, the scholarly vitality of the field masks something quite different: an intellectual vacuity, running hither-and-yon in search of what is in style. Jewish studies in universities reveal the absence of a clear-cut program by which the field unfolds, in accord with which a given subject is made into a course and is set into juxtaposition, and relationship, with some other course or courses, both in Judaic studies and in the disciplinary curriculum.

In fact we confront a field in search of itself. That is a mark of weakness, but also, as I said earlier, of strength. Diversity is strength; diffuseness, weakness. Response to rich stimulus makes our lives interesting; running in all directions all at once marks our intellectual life as trivial and modish. What is needed is a center of gravity, a source for order and intellectual community, a vehicle for educational stability. Now what I have said about Jewish studies in universities cannot be said about Jewish studies in Hebrew teachers' colleges and Jewish seminaries, where there is an accepted and worthwhile curriculum. There is a stable and solid program of learning. People do emerge, in general, predictably literate in some subjects, in accord with a reasonable standard of learning. They do know some few things very well: Hebrew language, Jewish texts of a classic and modern origin – things which fit together. In contrast to the niggardly smattering of facts and the excess of easy insight with which we equip our university undergraduates, the students who complete programs in the better Hebrew colleges and the more important seminaries and *yeshivot* do know both that they know some few things, and also that they do not know many other things.

For in knowing a few things well, they understand what knowing is, as our undergraduates do not. We who devote our lives to university studies of Jewish subjects have much for which we can be proud: we have confronted a new context in a generally responsible and responsive way. We have not taken for granted that we know what is needed, which is pretty much what is done in Jewish contexts for Jewish studies. We have listened and tried to learn about the unprecedented context presented by powerful institutions of general culture to which, for the first time in history, Jewish learning finds its way. We have taken seriously the unprecedented requirements of a wholly new setting for Jewish learning. We have made full use of the intellectual opportunities for our day.

But for this we shall be called to account: for educating a generation of young Jews and gentiles to think that it is much easier to enter into the disciplines of Jewish learning than it actually is. For that, and for one more thing: in all too many instances, for not educating at all but calling the result learning.

IV

In my judgment in the lamentable traits of Jewish studies in universities that I have outlined underscore one useful and important program of work at a school such as Dropsie University (or Brandeis University). I refer now to those types of institutions with large faculties which have a paramount commitment to Jewish learning, and also have freedom of vision and exemption from partisan and apologetic commitment. Here truly humanistic, interesting learning is possible. What is needed, specifically, is a faculty of true scholarly achievement, capable of serving as a source for broadening and deepening the learning of the scholars in colleges and universities. I refer to the need for a center for Jewish humanistic studies meant to serve, in particular, the overburdened professors of Jewish this, that, and the other thing, in the colleges and universities of the country. It would be a post-graduate center for broadening knowledge of some few things, and for deepening knowledge of some one thing. What is needed, in particular, is a place for use of sabbaticals, a center for advanced study of a rather particular order. Let me unpack this rather simple idea.

If there were no Dropsie University, perhaps, in this day and age, no one would think of creating it. But there is such a place. Its leadership does seek an important and critical task in American higher education. After a long period in which it lay moribund, Dropsie now takes up a new set of tasks, enters a new period in its own history. I salute that ambition. I cherish that fresh hope. I wish to encourage the dream of renewal and rebirth. For, as I said earlier, we must prize whatever we now have, lose nothing, but reform and renew everything. Every student, every institution, every professorship, every library and librarian, all faculties and administrations, even the bricks in the handful of buildings devoted to Jewish learning – these are all we have. They are the blood and bone of whatever intellectual and scholarly life American Jewry is going to have in our day. There is not apt to be much more than what we now have. But we must see that there will not be less.

So, to carry the argument forward, one important task I see for Dropsie is to frame a program (among its other programs, to be sure) for post-doctoral studies here in Philadelphia, with its remarkable Jewish intellectual resources, its universities and Jewish institutions. Such a center should provide residential fellowships for both senior scholars and junior ones. It should be conceived along the lines of the National Humanities Center in North Carolina and the various other centers for humanistic and scientific study in this country. These are places in which scholars are brought together for a year of common discourse and study. The result of a year of such study is that professors work together with professors, younger with older, accomplished people with beginners; in all a community of learning takes shape and begins to flourish.

Such centers for humanistic study are not merely places in which individuals pursue their personal research interests or ask questions of more learned people while they engage in private projects. On the contrary, that kind of essentially individual work does not require the locus of a center at all. What centers offer, which individual studies do not, is the formation of a timely community of people who wish to talk together and work together over a protracted period. These people have the time and energy and will to learn how to converse with and learn from one another. They are scholars who appreciate how individual labors must benefit, must be fructified, in a community of learning.

If such a center is to make its contribution to the stabilization of Jewish studies in universities, it must also make provision to continue the education of the professors themselves. For, as I indicated earlier, in the nature of our work all of us are called upon to teach many more things than we have studied. Without fear of contradiction by other equally informed people, we express our opinions about anything we like. In our area of work, we reign supreme but also alone, monarchs of a realm consisting, in the main, of not much more than ourselves. The result, as is clear, is that we opine about too much, and we take our measure too little. A program of systematic studies in fields we teach but have not studied is as important as a research colloquium. The particular nature of the field demands that we broaden ourselves, so as to become better informed teachers for our undergraduates.

Dropsie can turn itself into something we do not now have and do need: a center for Jewish studies in universities. To Dropsie the people who do the work in universities may retreat for renewal, for intellectual encounter with peers, for fresh exercises in systematic learning. For that purpose, what is needed is two sorts of professors. First is a resident corps of teachers for some of the disciplines and subjects required, yet not widely mastered, in universities. Second, is a revolving corps of teachers and students for the successive research colloquia to be organized over the years. These two programs, one in systematic study, the other in collective research on important and shared problems, will attract to Dropsie the people who today do the work, who actually meet the educational payroll so to speak. We who bear the full responsibility, but also the full power, for the character of Jewish studies in universities will respond to such an initiative. The labor of integrating the field, of providing it with a critical and vital center, of nurturing a common discourse about standards of teaching, the character of useful curricula, and a shared program of education and even of culture – that labor seems to me worthy of the resources at present subjected to the careful inspection of thoughtful and ambitious people.

What is needed is a center of gravity, a source of order and intellectual community. For the Hebrew colleges and seminaries, the established tradition of learning forms such a center and such a source. It is a tradition of a given order, for a given purpose. That tradition explains why, in those places, people do things in one way and not in some other. Rabbinical schools have a pretty clear idea of what they think rabbinical students should study. Hebrew colleges have a fairly standard definition for the subjects their students should learn. But we in universities and colleges do not. It is clear that our distinctive context is not going to, and ought not, provide us with a focus and center of gravity congruent to the tradition of learning of Jewish studies which is our subject.

V

So now the question is raised: With the various Judaic studies programs in universities, is Dropsie University still needed? I believe I have given one answer to the question. This is an answer relevant to the field of Jewish learning as a whole. If you want to know how Dropsie may find a place in the very center and heart of the vast enterprise of Jewish learning in this country and Canada, then seek the flaw at the center, the ache at the heart, of our common corpus of studies.

There is a university constituency to be served. It is made up of scholars of Jewish studies as well as scholars of other subjects with special knowledge and competence in Jewish studies of a narrower order. There is a major task to be done to take both of these types of scholars and improve their capacities to pursue learning and education in universities. It is not a task which is apt to be done in any other institution. Universities in general are not likely to deem Jewish studies so critical within the larger curriculum as to warrant the effort and investment required for the formation of a residential center for the Jewish humanities. Jewish seminaries and teachers college do not have the intellectual resources, the vision, or the understanding of context, to form such a center. That is because they are essentially removed from the life and problems of universities and do not grasp (or care to grasp) what these are.

Consequently, I perceive a special labor for which Dropsie may make itself especially qualified. Professor David Goldenberg writes to me, "I happen to think that the potential is here for a leading center of Judaic studies in America, because it is the only institution exclusively devoted to the subject and yet non-theological." I happen to concur in this judgment. That is why I offer for consideration this theory of a problem and how Dropsie may choose to meet it.

So to conclude: the constituency is the vast body of American college students who take our courses. The context is the study of Jewish subjects in universities. But the meeting of context and constituency has now to take place in yet another place, on yet another plane. Whether Dropsie constitutes the right place, whether this is the right time, and whether the lay leaders and president and professors are the right people – these are questions to be settled by the people themselves. I should not have raised these questions if I thought no response might come forth. The question is whether this is the time and the place for a national residential center for post-doctoral humanistic Judaic studies. I do not know the answer. But I do know that if it is not here, it is not apt to be elsewhere either.

8

The Tasks of Theology in Judaism: A Humanistic Program[1]

On the occasion of receiving the L.H.D.
The University of University, 1977

The principal task of theology in Judaism is to draw out and make explicit the normative statements of the acknowledged sources of Judaism and to learn how to renew discourse in accord with these norms.[2] It is, specifically, to delineate the worldview shaped within the experience and aspirations of the community of Judaism and to perceive the world within that view. The goal is that, in time to come, the sight of ages to come may be yet more perspicacious too. Vision

---

[1]Prepared for the occasion of receiving an honorary degree, L.H.D. (Doctor of Humane Letters), at the University of Chicago, June 9, 1978. Presented at the Divinity School convocation, June 8, 1978.
[2]Because of the occasion for which this paper is prepared, I have formed the paper in response in some small way to the thought of Professors Jonathan Z. Smith (Parts I and II) and David Tracy (Parts IV and V). The context of the whole, of course, is the difficult question of the role of theology in the humanities, thus provoked for me by the character of the degree. Part III derives its basic perspectives from my *History of the Mishnaic Law of Purities*, 22 vols. (Leiden, 1974-77), *History of the Mishnaic Law of Holy Things*, 6 vols. (Leiden, 1979-80), and *History of the Mishnaic Law of Women*, 5 vols. I enjoyed the critical counsel of professors Wendell S. Dietrich, John Giles Milhaven, John P. Reeder, Jr., Sumner B. Twiss, and Richard S. Sarason, Brown University; William Scott Green, University of Rochester; David Blumenthal, Emory University; and Marvin Fox, Brandeis University, to all of whom I express thanks and, for all, absolution as well for *my* sins.

received, vision reformed, vision transmitted – these are the tasks of theology in Judaism.[3]

I. Vision Received

The beginning of the work is to state what it is that Judaism teaches, to define both its principal concerns and its methods of expressing its ideas. The work of definition is to discover what it is that theology to begin with wishes to say. This descriptive task – the perception of the vision received – is theological in its purpose. But it requires the disciplines of hermeneutics, history of religions, and history. The tasks of theology in Judaism will be carried out at the intersecting frontiers among these useful disciplines, even though, as I shall explain, merely working along lines laid out by them will not yield a significant theological result.

Let us start with hermeneutics. The reason to begin here is that, when we wish to define Judaism, we first have to locate and encompass the whole range of texts which find a place in the canon of Judaism. For to define a religion is to state the substance of its canon, that is, to spell out the canonical ideas found in the canonical literature. And, second, the work of coming to grips with that range of canonical texts with which the theologian of Judaism must reckon is an exercise in the exegesis of exegesis. The theologian has to explain how these texts have been so read as to be received as everywhere pertinent. For Judaism is a religion of great age and diversity. To uncover the

[3]It is a commonplace that *halakhic* statements are normative and theological statements represent the private opinion of an individual. This paper is meant to restate the theological task in such a way that it too may be perceived, within the communities of the faithful of Judaism, as part of public discourse, not merely private opinion. At this time, however, I do not wish to enter into issues of Judaic dogmatics. The reason that the work of dogmatics, the restatement of available and required truths for the current age, need not now be done is that it is premature. For a long time we were told that, in any event, Judaism has no theology, and it certainly has no dogmas. While the dogma of dogma-less Judaism has passed away with the generation to whom it seemed an urgent and compelling proposition, it has left discourse about and within Judaism in disarray. There is a poverty of philosophical clarity and decisive expression amid a superfluity of conviction, too much believing, too small perspicacious construction. As one person put it, "There is no God, but Israel is his sole, chosen people." Of still greater weight, dogmatics lays the groundwork for the exercise of advocacy and apologetic. That exercise is a work of mediation between culture and revelation, between where the people are and where Torah wishes them to be. It seems to me self-evident that, until we have a richer and more responsible conception of what it is that awaits both advocacy and mediation, that is, Torah or Judaism, formulation of dogmas for defense is unimportant.

fundament of ultimate conviction everywhere present, and to do so with full reverence for diversity in the history of Judaism, we have to look for what is ubiquitous. And that, I think, is the process and the method: how things are made to happen ubiquitously and consistently. Discernment of process yields the rules which we may extract from the happening and the substantive convictions which lie behind the rules. For when we ask about process and method, our interest is not simply in formal, but also in substantive traits. Axiomatic to the "how" of process and method is the "what" of substance, the elements of worldview which generate both the process and the method.

At this stage in the work, it is not the task of the theologian to declare the truth. The truth, Judaism everywhere holds, is revealed in Torah. It therefore is to be discovered in Torah. The theologian has to locate that point, within the intellectual structure of the faith, at which discovery may take place. The work is to lay out the lines of the truth, the frontiers of Torah. Now if, in the present age, we take seriously the commonplace proposition that Judaism is a way of life, we are not going to find it easy to choose those people whose way of life defines Judaism and reveals Torah. The diversity among the Jews as a group is too great. Some Jews do not see themselves as engaged in an essentially religious mode of being at all. Others, whom we shall have to call by a separate name, Judaists, do see themselves as participants in a religious mode of being, Judaism. These religious Jews are themselves diverse. The way of life of all those who are Judaists is not uniform. In this regard, therefore, the sustained effort to uncover the fundament of the true faith by description of the way of life of the Judaists is fruitless. The status quo does not contain within itself the fundament of the true faith. To turn the way of life into a statement of theology or a source for deeper meaning is hopeless. All we should gain is a statement – at best – of culture. Once we admit that fact, we no longer have the choice of speaking of Judaism as a way of life in a this-worldly and merely descriptive sense. If, on the other hand, we turn to historical descriptions of the "authentic" way of life of Judaism, for instance, the *Shulḥan 'Arukh*, we no longer speak of the way of life of all of the living at all, but of a holy book which is part of a holy canon. We might, therefore, just as well turn forthwith to the canon. Or, to state matters more bluntly, Judaism is not going to be described by sociology. But Judaism must be described and interpreted.[4]

---

[4]Obviously, I cannot concede that Judaism is practiced today only by those who now carry out the teachings of Jewish law, e.g., as summed up in the *Shulḥan 'Arukh*. It does not seem to be descriptively valid since vast numbers of Jews also regard themselves, and are generally regarded as, Judaists who do not live

And yet, how the holy books are to be read for the work of theology is not clear. For they already have been read for a very long time, and remarkably little theology has come forth. The work of definition remains primitive. So, it is clear, the canon has to be read in some way other than the way in which, under the current auspices, it presently is read. The established hermeneutics of *yeshivot* and Talmud departments, and of philosophers of Judaism and ideologists as well, proves arid and productive mainly of contention when, to begin with, it is of any intellectual weight at all. And the exercise in repeating the holy words without understanding much, if anything, of what they say and mean cannot in this context be taken seriously. It is not reading or learning at all. Pretense and ritual are not the same thing, and ritual learning must include learning. So we have to find a way of reading the holy books congruent to both their character and our interest in them.

It seems to me that that requirement is met with two questions. First, *how* do these texts convey their message? What is it that we learn from the way they say things and the way in which people have learned and are taught to hear what they say? Second, *what* do they say which is pertinent to living as a Judaist today? That is, once the text comes into being, leaving its own particular moment of history and undertaking a journey beyond its concrete and specific context, the canonical text has to discover new life in other contexts. And the way that happens is through the urgent work of exegesis. The task is the comparison of the words of one text to the ways of another world and the finding of modes of harmonization and mediation between the one and the other.

Now when the theologian comes along, it is not to do the work of descriptive hermeneutics, of explaining solely how the diverse texts have been made to speak. What the theologian requires, for the much more complex work of generalization, is information about commonalities amid the diversities of exegesis, the exegesis of exegesis, so to speak. The theologian, first, has to uncover the processes and modes of thought. To know how a given text has been received is interesting. To know how the methods of reception, transmission, interpretation, and application of that text correspond to methods to be located in the reading of other texts is to know something important; the deeper structure of the processes of hermeneutics, the method

---

in accord with all of the law of Judaism all the time or ever. The choice then is (1) to declare that Judaism has no *halakhah*, or (2) to declare that all who do not keep the *halakhah* are not Judaists. Both propositions seem to me factually so far from the truth as to have to be set aside. The problem explored here then becomes urgent and unavoidable.

within the diverse methods of the received exegesis. The work of generalization must come. What is available for generalization, it is clear, is what is common among exegetical techniques of diverse and discrete documents. That is, as I have said, how all of them are read, through all times, and in all places.

When, of course, we speak of times and places, second, we arouse the interest of the historian of religions. For what do we know about the exegesis of a text if we cannot describe the contexts of ideas and circumstances of visions in which that exegesis is done, that is, the particular choices which have been made among a broad range of possibilities? Surely the impulse and motivation of the exegete have to enter into the account of the results of exegesis: What was the question which had to be answered in those times and for those groups of people? It is not enough to wonder what it is that we learn from hermeneutics, that is, *how* people say things about the commonalities of faith. We have also to know what it is that, under diverse circumstances, they wish to say: The *substance* matters as much as the method. Here is the point at which comparative and historical studies in religions come to the fore.

When it comes to the work of description not only does context have its part to play; so too does consideration of choice, that is to say, comparison. What things people *might* have said we must know in order to understand the choices which they *have* made and the things they *do* choose to say. So these two go together: the consideration of formal language, mode of interpreting and applying the canon which, all together, I hope we may call hermeneutics, and attention to the range of the choices selected for serious attention, the work of comparison of diverse contexts and expressions of a given continuum of religion or of diverse religions to, for analysis of which we generally call upon the historian of religions.

There is yet a third kind of thinking about religions which is to be invoked – an interest in the larger concrete, social, and historical framework in which Judaism comes to particular expression and definition, an interest characteristic of historians. When we have some clear picture of the procedures and methods of exegesis of the texts and of the choices available and made, we have yet to link out results, our conception of the dynamics of Judaism and of its processes, to that world of the Jewish people which took shape in these processes and out of these dynamics.

There is, I mean, an ecology of Judaism: a natural framework in which all elements interact with all other elements to form a stable, coherent, and whole system. For if Judaism is to be described as it has endured, it has to be described where it has endured: in the political-social and imaginative life of the Jewish people, in its mind and emotions. And that part of the task of description and interpretation is best done by historians of the Jewish people, those who (in the present context) take on the work of relating the social and historical framework of the group to its inner life of feeling, fantasy, and imagination. The question to be asked in this setting is how it is that the distinctive myths and rites of Judaism – its way of shaping life and its way of living – continued to possess the power to form, and to make sense of, an enduring world in diverse and changing contexts. When we consider that Judaism continued in a single, remarkably persistent system for nearly 2,000 years, from the second century to the nineteenth and even the twentieth, we must ask what has so persisted, amid time and change, to have continued to make sense of the world to the Jews, and of the Jews to their world. That perennial and enduring congruence between myth and circumstance, context and system, surely will enter into our definition of Judaism alongside the elements of process described and choice explained.

My main point is that the defining of the received vision of Judaism is through processes of exegesis, which govern feeling and imagination, make sense of context and situation, and persist with remarkable stability for a very long time. It is the discovery and statement of these rules of process which permit us to speak of Judaism. The received vision of Judaism is to be defined as those distinctive processes of exegesis of the canon which yield coherent choices, made time and again through the ages, repeated in one circumstance after another. The work of description is to be done through the disciplines of hermeneutics, history of religions, and history. But in the end, these through their combination do not constitute theology. They only define the parameters within which theology is to be done.[5]

II. Vision Reformed

Our three-part assignment, then, is to work out the hermeneutics of texts, to uncover the choices before the ones who wrote the texts and the many who received them and so to understand what the religious community selected against the background of what it thereby rejected, and, finally, to analyze the concrete contexts in which the processes of exegesis and selection took place.

First, we must determine what is the text, or the kind of text, upon which theological work is to be done.

---

[5]See Parts IV and V.

It seems self-evident that, in nineteenth- and twentieth-century theological discourse, a wrong choice has been made. For when we ask about the canon upon which theologians of Judaism draw in modern and contemporary times, the answer is twofold: modern philosophy of religion, on the one side, and the Hebrew Scriptures, the Written Torah, on the other. A few particularly learned theologians cite talmudic sayings too. Proof of this proposition is through a simple mental experiment. When you read the work of nearly all modern and contemporary voices of Judaism, what books must you know to understand their thought? And what do you *not* need to know? It is commonplace that you must know Kant and will do well to know Hegel. You also should know some stories and sayings of the Hebrew Scriptures, the Written Torah, and some tales of the Talmud and midrashim, the Oral Torah. Except for Abraham J. Heschel and Joseph B. Soloveichik there is not a single important theologian of the present or past century who cannot be fully and exhaustively understood within the limits just now stated – modern philosophy of religion, Written Torah, and a few pithy rabbinic maxims – because none draws systematically and routinely upon the other resources of the canon of Judaism. But the entire range of the holy books of Judaism speaks, in particular, through Heschel.

In my judgment Judaism cannot draw for definition solely upon the Written Torah and episodic citations of rabbinic *aggadah.* This is for two reasons. First, it has been the whole of the Dual Torah, written and oral, of Moses, "our Rabbi," which has defined Judaism through the ages and which must therefore serve today to supply the principal sources of Judaism. Second, the whole (Dual) Torah in fact is many, for the canon of Judaism – Torah – has received new documents in every age down to our own.[6] If, therefore, we conclude that the correct sources of

---

[6]This is the principal point of my conference address at the University of Chicago, April, 1977, printed as "Transcendence and Worship through Learning: The Religious World View of Mishnah," *Journal of Reform Judaism* 25, no. 2 (Spring 1978): 15-29. I was surprised that the Reform theologians and rabbis at that meeting did not see the congruence between this description of the open-ended canon of Torah and the Reform conception of progressive revelation. Instead I found myself criticized for laying too much stress on the importance of reason, as against emotion, in the processes of the unfolding of revelation. But since when is how we feel today a revelation of God's will and word for the world? Further, a definition of Judaism which draws principally upon the Written Torah read other than through the perspective of the Oral Torah, its full and exhaustive interpretation, is not Judaism either. That is to say, so far as there are rules which permit us to speak of Judaism, these rules must be observed. Otherwise what we do is make things up as we go along and call our invention Judaism. But so far as we claim to communicate with other

Judaic theology are formed of the one whole Torah of Moses, our Rabbi, we once more find ourselves at that point at which we began, with the question of canon and hermeneutics of canon – how it is delineated and interpreted.

The canon of Judaism defines the sources of theology of Judaism and sets forth the field within which the work of theological inquiry must be undertaken. One part of that canon is well known to, and shared by, others: the Written Torah. That part is not to be neglected because it is not unique to Judaism. Heschel, for his part, understood that, despite all that has been done to make the Written Torah alien to Judaism, the "Old Testament" remains the *Tanakh*, the Written Torah of Judaism. He deemed his most important book to be the *Prophets*. The second half of the Torah, the oral part, *aggadah* and *halakhah*, however, is not to be neglected – just as Heschel, for his part, understood it: the Mishnah, the Talmud, and the great corpus continuous with the Mishnah and the Talmud. Here, too, Heschel undertook work of surpassing intellectual ambition – in his *Torah min hashshamayim beaspaqlaria shel haddorot*, an essay in the conceptions of revelation of the authorities of Mishnah, and, in a still larger framework, in the character of religious epistemology in Judaism.[7]

---

ages and other people in our own age, we cannot simply make things up as we go along. When there is no shared realm of discourse, past and present, there is that capricious alternation of noise or silence which is, in the life of emotions, the prelude to death and, in the life of the intellect, the symptom of the end of reasoned discourse. Since theology is the work of and for intellectuals pursued through reasoned discourse about, in part, a realm of distinctive and rich emotions and educated feelings, we cannot afford the costs of ignorance and capriciousness.

[7]To complete our definition of the theological canon through our sketch of Heschel's remarkable choices, we have to refer to the entire intellectual range formed of the philosophers of Judaism of the Middle Ages, Maimonides and Judah Halevi being Heschel's particular but not sole choices, the metaphysics of the Zohar, which Heschel fully grasped, and those doctors of the heart and soul who created the Hasidic tales. Into this comprehensive framework of the Judaic canon, Scripture, Oral Torah, Zohar, philosophy, mysticism, prayerbook – rationality and feeling, revelation and reason – which Heschel took into his mind and made his own, Heschel also received the achievements of the nineteenth- and twentieth-century theologians of Christianity and philosophers of religion. His last book, and in many ways his most sophisticated, brought together the Kotzker and Kierkegaard, a tour de force not likely to have its parallel in our day. See the following: Abraham Joshua Heschel, *Torah min hashshamayim beaspaqlariah shel haddorot*, 2 vols. (London and New York, 1962-65) (English title: *Theology of Ancient Judaism*, vol. 1, *The Prophets* [1962; originally published in 1936 as *Die Prophetie*]). See also Heschel, *God in Search of Man: A Philosophy of Judaism* (Philadelphia, 1955), and *The Sabbath: Its Meaning for Modern Man* with wood engravings by

Thus far I mean to stress two points. First of all, the sources of theology of Judaism are the whole and complete canon of Torah. That canon is defined for us by the shelves of books deemed by the consensus of the faithful to be holy and to warrant study in religious circumstances, that is, to be part of Torah. The canon of Torah is sufficiently open so that the words of even living men may be received in faith and recorded in piety. Torah is an open canon: *The processes by which books find their way into that canon define the convictions of Judaism about the character and meaning of revelation.*

Second, I am able to point even in our own day to a theologian whose *ouevres* do conform to the criterion of breadth and rigorous learning as the Judaic canon by which all theology is to be measured, and by which most theologians, alas, are found shallow and ignorant.

Having indicated through the corpus of Heschel's work the character of the canon of theology in Judaism, I may now come to a further point. Even the most productive and by far the best theological mind in modern and contemporary Judaism missed the principal theological canon of Judaism. For Heschel neglected the chief source of Judaism as *halakhah*.

III. Vision Reformed, Vision Transmitted

The center of Judaism is its way of life. No accurate and careful description of Judaism omits that obvious point. We already have noted that merely describing how Jews now live is not to define the way of life of Judaism. That is a sociological fact. But it is now to be balanced against a theological conviction everywhere affirmed in the history of Judaism from the second century to the nineteenth and twentieth centuries. Judaism expresses its theology through the pattern of deeds performed by the practitioner of Judaism. We are what we do. Judaism is what Judaists are supposed to do. I cannot think of a proposition more widely held in ages past and in our own time than that the theology of Judaism *is* its *halakhah*, its way of living. If, therefore, we want to describe what Judaism teaches, we have to make

---

Ilya Schor (New York, 1951). I once told Heschel I thought the center of his work lay in religious epistemology, the sources of religious truth. He said to me, "No, you are wrong. The center is the question of ontology." This is stated by Fritz A. Rothschild (*Encyclopaedia Judaica*, 8:425) as follows: "Heschel's own work attempts to penetrate and illumine the reality underlying religion, the living and dynamic relationship between God and man, through the objective, yet sympathetic understanding of the documents of Israel's tradition and of the experience of the pious Jew." Note especially Abraham Joshua Heschel, *A Passion for Truth* (New York, 1973).

sense of what Judaism requires the practitioner of Judaism to practice.[8] But what is the meaning of the practice, and how is that meaning to be uncovered?

Under some circumstances Judaism borders upon orthopraxy (eat *kosher* and think *teraif* [unkosher]) and, under others, upon what Heschel called "religious behaviorism." That is, we find robots of the law, who will do everything required by the law and think nothing on account of the law – religious behaviorists. And we also find nihilists of the law, who do everything by the law and think the law allows thinking anything we like – ortho-practitioners. These corruptions of the faith are revealing. What seems to me worth noticing in them is that orthopraxy is deemed an acceptable option, while religious behaviorism is rarely recognized, let alone condemned. It is surprising that there is little effort (Soloveichik here is definitely the exception) and no wide-ranging, systematic, and *sustained* effort whatsoever (with no exception) to state the theology of Judaism principally out of the sources of the *halakhah*.[9]

---

[8]Joseph Dov Soloveichik certainly is to be invoked as a principal exponent of the position outlined here, e.g., in his "Ish hahalakhah," *Talpiyyot* (1944), pp. 651-735, and "The Lonely Man of Faith," *Tradition* 7, no. 2 (1965): 5-67. As Aaron Rothkoff wrote, "The man lives in accordance with the *halakhah*, he becomes master of himself and the currents of his life...he ceases to be a mere creature of a habit. His life becomes sanctified, and God and man are drawn into a community of existence, 'a convenantal community,' which brings God and man together in an intimate, person-to-person relationship. It is only through the observance of the *halakhah* that man attains this goal to nearness to God" (*Encyclopaedia Judaica*, 15:132-33). It is no criticism to observe that Soloveichik's observations, while profound, thus far are episodic and not systematic. Despite his formidable insights, the work of interpretation of the *halakhah* as a theological enterprise simply has not yet begun. Nor do I think it can be done by *halakhists* within the intellectually impoverished resources of their training. They are, to begin with, in no way humanists. Perhaps had Rosenzweig lived he might have done this work, just as he – nearly alone – turned to the *Siddur* as a principal source of theology.

[9]My description of Heschel's corpus seems to me probative. I can point in his works to systematic and profound reflection upon the theology of the whole of the canon of Judaism except for the *halakhic* part; that is, that part which, speaking descriptively, all concur, forms the center and the core. The fact that Heschel lived wholly and completely in accord with the *halakhah* is beside the point, just as it is beside the point that another great theologian of modern Judaism, Martin Buber, did not. What the two have in common is that through them *halakhah* did and does not speak, and, in the case of Buber, what to begin with is heard from *halakhah* is simply a negative fact, the existence of something *against* which theology will find its definition. What we do have as theology of *halakhah* in Heschel and Soloveichik is sermonic and not sustained; it is episodic and not systematic. (Here I shall mercifully leave unnamed a fair number of Orthodox and Conservative *halakhist*-theologians.)

The fact is, however, that so far as Judaism today is a living religion it continues its life though *halakhah*. One authentic monument to the destruction of European Jewry likely to endure beyond the present fad is contained in the response literature of the ghettos and the concentration camps.[10] That is where Judaism is lived, defined in the crucible of life and death. There is a theology of Judaism emergent from and triumphant over the "Holocaust." But we have yet to hear its message, because we scarcely know how to listen to Judaism when Judaism speaks idiomatically, as it always has spoken, in accord with the methods and procedures of *its* canon, in obedience to *its* rules, and, above all, in the natural course of the unfolding of *its* consistent and cogent processes of thought and expression. The *halakhah* endured in the crucible of Warsaw and Lodi when *aggadah* and theology fell dumb.

The coming task of theology in Judaism is to define Judaism through the theological study of the now-neglected canon of the *halakhah*. To begin with, the canon must be allowed to define its literary frame for theological expression. One of the chief reasons for the persistent failure of the philosophers of *halakhah* down to the present time to accomplish what they set out to do is the confusion of their categories. They work through the whole of *halakhah* on a given subject. They therefore present results entirely divorced from context, on the one side, and from dynamic processes of exegesis, on the other. So they tell us things, mere facts. That is, they end up with a description of merely what "the *halakhah*" has to say, without analysis or explanation of meaning – a clear account of the context in which, and setting to which, *halakhah* framed the message, and how the message was framed.

I say this of Heschel, however, in full awareness of the unkept promise of his *The Sabbath: Its Meaning for Modern Man*, which comes as close as any essay in contemporary theology of Judaism to take up in a systematic and existentially profound way (as against the intellectual ephemera of sermons), the intellectual premises of *halakhah*. There is in the corpus of Heschel no work which draws upon and responds to the *Shulḥan Arukh*. Maimonides' *Mishneh Torah*, the Talmud as Talmud (not merely as a storehouse of interesting sayings and stories), or, above all, and the source of it all, Mishnah and its companion, Tosefta. If it is not in Heschel, then, as I have said, it is nowhere else. I cannot point to a single systematic and sustained work of theology out of the sources of Mishnah and Tosefta, out of the Talmud as a *halakhic* monument or any significant part thereof, out of the monuments formed by the medieval commentaries and codes, down to the present day. For historical study of the social-religious meaning of *halakhah*, see Jacob Katz, *Masoret ummashber* (Tel Aviv, 1958), *Tradition and Crisis* (Oxford, 1961), *Exclusiveness and Tolerance* (Oxford, 1961).

[10]Some of this has been translated into English as *The Holocaust and Halakhah*, by Irving Rosenbaum (New York, 1976).

They therefore tell us about *halakhah*. They do not, however, convey a shred of wisdom or insight into the processes and methods of *halakhah* relevant to any given age of Judaism, past or present. But the *halakhah* did not and does not take shape in a timeless world. It is meant to *create* a world beyond time – a different thing. Its genius was to take shape in a very specific and concrete moment yet to transcend that moment and to address ages to come as well. We shall not know how that was done if we persist in ignoring the diversity of the context and canon of the *halakhah*. We have to confront the specificities of its books and their diverse messages and methods of all, the historicity and religiosity of the *halakhah*.[11]

Once the canon is suitably defined in its diversity and specificity, what is it that we wish to know *about* these documents? The first thing is to grasp the processes of their unfolding: the hermeneutics generative of the exegetical processes which occupy the *halakhic* thinkers of the ages. One significant issue must be how the *halakhic* process expanded its range and so was able to encompass and make its own each and every circumstance confronted by the Jewish people. For Judaism is a world-creating and world-explaining system. The system, as is obvious, works through law. The law, moreover, functions through processes of argument and discussion. These make intelligible and bring under control of rules of all of those fresh data of the world which, together, at a given point, constitute time and change. The system persists because it makes sense of all data and draws within its framework the

---

[11]Just as Heschel could address himself to the issues of religious ontology of the prophets, the rabbis named in Mishnah, Maimonides, and Judah Halevi, the Zohar Hasidic literature, prayerbook, and on down to our own time, so the theologian of *halakhah* will have to allow each and every document of *halakhah* to emerge in all its concrete specificity. But where to begin? Self-evidently, it is to Mishnah and its tractates and divisions that we look for *one* beginning. But if we do not also look to Scripture and its many and diverse codes of law, clearly etched along the lines of the Priestly Code and the Holiness code on the one side, and the earlier thinking of the Deuteronomica schools on the other, we shall miss yet other beginnings. And I think it is obvious that, for theology as Judaism to be compelling in our own time, it will have to contend with the testimonies of documents standing on the threshold of the canon even now; I mean, the Dead Sea Scrolls (see Lawrence H. Schiffman, *The Halakhah of Qumran* [Lieden, 1976]), the Targumim, and the other documents important to our own day and unknown or neglected before now. In outlining the limits of the *halakhic* canon, we want to inquire after the processes of thought and the reaching of concrete conclusions of the masters of *halakhah*, early and late. They who expressed their theology through law and only through law so shaped the norms, social and psychological, of age succeeding age. They surely must define Judaism, not merely the epiphenomena called its "way of life."

newest facts of life. When it can no longer deal credibly with the new world within its vast, harmonious framework of rational inquiry and reasoned dispute, of exegesis of the canon in light of the newest concerns of the age, and of the newest concerns of the age in the light of the canon, the system collapses. That is to say, faced by two facts which could not be brought within the intelligible framework of the system of Judaism, Emancipation and modern, political anti-Semitism, Judaism has considerable difficulty. Specifically, it did not succeed in shaping meaningful issues for argument in accord with its established methods and its rational agendum for reasoned debate. So the theologian will want to reflect upon both how the system works and how it does not work. There is a clear frontier delineated by the end of inner plausibility. There is a border defined by the cessation of self-evidence.[12]

IV. Vision Transmitted

At the outset I specified the first two principal tasks of the theologian in Judaism as those of definition and correlation: definition of Judaism – vision received; correlation of Judaism with the life of

---

[12]Alongside description and interpretation of the processes of exegesis must come a second arena for delineation: the range of choice permitted by the system and prohibited within the system. One may only eat certain few foods, but the problems connected with the eating of those foods are rich and engaging. Stated more broadly, the proposition does not change. There is a given way of life defined by the processes of exegesis of the law and through its diverse literature. That way of life has to be described in the context of humanity and of the humanities: what sort of people, society, and culture emerge when life is lived in this way and not in some other. The *halakhic* literature awaits this kind of mention: description of the life of emotion and of relationship; of the society of home, family, and town; of the choices made, and the alternatives avoided, by the individual and by the group. The whole is best framed by the *halakhic* corpus. Since, moreover, we have access to other great systems of religion expressed through distinctive ways of life – I refer, by one instance, to Islam, with its legal literature, its processes of exegesis, and its way of life, but I do not exclude reference to Buddhism, on the one side, and to Christianity, on the other, both of them profoundly *halakhic* constructions at important points in their history – there is a sizable task of comparison to be worked out. So alongside, and cogent with, the exegesis of exegesis, that is, the description of the processes of Judaism, another task must be done: The comparison of the results, the description of the history of Judaism within the history of religions. Through this work there is a chance to gain that perspective upon which definition must depend. And I need hardly dwell upon the centrality of the work of the historian of the Jews, able to relate the *halakhic* process to the concrete social and historical circumstances of the Jewish people. For the historian and sociologist of the Jews in the end provide the most interesting evidence about the concrete workings of Judaism.

Jewish people – vision reformed. At the end let me point out that these tasks are not to be done in isolation from one another, because the sources of definition of Judaism, the *halakhic* sources, address themselves to the life of the Jewish people and propose to reshape that life in accord with the paradigm of the holy: *You shall be holy, because I am holy.* In this context, there are two sources for theology in Judaism: first, Torah, whole, unending, a never-to-be-closed canon; and, second, the human experience of the Jewish people raised to the level of Torah through *halakhah.*[13] Theology in Judaism makes sense of life already lived. But theology in Judaism has to reflect upon a particular mode of life already lived: the life lived in accord with Torah, therefore with *halakhah.* What is to be defined and explained is the correlation between the (ideal, normative) human images of the *halakhah* and the actual shape of life lived in accord with the *halakhah.* What is this particular kind of humanity which is shaped within the disciplines and critical tensions of the law? What are the larger human meanings to be adduced in interpretation of this particular kind of humanity?

To answer these questions the texts which constitute the sources of theology in Judaism have first to be reread, systematically, thoroughly and, at the outset, historically, one by one. A fresh set of questions has to be devised – questions about, first, the inner issues addressed by the *halakhic* texts, second, the human meaning of those issues, when interpreted, third, against the particular times and settings in which the texts are framed, and, fourth, also against the continuing and enduring social and historical realities of the Jewish people. These are the four criteria of meaning yielded by correct interpretation.

To start at the end, we have to know about those ongoing considerations which must be taken into account by all normative

---

[13]What follows is a response to David Tracy, *Blessed Rage for Order: The New Pluralism in Theology* (New York, 1975), pp. 43 ff. I hasten to clarify that it is the model, not the substance, which I invoke as a clarifying exercise of intellect. Tracy describes the revisionist model as "philosophical reflection upon the meanings present in common human experience and language, and upon the meanings present in the Christian fact." Of acute relevance is Tracy's first thesis, "The two principal sources for theology are Christian texts and common human experience and language." If I may rephrase in this setting the outcome of my earlier propositions, it is that the principal sources for theology in Judaism are, first, the *halakhic* texts as they are lived out in ordinary life and, second, the common human experience and language which will help to make sense of the inner meanings of those lived texts. This is, I hasten to say, not a translation of Tracy's propositions into the setting of Judaism. It is an effort to respond to what seems to me a sound insight, arising on its own, within the context of Judaism.

statements on behavior and belief, those traits of society and imagination which characterize every context in which Judaism comes to expression and which, therefore, define the other limits of Judaism.

Next, we need to discern those particular and distinctive concerns of a given situation and to isolate what is fresh and unanticipated therein.

For once we have uncovered the concrete and specific context in which a major conceptual initiative is given shape in *halakhah*, third, we are able to enter into the human circumstance which will help us to understand the question – the existential problem – dealt with by a given initiative.

And, finally, it is at that point that we may bring to full articulation the inner issues addressed by the *halakhic* text. Then we do not reduce them to accidents of a given context. We confront them in their ultimate and whole claim to speak in the name of Torah and to talk of holy things, of God and humanity in God's image.

It is principally in the great *halakhic* texts that the humanistic concerns of theology in Judaism are encapsulated and awaiting discovery. So far as Judaism proposes to express itself through the deeds of the Jewish people and the society which they construct together, we require access to two things. First is philosophical reflection upon the meanings present in common human experience, and second is the language prescribed and expressed within Torah. That common human experience, so far as it is accessible to Torah, is shaped by *halakhah* – when *halakhah* is understood for what it is. So at the end let us state what it is and is not.

Halakhah is Judaism's principal expression, too long set aside since the splendid philosophical-*halakhic* accomplishment of Maimonides, is to express the theology of *halakhah* in its fullness and complexity. If we take *halakhah* as the crucial category for the worldview and methods defined as Judaism, in contrast to the other definitions of the principal sources of Judaism, then we want to know the range and perspectives of the vision of the *halakhah*. What the worldview is which shapes, and is shaped by, the ethos of the *halakhah*, the conceptions of humanity and of the potentialities of human society – these things await definition. But, I wish now to suggest, theology is something more than merely the making explicit of what is implicit and constitutive.

The work of the theologian – as distinct from that of the scholar of history or hermeneutics – must be constructive and creative. For we must grant to theologians what we do not want for scholars: the freedom as constructive religious thinkers to propose fresh perspectives on, and even alterations in the worldview and ethos of, the law. This freedom, we know, has been assumed and vigorously exercised by the great thinkers of the *halakhah* who understood the deep paradox of the famous play on words, *heru 'al halluḥot* – "freedom [is] incised upon the tablets of the law." If, as we tell ourselves, in discipline there is freedom, then to the theologians we cannot deny the greatest freedom of all: to speak in fresh and original ways within the *halakhic* frame, as they do within the frame of biblical and aggadic materials all the time. For, it is self-evident, affirming a *halakhic* definition of Judaism is a theological decision, in the rich sense of the term: the doing of normative and constructive theology.

Having specified the historical and hermeneutical work to be done, we therefore turn to adumbrate the constructive task. For, as I implied, theology is not solely the description of theology, the evocation of worlds past and remembered. If it also is not the invocation of worlds here now and coming in time, it is hardly needed. It is the first task of the theologian to describe and interpret that world of meaning. But it is the second, and still more important, task to carry forward the exegesis of the worldview of Judaism by continuing *halakhic* reflection upon the world. That is, theologians have the work of viewing the world and shaping a vision of what we are and can be.

For in its way *halakhah* in the end lays before us a conception of who the community of Israel is and what the community of Israel can be. *Halakhah* speaks of the holiness of the community of Israel within the holiness of God. Its themes and issues then focus upon the way of life of the community of Israel, to the end that the community of Israel may fulfill its promise and potential as the people of the Lord, the kingdom of priests, and the holy people. Now when theologians look at the world today and see the world within the disciplines of *halakhah* and the perspectives of the holiness *halakhah* means to nurture, their creative and constructive work begins. It is to lay down statements of continuing norms for a new context. It is to renew the ancient norms through the lessons of a new age. What, after all, do we deal with, if not an exploration of human nature and of the divine image impressed within human nature? And what is at the heart and soul of Judaism if not the inquiry into the image of God in which we are made, therefore into the potential sanctity of us and of the world we make?

We cannot, therefore, concede that the theological work is done for all time in the pages of Maimonides' *Mishneh Torah* or *Shulḥan 'Arukh*. We insist that the work is to be done in our own days, when decisions are made which bespeak a vision of who we are and what we can be, of what it means to be in God's image and to live in a community meant to express God's will. The ancient, medieval, and modern rabbis did and do more than a work of history and hermeneutics. On the basis of what their eyes are trained to see and their minds to perceive, in age succeeding age they forge anew and contemporary understanding of a new and unprecedented world. That was what was original for them: Maimonides does not merely quote the ancient sources, though *Mishneh Torah* is a melange of quotations. Through his reflection and arrangement he says something new through something 1,000 years old. What we have to learn is that the *halakhic* process contains the theological process of Judaism. When we understand how that process works we shall gain access to Judaism. The reason is that the *halakhic* corpus contains such vision as we have, and have to share, about the sacred potentialities of humanity and of the human community. The tasks of theology today begin in the exegesis of exegesis done. But they lead to the doing of the exegesis of this time, the interpretation of our world and of its days. The creation of worlds goes on in world without end. That is what, as Rashi says, it means to be "like God" – to create worlds.

Judaism is a religion about this world and about the human being. Its encompassing conceptions concern the human being, made in God's image and little lower than angels, and the community framed and formed by human beings, the arena for the working out of God's word and will. Distinctive to Judaism is the intensely practical and practiced law. The word is not abstract. The will is for the here and now. But the word is yet a word, the will is not solely about what I eat but how I understand and feel – and what I am. In the end, we always are what we are, that is, we are mortal and die. But before that, we may become something "in our image, according to our likeness," like God – only that we die. And there, in that painful tension between death and living, between our mortality and the promise and vision of the sacred in ourselves, is the sanctuary of life, the arena for our struggles and our anguish. In the pain and the suffering, in the living in the face of the dying, is the sacred. The achievement, the vanquishing and the being vanquished, too, are sacred. Holiness is the pathos, holiness, the triumph.

V. Cui Bono?

It remains briefly to address two questions, usefulness and relevance. At the outset there is a threefold set of tasks of theology in Judaism: (1) to define Judaism, (2) to discover the human situation to which Judaism responds, and, finally (3) to create those modes of advocacy and apologetics which will permit contemporary Jews to gain renewed access to that Judaism subject to definition. This third task may be captured in the question: To whom is such a theological enterprise as I have described going to be useful? And alongside there is a second question, important to those who will want to study, and even interpret, the theology of Judaism in the setting of universities, therefore in discourse with a diverse and plural intellectual constituency: To whom, outside of Judaism, are the results of this kind of theology going to be relevant?

The obvious fact is that the two questions are one. For Jews seeking to define and understand Judaism and scholars of religions with the same fundamental questions – What is this thing? How does it work? – part company only at the end. Jews have yet a Jewish question not shared by others: How shall I find my way inside, or, if inside, what does it mean to *be*, to live, inside? But these are the same questions once again. The study of religions must encompass attention to the study of theologies, and, given the situation of teacher and student, the study of religions is going to include much effort (perhaps too much) given to the understanding of theologies.

Now I think it is everywhere understood as a datum that in our classrooms there will be no advocacy but the academic kind, and surely no active theologizing. But there must be understanding, an exercise in interpretation, in the framework of the common humanity or the study of religions collapses into the recitation of facts, a rubble of trivial observations. To prevent the ruin of the work, we quite properly turn to anthropology and sociology, philosophy and psychology, drama, poetry, and art – indeed to each and every source of insight available to us in humanistic leaning. But if my proposal is a sound one, then we find yet another source of insight to which to turn: theology itself. If the work is done with a decent respect for the diversity of our students and for the rights of all of them to be what they are without our interference, then surely the insights sought in descriptive theological inquiry and exposition – the human meaning of the law – may turn out to crown the construction of meaning (if not the search for truth) at which we labor.

9

The University as a Locus for the Judaic Life of Intellect

Why the New Is Not Necessarily Better than the Old, but Only Different

On the occasion of receiving the honorary doctorate,
Dottore ad Honorem in Scienze Politiche (indirizzo storico-politico)
University of Bologna, 1988

Why Universities Are Different from All Other Centers of Learning, and the Example of Judaism

What we celebrate, on the occasion of the 900th anniversary of the University of Bologna through the conferring of this degree requires definition.[1] The occasion, I think, draws us back to questions of philosophy concerning continuity and change, permanence and transience. A university as old as this one has changed many times over 900 years, so we reflect on what has lasted, amid time and change, to make us want to celebrate the long history of a distinguished center of learning. These questions are framed through the metaphor of the river. So we ask: what precisely do we mean by a river? For both Indian and Greek philosophy, and also, as a matter of fact, the rabbis of the Mishnah, want to find out whether the river is all the water all the time and everywhere? or merely the spot at which we stand? And when is the river the river? Is it when it flows from beginning to end, or just in the here and now? These profound questions of continuity and

---

[1]Address at the University of Bologna on accepting the degree *Laurea ad Honorem in Science Politiche*, on March 17, 1988.

131

change, permanence and transience and essence and existence, capture our attention. For we have to find out what words mean in context, such words as learning and as university, for instance, and indeed we do well to undertake even the definition of context, address not only speculative minds. We today participate in something entirely concrete and not abstract, namely, the celebration of 900 years of something. But precisely what is that? The answer to that question will give food for thought about the next 900 years of this ancient, properly celebrated foundation, this University of Bologna – and also about what animates that university and justifies its near millennial endurance, which is learning.

We do not celebrate these buildings, or even the place at which they stand, for the university originally had no fixed location. Lectures were given wherever they were given, in convents, for instance, until the Archiginnasio Palace was built in 1562. So for nearly 500 years, one could not point to the University of Bologna. But there was a University of Bologna. Nor do we celebrate what was taught in Bologna for 900 years. For the contents of learning changed, in the nature of things, but so too did the categories. The university in its day was famed for the study of law; in the twelfth and thirteen centuries, thousands came here to study Roman law. But the subject of law was only one, and other subjects, medicine and philosophy and science, joined the curriculum in due course. So we do not celebrate 900 years of the study of some one thing. We do not even celebrate the coming together of teachers of a certain kind and students of a certain kind. In the present age young women as well as men assemble. But in the early centuries, mature men – no women – came here, and these were officers of the church or the state, archdeacons, heads of schools, canons of cathedrals, for example. So the University of Bologna at that time may be compared not to the University of Bologna today but to a War College for colonels and brigadier generals, undertaking vast new responsibilities in the military, or to a business school for the training of advanced executives in industry. If, then, we ask ourselves where is the river, what is the river, and what makes up the river, that is this university, we cannot easily answer that question. There is more change than continuity, and the transient seems all there is. Yet if you give me a moment of patience, I shall propose an answer and identify what we celebrate.

Before identifying what we rightly celebrate, however, let me focus briefly on the selection of a specialist in the history of religion whose focus is on Judaism and ask about what, in 900 years past and even today, has prompted that particular choice. The sources on which I work, the ancient writings of Judaism in the first seven centuries A.D., have never been studied in this university, though they were long studied by major intellects in Italy, and they are just now beginning to find a place here. So as a matter of fact we do not celebrate something done here, or even the counterpart to a component of the faculty here. And how I read these sources, which is as documents in the expression, by humanity, of its conception of the making of a world, a social world, hardly corresponds to any approach to the reading of any religious documents that has been taken in the 900 years of this university. True, the Talmuds and related writings form the counterpart, for Judaism, of the canon law and jurisprudence, studied with such remarkable distinction here by the noted jurists of Bologna Irnerius and Francesco Accursius (Accursio). Without a considerable labor of mediation by bilingual persons, they would have no more understood these writings than the succession of scholarly Talmudists would have understood the civil and canon law addressed so brilliantly in this place. But neither the famous Talmudists of Italy nor the celebrated canon lawyers of Italy will have understood the questions that I bring to the sources that, in one idiom or another, they studied. They wanted to know one thing, I something else, about the same thing.

The question now stands forth in stark clarity. We do not celebrate a place, however old. We do not celebrate a single tradition of learning, however deeply rooted in generations of successive masters and disciples. We do not in the person of this speaker celebrate a subject pursued at this university for endless centuries. Nor do we even mark a long-enduring subject, whether law, whether religion, though both law and religion form foci for distinguished intellectual effort in this place over a long period of time. Then what do these 900 years join together, which did not happen before, in this place, and did not happen somewhere outside of this place in the way that it happened here, within? And to these negatives I add the particular ones of the occasion at hand: we also do not celebrate a subject long taught here or even a reading of a kind of subject long undertaken here.

I may offer a particular way toward an answer to this question, what do we celebrate after 900 years of the University of Bologna that derives from my subject, and, if I am able to do so, then I shall have given toward commemorating the occasion something distinctive to myself. Such I conceive my task to be. I study books that celebrated their 900th anniversary when the University of Bologna (whatever we may mean by that) began. In 1088, the Mishnah, a philosophical statement in the form of a law code that bears comparison to Plato's Republic and Aristotle's Politics, was approximately 900 years old, having taken shape toward the end of the second century. So before you, and in celebration of your 900th anniversary, stands a representative of a tradition of learning that is twice the age of this ancient foundation. Not only so, but institutions in which the literature of ancient Judaism, beginning with the Mishnah, were studied enjoy a continuous history, if not in one place, alas, of nearly those same close to 2,000 years. My subject here is a very new one. But to that subject and its institutions, the University of Bologna, in its 900 years, is very new too, if no longer a mere parvenu. Consequently, you see me as a Judaic specialist as someone standing at the threshold of your palaces of learning, just as, with equal justice, you see me, as an American, as a new person, as indeed we Americans think that we are. But I see you, in the context of learning, as a chapter in a long story, a tale that began before, and that can continue afterward.

Nor is the story the one told by the Mishnah and its successor writings, which is not the only ongoing tradition of learning that, in the West, in Europe and in the Americas, finds its home, for the moment at least, in universities. There is, after all, philosophy. There is, after all, mathematics. There is, after all, music. The classics of ancient Greece and Rome may make the same statements in Greek and in Latin as I have in reference to writings in Hebrew and in Aramaic. Most of what we study here will see this new, this young, this scarcely-tried institution as a temporary home, this thing, this university, this Bologna. And, I should say, every professor of every subject may find roots to his or her subject of learning, however recent in its contemporary formulation, in the soil of remote antiquity. For mathematics, we now know, dictated the arrangement of the stones at Stonehenge, and the cave drawings in France and Spain, as much as the aboriginal wall-scratchings in Australia, as much as the ruins of the old cities of Africa, Zimbabwe, not to mention the remarkable Mayan monuments of the Yucatan and Aztecs of Middle America and of the Incas of the Andes – they all bespeak reflection, judgment, proportion, taste, composition: philosophy. And all these traditions of learning, each with its precision and its canons of rationality, every one of them flourished in intellect and in heart, but, for most of the history of humanity, not in universities.

When, therefore, we celebrate the 900th anniversary of this University of Bologna, our task is to remember not how old, but how new, this place really is: new, changing, transient, above all, transient – a river always flowing, always changing. Take the water out of the river and you have the banks, and they are, more or less, permanent. But then you have no river anymore. Everyone here, in every tradition of human knowledge, stands for something that humanity has pursued in other institutions than this type of institution, under other circumstances than this one, and in the service of different auspices from the ones that sustain and support universities as we know them and have known them for these 900 years of Bologna: church, state, industry, commerce, to name the more important auspices of learning today.

Learning transcends its auspices. Learning recognizes no limitations of an institutional sort. Learning is so natural to humanity as, in the end, to require nothing more than the intellect driven by curiosity and sustained by speculation. Accordingly, we have to ask ourselves what it is that marks as distinctive and as valuable the university as we have known it for the brief spell commencing nine hundred years ago in this place, among the ancestors of this people. Why is the university of the West, inclusive of the Americas, and now Africa and Asia as well, different from all other forms in which learning has found a home, in which, in more academic language, learning has been institutionalized in permanent and socially sanctioned form?

As I said, it is not because it is old, for it is young. It is not because the program of learning, the curriculum, is stable, because it is subject to change that, relative to the hundred thousand year history of humanity, happens every forty-five minutes. And it is not because the university is the best place in which to pursue curiosity and to sort things out, for that remains to be demonstrated. When we consider that nearly all of the great intellectual achievements in the history of humanity – by definition – took place outside of universities and were the accomplishments of persons who were not professors, paid to think great thoughts and write them down, we realize that fact. If we point to the formative intellects of the world as we know it, Darwin, Freud, Marx, to name only three, we must wonder who needs universities at all. For clearly, the great intellectual steps forward in the natural and social sciences were taken somewhere else, on the Beagle, or in the imagination of a despised Viennese Jew, or in the hall of the British Museum, open to a lowly foreign journalist.

What marks the university as different from all other modes of the institutionalization of learning? It is that as we have known universities from the very beginning, we assemble here to treat learning as shared, plural, open, diverse. The history of Bologna, with its greatness in law, is not the history of a law school but of a university, in which medicine, philosophy, natural and social science joined together. What we institutionalize in universities is the possibility of shared discourse and public exchange of knowledge among different people who know different things and seek to find a language common to those different things. What it means to study, in some one place, mathematics and botany, or sociology and religion, is that we judge it better to study these things in one place than in many places. And in the end, though not every day, that judgment addresses a deeper concern for explaining many things in a few ways. If chemistry did not speak to geology, or physics to mathematics, or economics to political science, then the premise of the university that learning many things helps us to understand them all in some cogent way proves flawed. But it is not flawed, for, as we know, economics without mathematics, and political science without history, and anthropology without psychology, are not possible. Learning flows across disciplinary lines, to the discomfort of the limited and the specialized, because humanity will not stay within bounds. The analytical mind, in mathematics, in times past turned to measure the dimensions of God. And so throughout: there are no limits to mind and imagination.

I do not think it will be difficult to identify the reason for that fact. It is this same quest to understand and make sense of things that is natural to our condition as human beings. And understanding, making sense, means putting many things together in some few ways. The mathematicians at Stonehenge had to make many observations indeed, gather accurate facts beyond number, to know how, at just one moment in the cycle of the solar year, light would enter one space, and not some other, and continue in one line, not some other. And those same mathematicians at Stonehenge had also to want to mark that moment, had to believe it mattered in so profound a way that the energies of an entire society, over a long period of time, could be invested in nothing better than the realization of that magic circle of stones that embodied the facts they put together. When we consider the caves in Ireland, the temples in Middle America, where, at some magic moment, the light over head strikes some one point, then but at no other time, when we contemplate the calculations in mathematics, the engineering skills, required to make a temple or dig a hole in such a way that, just then, things would be this way, not that, we realize what has always been at stake in learning. It is not the fact naked and celebrated in its raw state, but the fact explained by reference to some, indeed many other facts.

In universities we draw together many disciplines or fields of learning, *science* you say in Italian, in quest for not information but understanding. And by understanding, we mean, the capacity of many things to find explanation in some one way. What this means for those of us who study the particularities of a single human group, the Jews through time, or the Classics, or the anthropology of this tribe or the sociology of that class or locus, is simple. We all learn a great deal about some one thing. But only when we can intelligibly address others, who know a great deal about some other thing, are we able to join in that mode of discourse that marks the university as singular and, I think, unique. It is when we aim at facing problems in common, meaning at explaining many things in some few ways, that we join universities and belong nowhere but in universities. There the difference is to be explained, not (merely) celebrated. There the discourse is to be common, not (merely) distinctive and particular, whether to the discipline, whether to the data.

And how are we to do this? Let me close with a very simple answer. It is by treating the particular as exemplary, the unique as typical. So long as what we know we know only in its own terms and not by way of comparison, we celebrate the extraordinary and instead of explaining, simply paraphrase our sources. When we see what we know as suggestive, as data that serve as an example of a condition to be explored in diverse examples, and when we offer what we know as useful examples for the testing of hypotheses of common interest and concern, then we form universities. For how we treat knowledge indicates where we are, that, and not what the world calls us, or what we call ourselves. The entry of any subject requires displaying a passport: this is what I, knowing what I know, can teach you about you, knowing what you know – and therefore how I can learn from you as well.

What are those particular ranges of human experience that, in my judgment, the subject that I study illuminates in particular? The history and literature and religion of the Jews lay no credible claim to uniqueness in telling the story of humanity under stress, for Jews are not unique in suffering, nor in loyalty, nor in endurance, nor in hope, though they have special lessons to teach about the power of humanity to endure despite and against great adversity indeed. But there is something characteristic of the intellectual tradition of the Jews, the particular tradition to which I have devoted my life, that I think does have a distinctive contribution to make to public discourse in the university. It is an example of that very activity that, over all, the university is meant to nurture, seeing things whole, all together, and within a single, unifying field theory of explanation. The very quest for connections, for the explanation of many things in some one way, that characterizes *le science* – all human learning – in the Italian sense, that is to say, all forms of learning, finds in the very canon of Judaism a stunning expression and exemplification. For that canon makes the effort to put together everything worth knowing and to explain it all in some one way. Providing an account of the formation of the world and the history of humanity, telling the story of everything in some one way, that remarkable canon, represented by the culminating statement of the Talmud of Babylonia, provides us with an example, in the form of a piece of writing, of what a university, an institution of persons, is meant to comprise and compose: everything put together, all at once, in a cogent way, in a single intelligible statement. In its odd context, that document and the writings that it holds together form a singular instance of what it means for learning to come together into a single system of understanding, for facts to yield a rationality, and for data all together and all at once to make sense.

Our work of learning in the particular kind of institution that we form in universities is different from the work of learning in all other settings for learning in that one way: the intent not merely to describe but to explain, and to explain not merely this and that, but everything, all together and all at once. True, appeals to the perennial philosophy and to encompassing explanations differ from here to there, with the result that there are, after all, diverse disciplines within the university, as there should be, and various things that form the object of study by those disciplines. The diversity of the university is as critical to the definition as the unity of learning in cogent explanation that marks the academic intellect but no other. No one can imagine that a single inherited system of holding things all together all at once and making sense of everything in some one way can yet serve. Nor do I suggest that we close all faculties at the University of Bologna and invite all the professors and students to study the Talmud.

But you have chosen to honor me in particular, and that means, a person who studies something you do not study here at all, and who studies in a way that is scarcely replicated anywhere else in which what I study is studied at all. So, in accepting this *Laurea ad Honorem in Science Politiche*, I do so only because I claim that the thing I study exemplifies in an interesting and suggestive way the things that all of us are meant to do together, in this kind of place and in no other, in the way in which we do it and in no other way: many things, in some one way. The framers of the talmudic canon put together all knowledge, as they identified worthwhile knowledge, and they explained everything they knew in some one way. They produced not an encyclopaedia of knowledge but a single coherent and cogent statement of what they knew, set forth in a cogent and proportioned way. It was their theory of the whole, all together and all at once. When we can do that, we shall also have founded a tradition of learning that will endure, where it serves, as theirs has endured. I have meant only to make clear to the world within, to the Jewish people, and to the world beyond, to you, colleagues of Bologna, what these remarkable intellects accomplished in intellect, the seeing of many things in some one way, the explaining of everything in a system and a structure of balance, proportion, well-crafted composition. But then again, they claimed it came from God. And, I suppose, in context, knowing after all the source of our systems and our structures and our capacity to effect composition, we for ourselves can claim no less, if in different language.

Part Two
LECTURES ON JUDAISM IN THE
HUMANITIES:
LITERATURE, SOCIETY, AND PHILOSOPHY

10

Beyond Historicism, After Structuralism: Story as History in Ancient Judaism

The Harry Spindel Memorial Lecture
Bowdoin College, 1980

All learning should aim to contribute to general education. By general education I mean not common literacy in an established canon of writings, but insight accessible to people without regard to prior traits of culture, race, sex, class, or nation. I cannot raise a topic in the study of Judaism, therefore, without proposing to address issues of general intelligibility. These are issues of general education, the humanities, and religious studies. Even though the framing of an appropriate address for discourse is brief, it is critical in establishing context and preparing the way for questions of method and meaning. What I mean by general education is explained by Jonathan Z. Smith, who defines it as the "notion of providing *exempli gratia,* an arsenal of classic instances which are held to be exemplary, of providing paradigmatic events and expressions as resources from which to reason, from which to extend the possibility of intelligibility to that which first appears to be novel."[1] From Smith, also, comes a striking and pertinent definition of the humanities, which, at its origins, in fifteenth-century Italian humanism, was a word set in contrast with its opposite. "Humane

---

[1] I cite and draw on Jonathan Z. Smith, "The Devil in Mr. Jones: Religion from the Perspective of the Human Sciences." Smith's address, given at the University of Chicago in his role as dean of the college, will be published in a forthcoming book of essays in a series under my editorship.

studies" were to be contrasted with"divine sciences," the humanities with theology.

Now in that context, the study of religion could not be part of the humanities. Matters changed so that religion became a topic of generally accessible discourse only when the distinction was made between two parallel paths in the study of religion, a humanistic one for the academy, a theological one for the seminary.[2] So there are these two matters. First is the interest in general education, that is, in showing how one small matter exemplifies some larger concern of broad interest and accessibility. Second, there is the determination of finding a humanistic program for the study of religions. Combining the two is not difficult. What we have to do is precede each specific statement with a general one, and place an *e.g.,* between the two. That is, we should seek for what is general in what is particular, showing how the facts of a given culture, race, sex, class, nation, or religion, in particular, illuminate the condition of culture, race, sex, class, nation, religion, in general. In the case of the study of religion, we have to take seriously the heritage of the Enlightenment, which sees religion as a generic, distinct from the collectivity of specific, believing communities. The Enlightenment, moreover, maintains that any human fact lies within the range of reason and is susceptible to shared understanding. So, carrying Smith's excellent program forward, I wish to offer, as an exercise in exemplification, a problem in the analysis of ancient Judaism in its principal expression, that is, the Judaism of the Mishnah, Talmud, and midrashic compilations of the first six centuries of the Common Era. This I wish to do in such a way that I may contribute to general education in the context of the humanistic study of religion.

The Problem

The issue to be exemplified in the study of ancient Jewish texts is nothing less than our basic judgment upon the past and its relevance, that is, upon history and how it should be studied. What I wish to do is to show how we may discover questions appropriate to historical facts in our hands. I present an exercise in exemplifying the discovery of correct questions to be addressed to ancient sources. Stories drawn out of ancient Judaism will serve as our laboratory case, so Judaism will provide a paradigm of interpretation, a resource from which to reason. To state matters rapidly and superficially, modern culture rejects the claims of history. The scholarly aspect of culture – that is, culture as

---

[2]Drawn from Smith.

nurtured in universities – today works itself out essentially independent of the past and, it must follow, independent, too, of the material and social reality of the present. That is why architecture, music, philosophy, literature, and the reading of texts work out their programs of study without regard to the history of architecture, music, philosophy, literature, let alone the history of the study of these subjects. As Carl Schorske states, "The modern mind has been growing indifferent to history because history, conceived as a continuous nourishing tradition, has become useless to it."[3] Evidence for this fact is drawn by Schorske from developments in diverse fields of learning. New critics in literature, he points out, replace literary historicism with "an a-temporal, internalistic, formal analysis." Traditional political philosophy gives way to "the a-historical and politically neutralizing reign of the behaviorists." In philosophy, as Schorske says, "a discipline previously marked by a high consciousness of its own historical character and continuity, the analytic school challenged the validity of the traditional questions that had concerned philosophers since antiquity. In the interest of a restricted and purer functioning in the areas of language and logic, the new philosophy broke the ties both to history...and to the discipline's own past."

What is important is that the new methods of analysis in the humanistic fields, which stressed internal traits and autonomous, enduring characteristics of structure and style, made the break from history. That is, once it is recognized that creations of literature and art adhere to canons of logic unbound by context but expressive of a universal and timeless "logic," whether of language or of morphology, then history as the story of where things come from and what they mean because of where they come from no longer explains very much. And, as Schorske says, "the historian could ignore [these autonomous characteristics of structure and style] only at the risk of misreading the historical meaning of his material." Let me now cite Schorske's fine statement of the problem, before turning to the exemplification of the problem in the study of stories told by ancient rabbis in the Talmud. This extended statement constitutes that generalization, to which the study of Judaism supplies its e.g.:

> The historian will not share to the full the aim of the humanistic textual analyst. The latter aims at the greatest possible illumination of a cultural product, relativizing all principles of analysis to its particular content. The historian seeks rather to locate and interpret the artifact temporally in a field where two lines intersect. One line is vertical, or diachronic, by which he establishes the relation of a text or a system of

---

[3]Carl E. Schorske, *Fin-de-siècle Vienna. Politics and Culture* (New York, 1980: Knopf), pp. xvii-xxii.

> thought to previous expressions in the same branch of cultural
> activity....The other is horizontal or synchronic; by it [the historian]
> assesses the relation of the content of the intellectual object to what is
> appearing in other branches or aspects of a culture at the same
> time...[4]

Let me now restate the problem as I wish to confront it. For a long time, from the beginning of the nineteenth century, history was deemed to provide the principal road into the interpretation of artifacts of culture, whether literary or philosophical or political or religious. The means of description and of explanation were one and the same: this is what happened, so this is what it meant. Consequently, when confronted with the need to describe a religion, people took for granted the issue was an essentially historical one. Explanation followed from the mode of description. The facts adduced in a given order and by a given program carry with them the explanation induced by that order and demanded by that program. Explanation and interpretation then became subdivisions of history, and meaning emerged from explanation. So what happened in the past was deemed to bear within itself its own claim upon the present. Theories of society emerged from histories of society, and so in the other fields of learning. Since, in the nature of things, learning shapes culture, and culture governs society and its material reality, it would follow that what had happened imparted meaning upon what was happening. History became doctrine, "historicism" viewed from the perspective of values.

Attacks on an essentially historical, hence traditional, view of culture seemed to come only from barbarians like Henry Ford, who said, "History is bunk." The citadel of historicism would not fall before mechanics. The point at which the historical reading and explanation of the artifacts of culture proved vulnerable lay outside of the citadel entirely. The great theories never collapse; people simply walk away from them. In the case of historicism, moreover, we deal with a variety of specific versions of the matter, consequently with a sequence of settings in which an other-than-historicistic theory of explanation and interpretation would replace the established one. In one setting, it would be a philosophical attack. In another, the discovery of enduring structures of mind, beyond time and circumstance, would call into question the developmental and orderly description which then passed for interpretation. In still a third, the logic embodied in the genetic fallacy would be overturned, so that origins no longer were found adequately to explain even themselves. In a fourth, the end of the fallacy that beginnings explain all carried in its wake the collapse of

---

[4]*Ibid.*, pp. xxi-xxii.

the notion that historical description contains any explanation at all. And so it would go. In the end matters were as Schorske sets them forth: history seemed bankrupt, to everyone but historians.

The issue is now to be drawn more concretely. To ask the question as simply as I can: How shall we read a story or a text? What do we think is important about that story? So at the outset the matter of history as against ahistory concerns the very purpose of learning, the context of interpretation. Once we determine that our interests are other than historical, in the sense of history as the story of one-time events, as narrative, it is obvious that we shall interpret texts from an other than historical perspective. We shall want to know different things, so we shall observe different traits. The challenge to a historical reading of stories and texts comes from a simple fact. Historians do not deem important, or even notice, traits of literary structure which call into question whether stories are meant to contain history at all. There are structural traits pointing to the original meaning and purpose of making up and telling a story. These in their nature simply preclude the pertinence of simple analysis of historical, including philological, traits. History and philology are interesting but not urgent. The reason is that to ancient fables and tales, including those of a historical character, they present the wrong questions. So their results provide beside the point. That is one position of that structuralism to which Schorske alludes.

In what follows, I shall lead you through three positions: examples of (1) a historicistic reading of two Jewish tales of ancient times, (2) a structuralist reading on these same stories, and then, at the end, (3) a post-structuralist reversion to questions of a fundamentally historical character. But these are different ones from those asked at the outset. From asking what really happened "behind" a story (the kernel of truth), I shall move to questions of what is happening in a given social setting through the principal didactic message of a story. For before us is obviously not an account of one-time events, history in the old sense. Rather, revealed are persistent traits of social culture and of mind, history in a mode congruent to the character and purposes of the evidence. That is the structure of this paper.

The Problem Exemplified in Ancient Judaism

Story and History

These rather general remarks demand concrete and specific exemplification. For that purpose, I wish to take up two stories found in ancient rabbinic writings and to show how they have been used for historical purposes. By attending to the structural traits of these stories, I then shall show that the use of such stories for history misinterprets the obvious purposes of the tellers of those stories. This I shall do by demonstrating on the basis of the structural traits of those stories just what the storytellers wished to accomplish. In this way we shall see why historicism misreads the historical meaning of these materials. The reason is that asking what really happened, or assuming that what the story says happened really did happen, misses the point of the story. The original and generative purpose of telling the story is on the surface, accessible to us because it is revealed by the basic structure of the story, its emphases, organization, points of conflict, and resolution. Stories are not history in so simple a sense as is assumed by a narrowly historical reading of stories. The reason is that they do not contain evidence of one-time events but speak of enduring social truths – a different sort of history.

Let us first of all take up the two stories, then rapidly draw upon a part of the record of what has been said about and done with them by people to whom historical description, interpretation, and explanation constitute a single and simultaneous act: historians in search of a narrative of events. The first story deals with a miracle-worker and what he did ("one time"), the second with a rabbi and what he did ("on that day"). These are two distinct types of historical person in the rabbinic literature, the former, as the name states, capable of affecting nature, the latter the principal heroic type of the rabbinic kind of Judaism. At the outset let us simply see the stories as they appear, in English translation, in their original settings.

The first story is about Honi, the circle-drawer, and how he made rain.

A.   They said to Honi, the circle-drawer, "Pray for rain." He said to them, "Go and take in the clay ovens used for Passover, so that they do not soften [in the rain that is coming]." He prayed, but it did not rain.
        What did he do? He drew a circle and stood in the middle of it and said before Him, "Lord of the world! Your children have turned to me, for before You, I am like a member of the family. I swear by Your great name – I'm simply not moving from here until you take pity on your children!" It began to rain drop by drop.

B.   He said, "This is not what I wanted, but rain for filling up cisterns, pits, and caverns." It began to rain violently.

C.   He said, "This is not what I wanted, but rain of good will, blessing, and graciousness." Now it rained the right way, until Israelites had to flee from Jerusalem up to the Temple Mount because of the rain.

D.   Now they came and said to him, "Just as you prayed for it to rain, now pray for it to go away." He said to them, "Go, see whether the stone of the strayers is disappeared."

E.   Simeon b. Shatah sent [a message] to him, "If you were not Honi, I should decree a ban of excommunication against you. But what am I going to do to you? For you make demands before the Omnipresent so he does what you want, like a son who makes demands on his father so he does what he wants. Concerning you Scripture says, *Let your father and your mother be glad, and let her that bore you rejoice* (Prov. 23:25)."[5]

For the present, it suffices to note that the principal action of the story is in a sequence of three events (B, C, D), rain drop by drop, violent rain, and the right kind of rain – but for too long. The story trails off, and Honi ceases to be the chief actor, at D. The message of Simeon, E, is totally without preparation. It appears to be tacked on, and the saying stands outside of the narrative materials, to which it does not make reference.

Let us now turn to the second story, which is of a more obviously historical character. This story deals with the destruction of the Temple in Jerusalem in A.D. 70 and establishes a link of continuity between that Temple and a schoolhouse of Judaism located in Yavneh (Jamnia), a town just off the southern coast of the Land of Israel. The second hero is Yohanan ben Zakkai, who (as this story tells us) is the one who effected the movement from the doomed Temple to the nascent schoolhouse, from cult to learning, from priest to rabbi, and from independent state to subordinated, autonomous holy nation. (But this view of the focus of the story is wrong, as I shall suggest in a moment.)

A.   When Vespasian came to destroy Jerusalem, he said to the inhabitants, "Fools, why do you seek to destroy this city, and why do you seek to burn the Temple? For what do I ask of you but that you send me one bow or one arrow, and I shall leave you?" They said to him, "Even as we went forth against the first two who were here before you and slew them, so shall we go forth against you and slay you."

B.   When Rabban Yohanan ben Zakkai heard this, he sent for the men of Jerusalem and said to them, "My children, why do you destroy this city, and why do you seek to burn the Temple? For what is it that he asks of you? He asks of you one bow or one arrow, and he will go off from you." They said to him, "Even as we went forth against the two before him and slew them, so shall we go forth against him and slay him."

C.   Vespasian had men stationed near the walls of Jerusalem. Every word which they overheard they would write down, attach [the message] to an arrow and shoot it over the wall, saying that Rabban Yohanan ben Zakkai was one of the Emperor's supporters. Now, after Rabban Yohanan ben Zakkai had spoken to them one day, two days, and three days, and they still would not

---

[5]Mishnah Taanit 3:8.

listen to him, he sent for his disciples, for Rabbi Eliezer and Rabbi Joshua. "My sons," he said to them, "arise and take me out of here. Make a coffin for me that I might lie in it." Rabbi Eliezer took the head end of it, Rabbi Joshua took hold of the foot, and they began carrying him as the sun set, until they reached the gates of Jerusalem. "Who is this?" the gatekeepers demanded. "It's a dead man," they replied. "Do you not know that the dead may not be held overnight in Jerusalem?" "If it's a dead man," the gatekeepers said to them, "take him out." They continued carrying him until they reached Vespasian.

D.   They opened the coffin, and [Rabban Yohanan ben Zakkai] stood up before him. "Are you Rabban Yohanan ben Zakkai?" [Vespasian] inquired; "Tell me, what may I give you" "I ask of you only Yavneh, where I might go and teach my disciples and there establish a prayer [house] and perform all the commandments." "Go," Vespasian said to him, "and whatever you wish to do, do."

E.   Said [Rabban Yohanan] to him, "By your leave, may I say something to you?" "Speak," [Vespasian] said to him. Said [Rabban Yohanan] to him, "Lo, you [already] stand as royalty." "How do you know this?" [Vespasian asked]. [Rabban Yohanan] replied, "This has been handed down to us, that the Temple will not be surrendered to a commoner, but to a king; as it is said, 'And he shall cut down the thickets of the forest with iron, and Lebanon shall fall by a mighty one' (Is. 10:34)." It was said: no more than a day, or two or three days, passed before a pair of men reached him from his city [announcing] that the emperor was dead and that he had been elected to succeed as king.[6]

This story is in five parts: two before the escape from Jerusalem, the escape itself, then two parts after the escape. The focus of interest in the protagonists runs from Vespasian to Yohanan, then, at the other end, from Yohanan and what he wants to Vespasian and what he wants. We shall not be detained by the problem of chronology or by trying to correlate the tale with the chronicle of Josephus concerning the war against Rome.[7] To do so would foreclose discussion of what is important about this story, that is, what question to begin with is to come to bear upon it.

Beyond Historicism

The two tales before us have performed long and honorable service for historians. Both of them pop up in all historical accounts of the history of the Jewish people in the Land of Israel. Honi appears as a miracle-worker. Yohanan ben Zakkai figures in every account of the destruction of the Temple. So the events depicted are things that really

---

[6]Abot deRabbi Natan, chapter four.
[7]This is discussed, with full bibliography, in my *Life of Yohanan ben Zakkai* (Leiden, second edition, 1970: E.J. Brill), pp. 145-173.

happened, at the time at which the storyteller says they happened, to real people. These report one-time events. The sayings attributed to the participants in the story really were said, by the people to whom they are assigned, at some one time, and for some one purpose. History is particular. It tells not about the ongoing struggles and values of a social group. It reveals not enduring traits of culture. Reality is specific, and, as I said, it happens once for all time. True, a certain skepticism about obvious miracles will figure. It is conventional to avoid total gullibility about Honi's power. But that skepticism serves a limited purpose. Concerning the story about Yohanan and Vespasian there are no reservations whatsoever. When we have accomplished the proper exegesis of the story, with stress on philology, lo and behold, we have history. So the methodology of history governs the interpretation of these stories. In this context it is appropriate to cite the wise observation of William Dever, "'Methodology' in archaeology, as in any theory of human inquiry, grows directly out of theory: how you look at the evidence depends on what you want to know and why you think it may be important."[8]

Now let me briefly substantiate this statement of how the two stories have been used. First, the story about Honi has routinely served to prove the character of Jewish magical praxis in the time in which Honi is supposed to have lived, three hundred years before the redaction of the Mishnah, in which the story first appears and is preserved. To take one among innumerable examples, Joshua Trachtenberg writes, "One of the most picturesque of ancient Jewish miracle-workers was Honi HaMe'agel (first century B.C.E.), whose penchant for standing within a circle while he called down rain from heaven won him his title, 'the circle-drawer.'"[9] In this sentence we see that the story is deemed fact, historical fact, about a one-time event and a person who lived in a particular place. The article on Honi in the *Encyclopedia Judaica*[10] begins, "Renowned miracle worker in the period of the Second Temple....The Talmud recounts wondrous tales as to the manner in which his prayers for rain were answered." So far as I know, these "tales" in fact add up to the *one* which we considered. To be sure, the story occurs in diverse compilations, from the Mishnah onward. So I suppose we are expected to count each time the story is told as evidence of yet another miracle of rainmaking. Later in the same article, the author states, "Honi appears as a charismatic personality and the

---

[8]William Dever, in *Biblical Archaeologist* 43, 1, 1980, p. 42.
[9]Joshua Trachtenberg, *Jewish Magic and Superstition* (Philadelphia, 1961: Jewish Publication Society of America), p. 121.
[10]Unsigned article, *Encyclopaedia Judaica* (Jerusalem, 1971: Keter), 8:964-965.

people considered him undoubtedly a kind of folk prophet with the ability to work miracles. Even Simeon b. Shatah, despite his displeasure with Honi's self-confidence and his wish to place Honi under a ban, was compelled to give way to those who regarded Honi as a 'son who importunes his father.'" To be sure, this paraphrase reads into the tale more than is there. But what is important in this routine account is the frame of reference. It is entirely historical. The story *is* history: a one-time event, a particular person. Honi is not made to typify or to express an established ideal, value, or philosophy. He does not serve as an expression of social conflict or class phenomenon. He is a person. He lived at a given time (first century B.C.E.). He did certain things. He is important because we know who he was and what he did.

The story about Yohanan ben Zakkai's emergence from the dying city of Jerusalem, through a coffin, to a new mode of life in Judaism, invariably yields a history of a concrete event. Let me cite one important instance of how the story is utilized:

> It is the accepted view among scholars regarding the negotiations between Vespasian...and Rabban Johanan b. Zakkai that the latter, when he foresaw the destruction of Jerusalem and the burning of the Temple, sought to take preventive measures to avert the collapse of the nation and its Torah by establishing a "spiritual center," which would assure the continued existence of the Jewish people, even when its residual political independence was gone and its homeland destroyed...[11]

Gedalyahu Alon, who wrote these words, goes on to address this question to the story we read (and some of its parallels): "What prompted Rabban Johanan to go particularly to Jabneh?" The reason the question is to be asked is that Alon assumes the story can answer it. The story takes for granted there was some reason to go to that place, and Alon takes for granted the story tells us what really happened. As it happens, Alon takes Yavneh to be a kind of concentration point for Jews who had surrendered to the Romans or were friendly to begin with: "[They] went to Jabneh not because they particularly desired this place, but because they were sent against their will...Rabban Johanan's main request to Vespasian that he should be allowed 'to study Torah [at Jabnet] and make fringes and perform there all the other precepts' simply means that their captors should not make the conditions of their confinement unduly stringent, as they were, apparently, wont to

---

[11]Gedalyahu Alon, *Jews, Judaism and the Classical World* (Jerusalem, 1977: Magnes Press of the Hebrew University), p. 269.

do with others..."[12] Now what is important is on the surface. Alon is certain that he discusses an account of words really said, of deeds truly done, on some one day, between two concrete, historical personalities. The story is history. Our work is to interpret the language and details of the story. Properly interpreted, these will tell us history: what Yohanan ben Zakkai did and why he did it, what Vespasian said and why he said it – on that day.

So the details of the story to which historians draw our attention concern what was said, what was done. In fact, as I shall now show, that is a false perspective on the character of each story. It presupposes that the story asks one set of questions, serves one set of purposes. But the story addresses a different purpose from the narrowly historical one. Each one is didactic. Each is an artifact of social culture and makes a point which is representative of a social group, a fundamentally theological and secondarily exegetical lesson. The storyteller makes no pretense at narration of things which really happened. The reason is that his plan is to create not a narrative but a drama. He wishes not to tell a one-time event but to create a paradigm. In fact, as we shall now see, the story about Honi portrays the relationship between the sage or rabbi and another type of heroic figure within the Jewish community, and the story about Yohanan ben Zakkai and Vespasian expresses the relationship between the sage or rabbi and another type of heroic figure among the nations of the world. So in their deepest structure both stories take up the problem of the relationship of a rabbi to another focus of power. As I shall spell out, each story answers the troubling question of how the rabbi relates to some other, competing type of powerful social character. The stories express the tension between rabbi and holy man, rabbi and emperor. They resolve that tension by explicit claims of priority for the source of the rabbi's power, knowledge of Scripture. The historical question to each is social. The issue unpacked through examining each is the mediation of social power ("at some one-time," "on that day" indeed!). Let me now spell this out.

Story and Structure

The importance of seeking the basic structure of a story is in discovering the essential purpose originally and perpetually served by the story. However interesting are matters of detail, it is when we can state the main point of a story that we enter into its meaning to the person who made it up. The beginning of interpretation lies not in explaining a mere detail, for instance, what Yohanan ben Zakkai

---

[12]*Ibid.*, pp. 294-295.

really asked for, or really got, from Vespasian. The first and determinative step of interpretation is to find out the purpose of a story: the source of its conflict and resolution, the center of its action, the provocation of telling one detail and ignoring some other. These things we see when we uncover the basic, irreducible units through which the story unfolds. The power of a structuralist interpretation of literature is to chop away secondary matter and cut right to the heart. It is to uncover the logic of a story, unbound by context but timelessly revealed so that we, far away and long afterward, can see what the story originally meant (and may continue to mean). That is why so many find compelling the inquiry into structure and interpretation through canons of timeless logic. Structures by definition are timeless and enduring – the opposite of one-time events.

Now historians take for granted that the purpose of telling the tales before us is to relate things which really happened, one-time events, history as historians write it. We have therefore to ask whether the traits of the stories sustain this view. That is to say, when we look into the way in which the story is told, do we discern an interest in an essentially one-time event? To put matters simply: the point of entry is the focus of concern, the main point made by the story. I shall now show that both stories are so constructed as to do two things.

First, there is the principal purpose, which is didactic. The storyteller wishes to make certain points through *how* he tells the story. He is confident the person who hears or reads the story will grasp these points and so apprehend his purpose.[13]

Second, there is a secondary (but culturally primary) purpose, which is to link persons and events to the present age to those of Scripture. That is, the story not only has a didactic purpose, *vis-à-vis* the life of the community to which the story is addressed and for which it speaks. It also reveals a deeper, exegetical program, *vis-à-vis* the hero of the story itself. The true power of the rabbi lies in his

---

[13]So long as rabbinic culture remained intact, the storyteller was right. The stories were understood in exactly what context in which they originally were told, and for precisely that purpose for which the storyteller told them. Only when, in the nineteenth century, graduates of yeshivas entered universities to do Semitics or history were the stories asked to provide a kind of history which they never claimed to present. Read as history, the wrong details are interpreted. But historical questions are not wrong. They are merely irrelevant to the character of the data to which, in this instance, they are addressed. My students and I read a fair part of the literature of history founded on asking narrowly historical questions of Talmudic tales and fables and present the results in *The Formation of the Babylonian Talmud* (Leiden, 1971: Brill) and *The Modern Study of the Mishnah* (Leiden, 1973: Brill).

knowledge of Scripture – and not in his power to work wonders or to dominate the affairs of nations and governments. Directed within the community of rabbis themselves, the stories project a picture of what a rabbi should be, which is a master of Scripture and of Torah, and show that through Scripture and Torah the rabbi can dispose of the conflicts of supernature and politics alike.

The inner structure of the story is blatant and expresses a highly conventional program. Only if we ignore that inner structure are we able to maintain that the story speaks once for all time, and not – as in fact it does – through lasting structures of recurrent events of power-relationships and enduring patterns of conflict. So the stories are not history, but old history newly reenacted. And, as I shall tentatively propose, Honi emerges as a kind of Balaam, and Yohanan ben Zakkai as a kind of Jeremiah. So "history" is told about what endures. That is, it is a kind of social science.

1. *The Structure of the Story About Honi*

I discern four scenes in the story of Honi, but the critical action takes place in a triad: three kinds of rain, too little, too much, just right but far to much. Everything else serves to set up this sequence of action or to make sense of it. These are the scenes.

One. They come to Honi and say, "Pray for rain." He boasts: "Go take in the ovens so the clay will not soften in the rain – which I, Honi, will now bring down by my prayers." What happens? Nothing.

Two. Honi draws a circle and stands in the middle. He reminds God that the Israelites are God's children. Then he underlines who he, Honi, is. He is a child of God more than the others. How so? "Everyone knows that I am like a member of the family before you." Honi swears that he, the child of the family, will punish the head of the family. How? By standing in one spot until the head of the family does what Honi demands. What happens? God plays a joke on Honi: "It began to rain drop by drop."

Three. Honi complains that this is not the kind of rain that will move hm outside of his circle. "This is not what I wanted!" So God plays another joke on Honi. God gives so much rain that the rain threatens to wash everything away – like the rain of the Flood in the time of Noah.

Four. Honi complains again that this, too, is not the kind of rain he wanted. Now he gets what he wants. God's last joke on Honi is that God still makes it rain too much. The people who came to Honi to ask him to make it rain now come and tell him to make it stop raining. Honi tries another boast: "Go see if a certain stone is under water." This is as if to say, "If the stone is now submerged, I'll turn off the rain." What happens? Nothing, just as at the outset. Now the story ends. Honi leaves the action. This ending is extremely sudden. Honi now should do something else. Honi does nothing. Why not? Because the point is clear. The storyteller now makes a comment on the story. He needs no more evidence about Honi. Honi's true character and power, and God's opinion of Honi, are self-evident. But the storyteller repeats in words the point he already has made in the actions and dialogues he has described. That is why we meet Simeon b. Shatah, "a leading sage" in the time in which Honi is supposed to have lived. What Simeon says is pretty much what Honi has said about himself. But he draws conclusions from the facts. He says that Honi is indeed special. If anyone else tried Honi's stunt, the sages would drive him away. But Honi is what he says he is: "a spoiled child in the heavenly household." Then the storyteller concludes by citing a verse of Scripture that underlines the special, familial relationship between Honi and Heaven.

The relevance of the biblical story of Balaam, prophet of the gentiles, is clear. Balaam enjoys a special relationship to God; he is a prophet. At the same time Balaam is the object of a joke on the part of Heaven. He goes to curse Israel, but ends up blessing it. He is a prophet who cannot even discern what a dumb ass can see. His power turns against himself. He is an object of ridicule. He who boasts that he can control Heaven is manipulated by Heaven – derisively so.

2. The Structure of the Story About Yohanan ben Zakkai and Vespasian

The first thing we must notice is that at the center and heart this is not a story about Yohanan ben Zakkai's escape from Jerusalem. That is not the source of the story's critical tension. The escape is not what makes the story work. The story is about the contrast between Yohanan ben Zakkai and Vespasian. Therein lies its generative tension. The story is long. But each part of it is needed. In fact, it is a play in five separate acts: two before the climax, which are matched against one another; then two after the climax, also matched against one another. And there is one in the middle – the climax of the whole story. Each scene is complete in itself. But one flows right on to the next. These "scenes" are conversations. At each point at which someone new begins to say something, we count a scene.

One. Vespasian talks to the inhabitants of Jerusalem. He tells them he simply wants them to submit. He will leave them alone. They tell him that they have done it before, and they can do it again.

Two. Yohanan ben Zakkai talks to the same people. Now he says to them, in the very same words, precisely what Vespasian said. He does make one important change. This shift is so important that the repetition of the same words as Vespasian said is absolutely essential to underline the differences. Vespasian called the people *fools.* Yohanan calls them *My children.* But the storyteller has precisely the same ending for both conversations. The people say the same words to Yohanan that they said to Vespasian. They see no difference between sage and general, life and death. This scene ends with a transition, a bridge between what has just happened and what is going to happen. Vespasian has "men inside the walls," spies. They write down on a piece of paper and shoot over the wall whatever they think Vespasian would want to hear.

Three. The next conversation is the climax of the story and makes its main point. People talk to one another in a dialogue. But the main point now is not the conversation but the scene itself. The scene is striking. Yohanan ben Zakkai wants to get out of Jerusalem. The storyteller assumes we know something he has not told, which is that one cannot walk out of the city. He can only get out if he is dead. The reason – again we are not told – is that the people in control will not let anyone out. Since we already know that, so far as they are concerned, Yohanan ben Zakkai, the great sage, is no different from Vespasian, the Roman general, we are prepared for this fact. Yohanan lies down in the coffin. His students, Eliezer and Joshua, carry out the coffin. The gatekeepers ask who is leaving, and they are told it is a corpse. They are treated like ignorant people, "Do you know...." Once they are told the facts, they let the coffin go through. Now Yohanan ben Zakkai is brought to the Roman camp, right up to Vespasian's tent. Why the Roman soldiers would let the Jewish sages carry a coffin through their camp, and what they thought was happening, we are not told. The storyteller will tell us only what we must know, so that he can make his points through what he says, and through what he does not say. The simple climax is that Yohanan rises from the coffin. The coffin is for the dead. Yohanan has gone down into death. And he has risen again, from the dead. He has left the dying city, the city that soon will be dead and full of corpses. He has come to the heart of the enemy's camp. There, in the face of the cause of death, he rises from the dead. It is a stunning set of contrasts, a long list of them. Then we have two further conversations.

Four. Yohanan and Vespasian talk. In fact, they have two conversations. In the first one, Vespasian speaks first and controls the conversation. In the second, Yohanan speaks first and runs things. In the first conversation Vespasian recognizes Yohanan without being told. He immediately knows it is Yohanan, which is why he asks whether it is Yohanan. If he did not know it was Yohanan, he would not have known to ask. Then he wants to do something for Yohanan because

Yohanan is known as a friend of Vespasian. Yohanan asks for three little things. He wants to go down to a coastal town named Yavneh, which is no longer a battlefield. There he will (1) teach Torah to his disciples. And he also will (2) establish a prayer house. And, finally, he will (3) do all the commandments. In fact, these three things sum up all of Judaism as the sages shape it. Judaism is a religion that involves (1) study of Torah, (2) saying of prayers, and (3) doing all the commandments. So these "three little requests" to Vespasian are hardly so small as they seem. But to Vespasian they will not appear great. For he is engaged in a great war in the Land of Israel and a great adventure in Rome, as well. He wants to become emperor. He will be an important person. It is easy enough for him to do a little favor for Yohanan.

Five. At the end, Yohanan reciprocates and does a favor for Vespasian. It is also – in Yohanan's eyes – just as slight a favor for the Roman general as the right to go to Yavneh was in Vespasian's view. The thing that matters most to Yohanan is to go to Yavneh and there to teach his students and establish his prayer house and do the commandments. The thing that matters most to Vespasian is to become emperor. So Yohanan tells Vespasian that in a short time he will be made king. But the reason he will be made king, even though Vespasian does not know it, is Vespasian's position, here and now, before Jerusalem. Yohanan believes Vespasian is going to take Jerusalem. He therefore knows that Vespasian soon will be emperor. How does he know it? Because Yohanan is a master of the Torah. And in the Torah is a verse that says that "Lebanon" will fall by "a mighty one." Now in Yohanan's mind, "Lebanon" refers to the Temple. Perhaps this is because it was built out of cedars cut down in Lebanon and brought to Jerusalem in Solomon's time. Lebanon will fall to a mighty one – that is to say, in Yohanan's understanding of what Isaiah had said a long time ago, to an emperor or a king. So because of Yohanan's mastery of the Torah, he is able to tell Vespasian what is about to happen in faraway Rome. The end of this part of the story is predictable. What Yohanan said would happen, did happen.

Now let us stand back and go over the five scene of the play:

One. Vespasian and the men of Jerusalem.

Two. Yohanan ben Zakkai and the men of Jerusalem.

Three. Yohanan lies down in a coffin and rises up from the coffin.

Four. Yohanan does a favor for Yohanan, and gives him what he wants most of all.

Five. Yohanan ben Zakkai does a favor for Vespasian, and gives him what he wants most of all.

So that is the story – a powerful and beautifully constructed drama. It would not be possible to tell the story more simply, or to say more things in the telling of it. The irony of the story is clear. Vespasian thought that he was going to conquer the Jews. But the Jews came out able to rule themselves. Even though they ultimately gave over that bow and arrow, which meant they accepted Roman rule, "our sages" saved them and organized a government for them. Vespasian thought that he was going to become emperor because he was strong. But Yohanan ben Zakkai told him the truth, which is that he would become emperor only because he had the "merit" of taking Jerusalem and burning the Temple. Yohanan was saying that the conqueror of the Temple was able to do it because of one thing alone. God had permitted it. The storyteller's secondary point comes at the end, when he has Yohanan cite the verse of Isaiah to Vespasian. The storyteller believes that Yohanan ben Zakkai knew what was going to happen because Yohanan knew Scripture.

That brings up a second matter, the biblical passages of which the tale reminds us, without citing them at all. Specifically, in the biblical book of Jeremiah, we see another example of someone who in a time of siege tells the people to surrender. Jeremiah believes that Nebuchadnezzar, king of the Babylonians, is the rod of God's anger. He is going to take Jerusalem and destroy the Temple because God wants to punish the Jews for their sins. Jeremiah predicts that Jerusalem will fall to Babylonia. Jeremiah chapter twenty shows Jeremiah is at odds with the Jerusalemites of his day. The same is clear in chapters twenty-one and twenty-two and elsewhere in the prophecies of Jeremiah. Further, when the Babylonians do take Jerusalem, Jeremiah is well treated (chapter thirty-nine). And there is one final point. Jeremiah makes provision for the future. He buys a piece of ground, even when everyone thought that it was all over for the people of Israel in their Land. He did this to make sure people knew that there was hope and a future for the people and Land of Israel. In the light of these pages in Jeremiah (and many others, which say much the same thing), the story about Yohanan ben Zakkai and his dealings with Vespasian takes on depth. We realize that Yohanan is represented as a kind of Jeremiah, a living Scripture.

After Structuralism

Recognizing the structures of the narrative, perceiving the didactic and polemical purpose served by each one, we stress internal traits. That is how we have located those enduring characteristics of structure and style which show us the logic of the story. So we find ourselves wholly indifferent to a reading of the story as history. The story is something other than history. Those who read this material as history misread the purpose of the storyteller. Yet those who would abandon the historical dimension in interpreting these stories, who take up the structuralist position on interpreting them and treat them as utterly ahistorical, also err. It is not the naive and childish error of gullibility, such as historians of the old sort commit. It is error of a different order, as I shall now try to explain.

What is wrong with a mode of interpretation based principally upon the recognition of underlying structures of a story and leading to an ahistorical account of how the story works is that it is inadequate. Structuralism asks the right questions. It does not stand still to hear all the answers its questions precipitate. For if we conclude the work of interpretation with an account of the way the story is put together, we omit all reference to what remains critical in the interpretation of the story. To state matters simply: if we do not know who told a story, to whom, and for what purpose, if we cannot account for social context, we do not yet fully understand that story. Structure without context, that is, the social and economic, material context defined by concrete history, is insufficient either for description or for explanation.

Let me elaborate on this point. Internalistic, formal analysis is suggestive, but not exhaustive, of the layers of meanings of the story. Creations of literature express a logic unbound by context – but logic itself always is social and contextual. If we relativize all principles of analysis, we shall simply not fully make sense of the story we claim to interpret. There always are both diachronic and synchronic dimensions of interpretation, just as Schorske says. Nothing exists by itself. Someone tells a story. Someone hears, understands, and preserves it. Someone tells it later on. The very existence of sources for historical study bespeaks a historical process and a social continuum. That is why structuralism is impoverished – as much as is historicism.

We may amply describe a structure within the framework of religions and show how a system is constituted and how it functions. We may notice the fundamental concerns of the stories we have examined and show how the way in which the story is told highlights what the story wishes to tell us. But without careful attention to the historical context in which the story, as part of a system of values, actually functions, we still cannot explain what is important about the story. That is, we do not know how to describe and make sense of the system, the worldview and way of life, of which the story is a part. What is still more important, through (mere) structuralism we cannot account for changes within the system itself. Literature is part of society, and if we do not know what particular stimulus made it necessary or even inevitable that a story such as the one before us should be told, we cannot make sense of it.

Those structuralists who wish to provide systemic descriptions and literary analyses essentially outside the context of society and its history and change tell us something remarkably evanescent. They explain the condition of status. But ours is a world of change. Structuralism outside of the history of society and the framework of changing culture explains a system as it exists for a single moment. But systems unfold in history. True, the explanation is the thing. Out of structuralism come compelling explanations, stunning questions. But what is to be said of the explanation for the character of a system, when in yet a little while the system will change? Surely an explanation offered to account for the character of the system also must change. This means that the evidence of a system must be located, for interpretation, in the historical context of the social and material life of the people within the structure, in the present case, the people to whom the stories were told and who retell them.

So the challenge in reckoning with the sorts of tales before us is to move not merely past the ruins of historicism but beyond structuralism. A story of the ruined Temple or of drawing a circle and standing in it obviously is misread when narrowly historical questions define the mode of reading. The field of "Jewish history," consisting as it does in the discovery and recitation of facts (for ancient Judaism, pseudo-facts, in my view) is incompetent to deal with the sorts of tales we have read (and much else). But there is no salvation in structural anthropology and history of religions formed outside of a social, material context. That is so however much we must learn from those joined fields about the interpretation of facts, the description and analysis of systems, and the comparison of systems to systems, and of religions to religions. On the one side, history done by historians consists of accounts of one thing after another. On the other, history of religions yields vapid generalization. It often is helpless in the face of the specificities of facts and texts. Anthropology of religions, not unlike history, provides us with interminable catalogues of trivia on the one side, and compelling and enduring explanations of what are, in fact, fleeting structures, on the other. So we stand between the triviality of history and the evanescent taxonomy, divorced from all context, of structuralism.[14]

---

[14]That is, between the critics of Mary Douglas and Mary Douglas, so to speak. Her principal contribution, as I see it, is to insist on finding the principle of selection for a given system. This can be done for ancient Judaism represented by the Mishnah, as I have shown in my forthcoming *Judaism: The Evidence of*

I think in the end we have to fine another way. For each party performs a magic of reductionism. The historical side effects the reduction of constants and structures to details. It utterly misses the general in the search for the particular. Event is made to exclude insight or to yield mere homily. The one-timeness of historical narrative, the particularity and cultural narrowness of historical work, the focus on some few aspects of a world and a system – these guarantee that history in its conventional mode will yield triviality. They assure it will collapse, as it does, into mindless antiquarianism. But the other mode, the antihistorical description and interpretation effected by structuralism, reduces the flesh and blood of reality to neat matchboxes ("grid-group" in Douglas is only a caricature of the matter). Still, if I must choose, let my lot fall with the people who take seriously the ebb and flow of time and society, who explain change and culture. The others essentially are reactionary. For all their talk of deep structure, their taxonomies are profoundly irrelevant to the encounter with the world of material reality and social being. Stories such as those before us emerge from society and serve the purposes of society. They serve the brokerage of power and speak of conflict. That may not be why they were told to begin with; of that we cannot be certain. But it certainly is society – a group of people – which preserved and handed on these stories, and the reason is that society, a particular one of rabbis to be sure, understood and valued these stories.

Story as History in Ancient Judaism

The analysis of the structure of the two stories indicates the purpose of the storyteller. It is not to report things which really happened (surely an anachronism for ancient times), but to make important points of a theological-didactic character. Consequently, to adduce these stories in evidence of things which really happened as these stories say they happened is absurd. The reason is that the point of the story is missed, the wrong question asked. To be sure, last-ditch defenders of the historicistic hermeneutic will invoke the distinction

---

the Mishnah. But no "system" is isolated from the historical context defined by the ongoing society framed and formed by said system. Douglas' taxonomic approach to the interpretation of Leviticus seems to me sound, but her explanation of its systemic pertinence, that is, of the principle of selection, is too general. It therefore is inadequate to the sequence of contexts in which the taxonomy endured, even while the system changed. The strength of structuralism, as represented by Douglas, is its emphasis on the issue of discovering the principle of selection; the pathos is the incapacity to confront history – time and change in systems and societies. That is why the ultimate appeal is to rather self-evident generalities.

between the historical kernel of truth and the ahistorical husk of fable. But that distinction, imposed on stories such as these, produces capricious and subjective results. Some people eat the kernel, while others (as in the case of Alon) swallow the husk too. Not only are we left without clear and consistent, systematic modes of reading these fables and tales. As I have shown, we also, and especially focus on what is unimportant and miss what is important. Reading these stories as narrative history is wildly irrelevant to the point of the stories themselves. And, as I shall now suggest, it also obscures the kind of history the stories may be made to reveal, objectively, systematically, and consistently.

The two stories present history. It is a history of ideas and of religion, the history formed within the creative imagination of a group within Israelite society. If we know when, where, and to whom, it was important to make up these two stories, we shall have insight into questions troubling the group which expressed itself through these stories. For what we have are statements of the system and structure of rabbis. The obvious purpose of the story about Honi is to ridicule those whom rabbis envy, whose supernatural power they concede. Wonder-workers find no place within the rabbinical framework for the reason expressed by Simeon b. Shatah's saying. The simple purpose of the story about Yohanan and Vespasian is to draw the contrast between the two sorts of powerful men, sage and emperor. So, as I said, at both sides of the margins of Israel the rabbi is represented as the dominant and critical figure. Within the community he confronts the miracle-worker. On the other side of the border he deals with another kind of power. He masters both, because in each case what he wants is what one should want – not the power over supernature enjoyed by Honi, not the power over armies and empires enjoyed by Vespasian, but the power of the Torah which stands above supernature and nature.

Moving from these self-evident didactic purposes to the class or group of Israelite society represented by the stories, however, requires information not readily at hand. If we want accurately and fully to make sense of these stories as history, we have to locate the telling of the stories within history (when?), on the one side, and the preservation and retelling of them within a particular social group (by whom?), on the other. Let me ask some obvious questions to illustrate this point: When were miracle-workers a pressing problem to sages, so that a story about one of them would prove important? At what point did the rabbinical estate or movement become so remarkably self-conscious as to seek to locate itself at the limns, at the critical turning, of Israelite history? These two questions suggest what is needed to turn the stories into data for cultural and intellectual history. But it should be clear that the stories constitute not only artifacts of culture. They serve also to testify to social facts, to the material reality of relationships of institutions – rabbinical institutions. The storytellers speak of the exercise of power. Indeed, what makes the stories critical is their focus upon the two kinds of power rabbis in general did not exercise, supernatural and political. The power of the stories is their capacity to explain what kind of power rabbis do enjoy and why that sort of power is the most important sort. Since history is the tale of power and its disposition, these stories must stand as quintessentially historical facts.

Let me offer an example of how we might make use of those facts. It is meant to exemplify not results but modes of thought, ways of putting things together. If we postulate that polemic generally takes up threats near at hand, we must ask ourselves whether from the fact we may reconstruct the context.

In the case of a story about how miracle-working is true but undignified, we may wonder whether, within rabbinical circles, there were men who aspired to validate rabbinical teachings through the making of miracles, as people said, for example, the teacher, Jesus, also was a wonder-worker. Since the story surfaces in the Mishnah, toward the end of the second century, we may notice that miracle stories about second-century sages except Honi are not told in the Mishnah, a document of that time. But rabbis of the third, and, more so, of the fourth century, are widely portrayed as wonder-workers. Stories also are told in the strata of literature of that later period about how first- and second-century rabbis did miracles.

In the case of a story abut the rabbi and the emperor, we may, in like manner, wonder whether, within rabbinical circles, were men who aspired to vindicate rabbinical teachings through taking up political positions and forming an essentially political movement. Since the story surfaces in Abot deRabbi Natan, a secondary expansion of Abot ("the sayings of the fathers"), generally assigned to the period of the fourth or fifth century, we may notice that at precisely that same time a rapprochement appears to have taken place between the rabbinical estate of Babylonia and the exilarch who ruled the Jews of Babylonia with Iranian recognition. Rabbis of the later fourth and fifth centuries associated themselves with the exilarchate in ways in which those of the third and earlier fourth did not. Stories about hostility between rabbi and exilarch are told about figures of the earlier, not the later period.[15]

---

[15]My *History of the Jews in Babylonia* (Leiden, 1965-1970: E.J. Brill) I-V presents extensive accounts both of wonder-working stories told about rabbis and also of

So one might speculate that both stories address for different periods growing tensions within the rabbinical circles themselves. Both take up positions against directions in which, in fact, the rabbinical movement for a time would move, toward wonder-working, toward politics. But both stories express the principal and ubiquitous value of the rabbinical movement, that is to say, the primacy and priority of Torah-learning. Both rapidly lose their narrow and polemical cloak. It goes without saying that these are mere suggestions of how to think about the tales in their social and historical context. If the proposed context changes, so will our speculation.

Conclusion

The stories focus upon the relationships of powerful people: rabbis and rainmakers, rabbis and emperors or generals. They mediate between the rabbis' kind of power and other kinds, acknowledged to be equally compelling. Telling these stories is urgent, specifically, in the society of rabbis or sages. The context of the telling and retelling is the larger setting of the life of the community of Israel, in which the rabbis claim, and eventually attain, considerable power of a material and substantial order. The tensions and contrasts which form the center of the two stories and make them work reveal facts about the social relationships in which those who told and heard the stories located themselves. A power other than supernatural or political, as represented by the rainmaker and the general, infuses the sage or rabbi. That power, the stories underline, derives from mastery of Scripture, of Torah. So far as history is the story of social conflict and the adjudication and mediation of diverse kinds of, and claims to, power, these stories tell us history. True, it is not, and cannot be, the history of a first-century B.C.E. wonder-worker or a first-century C.E. prophetic sage.

The story about Honi surfaces in a document redacted at the end of the second century; the one on Yohanan first occurs in a document probably to be located in the fourth or fifth century. Some day, when we know more about Israelite society and its larger setting in these periods, as well as about the unfolding of the literature, institutions,

---

stories expressive of hostility between exilarchs and rabbis. These are divided by periods (demarcated by the lives of the sages about whom they are told), and there clearly is a rise in the numbers of wonder-working tales from third through fifth centuries, on the one side, and a decline in the number of stories about hostility between rabbis and exilarchs, over the same period. Much more work is possible along these lines. And, of course, Abot de R. Natan to begin with is generally thought to be Palestinian and not Babylonian (!).

and structures of the rabbinic estate and movement, we shall have access to still deeper layers of meaning, for a given place, time, and social group, contained and expressed in these stories. For these stories do constitute facts of history. If they are not factitious for the history of the period *of* which they speak, then they surely testify to the social relationships and imaginative life – the history – of the periods *to* which they speak.

11

Revelation and Reason, Scripture and Mishnah: Their Relationship at the Beginning of the Judaism of the Dual Torah

Lecture, University of Florence
January 20, 1989

When we formulate the question of the relationship of the Mishnah to Scripture, we adopt the language and categories that the authorship of the Mishnah wanted us to use. For (to personify that authorship in the name of Judah the Patriarch) what the Patriarch accomplished through remarkably adroit imposition of uniform rhetoric and logic upon the discussion of discrete topical materials was precisely that: to treat everything as one thing. Hence we rightly identify "the Mishnah" as a single work. We see it as uniform because whatever topic it discusses among its sixty-one relevant tractates (I omit reference to Pirqe Abot as outside of the entire rhetorical, logical, and topical program of the document, and to Eduyot as a mere reprise), the authorship of the Mishnah does what appears to be the same thing. That is to say, that authorship formulates its ideas within a strikingly limited formal repertoire. It appeals for cogency to a narrow range of logical possibilities, generally limited to what we know as *Listenwissenschaft*, that is, the making of lists that in detail register a single general rule (about which I shall have more to say), and, throughout, preserves a remarkable cogency of style.

But what if we introduce analytical variables of our own making? Then the unity and uniformity of the Mishnah prove to conceal considerable diversity. The sixty-one tractates of the Mishnah, each analyzed on its own, turn out to yield as much diversity in structure – e.g., relationship to other writings – as they do in topic. And we must not be deceived by the authorship's genius in its uniform formalization of the whole to assume that the topical differentiation that that same authorship has adopted for its organizing principle effects difference merely at the surface of things. For while the Mishnah's authorship has made things appear as though all that differs, in the vast cogent writing, is subject matter, subject matter matters. That is to say, differences on topic from one tractate to another (and one division to another) prove very real and contradict uniformity in rhetorica and even in prevailing logic.

And if that is the case, it must follow, the relationships between the document and other writings also have to be characterized with nuance and full recognition of the differentiated components of the whole. That is especially the case when, as I shall explain, our analytical variables appeal, in part, to the quite varied relationships between components of the Mishnah and Scripture. It becomes impossible to make a single statement of the relationship of the Mishnah to Scripture that serves to characterize all tractates. But it becomes quite possible to form groups of tractates, each set of which bears its own distinctive relationship to Scripture.

Since our interest lies in how tractates relate to Scripture, we shall adopt that criterion as our point of analytical differentiation. Simple logic dictates that, when we ask about relationships, there can be only three classes of relationship: total, none at all, and something in the middle. Here too, we can postulate as a matter of theory that a Mishnah-tractate may stand in a totally dependent relationship with Scripture, may have no relationship at all to Scripture, or may fall somewhere in between. That is a matter of theory. Now let me spell out the theory in terms of concrete facts. There are three possibilities in a relationship between a Mishnah-tractate and a passage of Scripture. First of all, Scripture supplies the topic and also provides the analytical program of the authorship of a Mishnah-tractate, chapter, or pericope. Therefore nothing within the Mishnah's treatment of the topic goes beyond the logical program of the theme Scripture provides within the details that Scripture sets forth. Second, Scripture sets forth a topic but does not then dictate the inner logic by which the topic will be worked out in a series of illustrative cases, as is the fact in the first relationship. Therefore the subject matter is scriptural, but the treatment of the subject entirely autonomous of Scripture. Third, even the subject matter is unknown to Scripture or is so casually and elliptically treated in Scripture that the Mishnah-tractate, theme and logic all together, is wholly autonomous of Scripture.

First let us consider how a Mishnah-tractate may stand in total dependence upon Scripture. Precisely what I mean by that classification requires definition, since it is not a subjective judgment. Let me give a single example of the first of the three relationships, since, from the viewpoint of the analysis of the Mishnah-tractates' agenda, that is the single operative classification. For that purpose I present first the relevant passages of Scripture, then the Mishnah's treatment of those passages. I believe it will be self-evident to readers that nothing in the Mishnah's discussion moves beyond the requirements of the exposition of the scriptural topic within the lines of analysis defined by Scripture. Here is the relevant scriptural passage, Deut. 23:25-6:

> When you go into your neighbor's vineyard, you may eat your fill of grapes, as many as you wish, but you shall not put any in your vessel. When you go into your neighbor's standing grain, you may pluck the ears with your hand, but you shall not put a sickle to your neighbor's standing grain.

This is further read in light of the statement, Deut. 25:4

> You shall not muzzle an ox while it is threshing.

On that basis, the rule is that workers are permitted to nibble on grain or grapes on which they are working. What follows is the Mishnah's treatment of this same topic.

7:1

A. He who hires [day] workers and told them to start work early or to stay late –

B. in a place in which they are accustomed not to start work early or not to stay late,

C. he has no right to force them to do so.

D. In a place in which they are accustomed to provide a meal, he must provide a meal.

E. [In a place in which they are accustomed] to make do with a sweet,

F. he provides it.

G. Everything accords with the practice of the province.

H. M'SH B: R. Yohanan b. Matya said to his son, "Go, hire workers for us."

I. He went and made an agreement with them for food [without further specification].

J. Now when he came to his father, [the father] said to him, "My son, even if you should make for them a meal like one of Solomon in his day, you will not have carried out your obligation to them.

K. "For they are children of Abraham, Isaac, and Jacob.

L. "But before they begin work, go and tell them, '[Work for us] on condition that you have a claim on me [as to food] only for a piece of bread and pulse alone.' "

M.   Rabban Simeon b. Gamaliel says, "He had no need to specify that in so many words.

N.   "Everything [in any case] accords with the practice of the province."

7:2

A.   And these [have the right to] eat [the produce on which they work] by [right accorded to them in] the Torah:

B.   he who works on what is as yet unplucked [may eat from the produce] at the end of the time of processing;

C.   [and he who works] on plucked produce [may eat from the produce] before processing is done;

D.   [in both instances solely] in regard to what grows from the ground.

E.   But these do not [have the right to] eat [the produce on which they labor] by [right accorded to them in] the Torah:

F.   he who works on what is as yet unplucked, before the end of the time of processing;

G.   [and he who works] on plucked produce after the processing is done,

H.   [in both instances solely] in regard to what does not grow from the ground.

7:3

A.   [If] one was working with his hands but not with his feet,

B.   with his feet but not with his hands,

C.   even [carrying] with his shoulder,

D.   lo, he [has the right to] eat [the produce on which he is working].

E.   R. Yosé b. R. Judah says, "[He may eat the produce on which he is working] only if he works with both his hands and his feet."

7:4

A.   [If the laborer] was working on figs, he [has] not [got the right to] eat grapes.

B.   [If he was working] on grapes, he [has] not [got the right to] eat figs.

C.   But [he does have the right to] refrain [from eating] until he gets to the best produce and then [to exercise his right to] eat.

D.   And in all instances they have said [that he may eat from the produce on which he is laboring] only in the time of work.

E.   But on grounds of restoring lost property to the owner, they have said [in addition] :

F   Workers [have the right to] eat as they go from furrow to furrow [even though they do not then work],

G.   and when they are coming back from the press [so saving time for the employer];

H.   and in the case of an ass [nibbling on straw in its load], when it is being unloaded.

7:5

A.   A worker [has the right to] eat cucumbers, even to a denar's worth,

B.   or dates, even to a denar's worth.

C.   R. Eleazar Hisma says, "A worker should not eat more than the value of his wages."

D.   But sages permit.
E.   But they instruct the man not to be a glutton and thereby slam the door in his own face [to future employment] –

7:6
A.   A man makes a deal [with the householder not to exercise his right to eat produce on which he is working] in behalf of himself, his adult son, or daughter,
B.   in behalf of his adult manservant or womanservant,
C.   in behalf of his wife, because [they can exercise] sound judgment [and keep the terms of the agreement],
D.   But he may not make a deal in behalf of his minor son or daughter,
E.   in behalf of his minor boy servant or girl servant, or in behalf of his beast, because [they can] not [exercise] sound judgment [and keep the terms of the agreement].

What we see is a very systematic and orderly exposition of the theme, with little initiative beyond the limits of the simple logic imposed by that theme. That is to say, first, we follow the established custom, M. 7:1. Second, we define precisely what one is permitted to eat while working, M. 7:2. Third, we explain how one is permitted to take produce, and the limits of what it means to work on produce, M. 7:3. M. 7:4 then proceeds to take up interstitial cases, e.g., working on figs and eating grapes. M. 7:5, 6 ask about limits set to one's nibbling. M. 7:7 finally addresses special cases, e.g., working on produce that no one may eat.

Anyone familiar with the way in which the authorship of the Mishnah analyzes any problem or addresses any theme will find a perfectly standard program of definition and exposition, consisting of a labor of extension and limitation of the rule. While this mode of thought in general may be deemed philosophical, it bears no abstract philosophical principle, e.g., a doctrine applicable to a vast variety of cases, whether of a metaphysical or an ethical or a legal character. The mode of thought may be deemed philosophical in a rather general way, but it is not distinctive to philosophy in any limited sense by which we may define philosophy. That distinction between mode of thought and medium of thought will gain greater clarity in later parts of this study. At this point it suffices to note that the treatment of the topic at hand is simply how the Mishnah's authorship treats any topic of Scripture on which it has no particular perspective or in which it discerns no problematic external to the logic limits of the topic as Scripture sets it forth.

Second, let us consider what it means for a tractate to appear totally autonomous of Scripture, that is to say, in its entire repertoire of ideas and problems never to allude to Scripture. For that purpose I allude to a variety of tractates that take up issues that Scripture does not supply, topics Scripture does not treat, or problems Scripture does not imagine.

My first candidate is Mishnah-tractate Kelim. This tractate is wholly devoted to the exposition of problems of classification, inclusive of connection and intentionality as issues of classification. Tractates on cleanness and uncleanness by definition form exercises of classification, since the ultimate taxa are unclean or susceptible to uncleanness and clean or insusceptible. But the exemplary power of detailed discourse to invoke fundamental principles of classification and to set forth the complexities of physics of connection is hardly exhausted by the generalizations, unclean or clean. Indeed, throughout, these form the mere result, but never the engaging problem of principled discourse. Mishnah-tractate Kelim deals with the status, as to cultic cleanness, of useful objects, tools or utensils. Its main point is that when an object has a distinctive character, form, use, or purpose, it is susceptible to uncleanness, so that, if it is in contact with a source of uncleanness, it is deemed cultically unclean. If it is formless, purposeless, or useless, it is insusceptible. Three criteria govern the determination of what is useful or purposeful. First come properties deemed common to all utensils, whatever the material. Second are qualities distinctive to different sorts of materials. Third is the consideration of the complex purposes for which an object is made or used, primary and subsidiary, and the intention of the user is determinative. These principles generate differing formulations of problems in the unfolding of a vast tractate. None of this comes from Scripture or addresses topics or problems known to Scripture.

Other tractates with no topical dependence whatsoever on Scripture include Mishnah-tractate Berakhot, where there is scarcely a single scriptural passage that plays a generative part in the formation of this tractate, even though some of the prayers that are recited make mention of verses of Scripture; Demai, in which not a single fact in this tractate derives from Scripture; Ketubot, in which, except for chapter three, the factual basis for this tractate is not scriptural; Moed Qatan, for which there are no pertinent verses of Scripture. Scripture knows restrictions on labor only for the opening and closing sessions of the festivals of Passover and Tabernacles, so Ex. 12:16, Lev. 23:7-8, 35-36, Num. 28:18, 25, 29:12-35; Qiddushin, for which, in the aggregate Scripture does not define the facts that form the expository center of this tractate; Tohorot, of the considerations and conceptions of which Scripture knows nothing; and so on and so forth.

To make the point simple, I conclude with reference to Mishnah-tractate Middot. Its specification of the layout and measurements of the Temple bears no clear and systematic relationship to Scripture's treatment of the same subject. Scholarship generally holds that it follows the pattern of Solomon's Temple with some adaptations of Ezekiel's, so F. J. Hollis (*The Archaeology of Herod's Temple. With a Commentary on the Tractate Middoth'* (London, 1934), p. 354), "The use made of Holy Scripture in the tractate is not such as to give the impression that somehow or other the words of Scripture are being followed...but rather that there was a fairly clear recollection of the Temple as it had been, with Holy Scripture appealed to to illuminate the fact, not as authority to prove it."

The point is now clear that there are tractates that totally depend for the entirety of their program and analytical problematic upon Scripture, and there are tractates that to begin with address subjects or themes of which the written Torah is simply ignorant. What about the middle range? Here we come to tractates that ask of a topic supplied by Scripture questions that Scripture in no way adumbrates. Let me give three examples of what I mean. Mishnah-tractate Makhshirin forms a well-crafted essay on the interplay of intentionality and classification. The prooftexts, Lev. 11:34, 37, establish the fact of the matter, but in no way permit us to predict the problematic of the Mishnah's treatment of that topic. The order of the tractate is so worked out that each point in the development of the study of that problem is in proper place. We start with the issue of the classification of liquid, with special attention to water capable of imparting susceptibility distinguished from water not capable of doing so: the wanted, the unwanted. This forthwith invites the issue of intentionality. Then, and only then, do we proceed to the consideration of the status of water used for one purpose and water used for a subsidiary purpose, and that leads directly into the question of whether what one is assumed to desire is taken into account at all, or whether we deem evidence of prior intentionality only post facto action. So there is no way of ordering matters to produce an intelligible sequence of problems other than in the way we now have them, and this tractate is philosophical not only in its topics but in its very structure.

A second example is Mishnah-tractate Nedarim, dealing with vows, on which Scripture sets forth rules. But nearly the entire tractate addresses a philosophical problem, specifically, the authorship provides lessons in showing how species relate in a common genus, or how the components of a common genus are speciated. That is so prominent a theme that were we to want to teach the method of classification through genus and species, this is the tractate that would provide rich and exquisitely executed examples of that method. The secondary interest, not surprisingly, is in the consideration of intentionality, on the one side, and the resolution of matters of doubt, on the other. These are subordinate to the main concern of this profoundly philosophical tractate.

A third example is Mishnah-tractate Negaim, addressing Leviticus 13 and 14. This Mishnah-tractate is a deeply philosophical treatment of a subject on which Scripture has supplied a rich corpus of information. As is common in tractates on uncleanness, the basic intellectual framework is defined by problems of classification of diverse data, yielding a single outcome: unclean, clean. The classification involves hierarchization, on the one side, and the resolution of doubts as to data (never as to the pertinent rule) on the other. That is the focus of interest of the bulk of the tractate, and we find ourselves in the same realm of inquiry as in Niddah, on the one side, and Miqvaot, on the other: classification and the resolution of doubt, mostly the former. This tractate provides a splendid and compelling exemplification of the power of classification to frame and solve problems. Specifically, classification makes possible hierarchical classification, which for its part renders plausible argument on shared premises yielding firm results. The power of hierarchical classification in framing issues is shown at M. Neg. 13:10: They said to R. Judah, "If, when his entire body is unclean, he has not rendered unclean that which is on him until he will remain for a time sufficient to eat a piece of bread, when his entire body is not unclean, is it not logical that he should not render what is on him unclean until he remains for a time sufficient to eat a piece of bread?" Tosefta's reply shows what is at stake: "Said to them R. Judah, 'The reason is that the power of that which is susceptible to uncleanness also is stronger to afford protection than the power of what is insusceptible to uncleanness is to afford protection. Israelites receive uncleanness and afford protection for clothing in the house afflicted with plague, and the gentile and beast do not receive uncleanness and so do not afford protection..." The same uses of hierarchical classification are shown at M. 13:11: "Whatever affords protection with a tightly sealed cover in the Tent of the corpse affords protection with a tightly sealed cover in the house which has a plague, and whatever affords protection merely by being covered over in the Tent of the corpse affords protection merely by being covered over in the house which has a plague," the words of R. Meir. R. Yosé says, "Whatever affords protection with a tightly sealed cover in the Tent of the corpse affords protection when merely covered over in the house which has a plague, and whatever affords protection when merely covered over in the Tent of the corpse even uncovered in the house which has the plague is clean." This argument and its numerous parallels are possible only within a system of classification, in which all thought is channeled into paths of comparison and contrast, inquiries into the genus and the species and the comparison of the species of a common genus, then the hierarchization of the results, one way or another.

Enough has been said to show how readily we differentiate among the relationships between various tractates of the Mishnah and Scripture. We can now not only describe those relationships, we may also analyze and interpret them. The analysis may be appropriately brief, since much that has already been said has suggested the analytical program I have devised. It is clear where tractates are "scriptural," merely repeating in the Mishnah's rhetoric and within the Mishnah's logic of cogent discourse what Scripture says in its rhetoric and within its logic of cogent discourse. Where tractates are not scriptural, I have now indicated, they are philosophical. This is in two aspects. An interstitial tractate – one that is scriptural in topic but not scriptural in its treatment of its topic – will ask philosophical questions of classification of a subject that Scripture has described within a different program of questions altogether. A good example of that type of interstitial tractate is Mishnah-tractate Negaim, which, as I said, wants to teach lessons of the rules of classification. Another is Mishnah-tractate Makhshirin, which proposes to investigate the relationship between one's action and the taxonomic power of one's intentionality. As to the third category, what differentiates an interstitial tractate from a completely non-scriptural tractate is simply the topic. A completely non-scriptural tractate commonly will pursue a philosophical reading of a given topic; what makes the tractate non-scriptural is the fact that Scripture does not know its topic.

In setting matters forth, I have now to indicate the proportions of the document that are scriptural, those that are (in the definition just now given) interstitial, and those that are utterly non-scriptural. Among the 61 tractates of the Mishnah, seven are neither scriptural nor philosophical (again: in terms now clear). Of the 54 others, 41 are philosophical (whether dealing with a scriptural topic or not dealing with a scriptural topic), and 13 are wholly scriptural, in the model of Yoma, for instance, or Pesahim. Of the 54 tractates that may be classified as either wholly scriptural or fundamentally philosophical, three-quarters are philosophical. Of all 61 tractates, two-thirds are philosophical. And that brings us back to the point at which we started, Rabbi Judah the Patriarch's presentation of the Mishnah as a single, seamless, internally harmonious, unitary document. To state matters simply, what Rabbi has accomplished in his formalization of the whole is the union of philosophy and revelation. I say this in a very concrete and not in an abstract sense. He has joined profound discourse on the nature of classification, the relationship of genus to species and the comparison and contrast of species, the role of intentionality in the taxonomic system, the disposition of interstitial cases in which a variety of taxic indicators come into play – Rabbi has joined a profound discourse on the nature of classification with a loving and detailed repetition of the facts of Scripture as these concern certain topics. The result is a document, the Mishnah, in which we are taught both philosophy and Scripture. Rabbi demonstrates through the Mishnah that revelation and reason, that is to say, Scripture and Mishnah's framing of philosophical principles of classification on which all knowledge rests, are shown to form a single, seamless skein of truth.

These results must strike as familiar – but also dissonant those familiar with the great work of Moses Maimonides, the pinnacle of Jewish philosophy, who set out to do precisely what I claim Rabbi has already done in the Mishnah. For, we are all taught in our elementary lessons, Rambam wished to unite reason and revelation, Aristotle and the Torah. And, it is clear, I maintain that Rabbi has done that in the Mishnah. He has chosen an aesthetic medium for his achievement – presenting within a single rhetoric and logic the entirety of the (written) Torah, revelation and of the philosophical principles of knowledge (classification of data into intelligible patterns, discovery of the rules and logic of things) of (Aristotle's) philosophy. When we turn our attention to Maimonides, we see a different choice as to how to accomplish the same purpose, and it is a choice, we now realize, that he did not have to make. Maimonides represented revelation, the Torah, in the Mishnah Torah, and he further portrayed reason, philosophy, in the *Guide to the Perplexed,* each document appealing to its own aesthetic choices as to rhetoric and logic of cogent discourse. The one is modeled after the Mishnah, the other has no antecedent in the received canon of the Dual Torah to which Maimonides appealed. Accordingly, it would appear to this outsider to Maimonidean scholarship, Maimonides invented a medium for representing philosophy, preserving another medium for representing the law. It was through the overarching intellectual system that he created that the two writings were shown to be seamless and harmonious.

If that picture, drawn by an outsider, is accurate, then we may identify a fundamental misunderstanding, on the part of Maimonides, of the character of the Mishnah, that is to say, the oral part of the one whole Torah revealed by God to Moses at Mount Sinai, and therefore of the Torah itself, and, it must follow, my ultimate goal is to correct the historical error of Maimonides, who identified Aristotle and his philosophical method as the source of correct knowledge, science, in his day. But in his misreading of the requirements of theology and philosophy of Judaism, he supposed to present philosophy outside of the framework of law, and law without sustained and specific engagement with philosophy. This came about because he did not realize the full extent to which the Mishnah, Maimonides' correct choice of the foundation document of Judaism after Scripture, stood squarely within the Aristotelian philosophical tradition. Specifically, when Maimonides systematized philosophy in his original *Guide to the Perplexed* and law in his imitative *Mishneh Torah*, he misunderstood the fact that the law, for the Judaism of the Dual Torah, constitutes the medium for theological and philosophical reflection and expression. And that is the fact, even though at numerous specific examples, he introduced into the explanation or elucidation of the law philosophical considerations. All of these preliminary impressions await sustained clarification, but they do serve to place this project into perspective.

In his separation of the presentation of law from philosophy, he tore apart what in the Mishnah had been inextricably joined in a lasting union, which was (and is) the law of that Judaism and both its theology and also its philosophy. Seeing the law in *Mishneh Torah* as a problem merely of organization and rationalization, Maimonides did not perceive that that same law contained within itself, and fully expressed, the very same principles of theology and philosophy that in the *Guide to the Perplexed* are invoked to define what we should call Judaism. Maimonides therefore did not grasp that the law in the very document that, in his (correct) judgment contained its classic formulation, that is, the Mishnah, also set forth precisely those principles of philosophy that, in Aristotle's system as Maimonides adapted it, would frame the proposed philosophy and theology of Judaism of *The Guide to the Perplexed*. Then, in the *Guide* Maimonides (mis)represented philosophy and theology by divorcing them from their legal media of articulation, as though these could come to expression entirely outside the framework of the legal sources of Judaism. So the greatest scholar of the Mishnah of all time and the greatest Aristotelian Judaism has ever known misperceived the profound intellectual structure of the Mishnah.

The reason for this error, in my view, is that Maimonides did not understand the deeply Aristotelian character of the Mishnah, which is the initial and definitive statement of the law of Judaism. And that is the error that I am in the process of correcting in this paper and in the companion studies and volumes of which it forms an offshoot and a by-product. I am showing, point by point, that the economics, politics, and philosophy, that is, the social order set forth by the Judaism of the Mishnah, finds its intellectual home in Aristotle's philosophy, method and (in the main) results as well. The modes of thought and the basic categorical structures correspond to those of Aristotle. This has already been accomplished in my *Economics of Judaism* and *Politics of Judaism*. Now when we realize that the Mishnah stands squarely within the Aristotelian philosophical tradition in its economics, politics, and philosophical principles (a proposition, as I said, I already have shown for the first two of the three main lines of social thought), then we can understand what happened to mislead Maimonides. And from Maimonides onward, the law has served only episodically and notionally, not systematically and totally, in the formation of the theology and philosophy of Judaism. The scholars of the law in the main knew no theology and could not understand philosophy; the scholars of theology and philosophy, whether or not they knew the law, did not understand in a systematic way that the law would provide the very principles of philosophy that they thought the classic sources of Judaism did not afford. Seeing the law of Judaism, from the Mishnah forward, as essentially distinct from the philosophical science of Aristotle, Maimonides and everyone since then, if they dealt with law at all, simply arranged the law and turned to the philosophy and theology.

What Maimonides should have done, which I therefore am in the course of doing, was in a systematic and rigorous manner to show the philosophy within the law. That means not merely that the law has or exhibits a philosophy. Everyone recognizes that simple and commonplace observation. At numerous points in his *Mishneh Torah* Maimonides articulates the principle at hand; and, as to theology, this is encompassed within the *Mishneh Torah Sefer Ahabah*. But the fundamental modes of thought and some of the principal problems of reflection of Aristotle guide the intellectual processes of the Mishnah, and that fact Maimonides did not grasp; if he had, he would have worked out the *Guide to the Perplexed*'s main points within the very framework of legal exposition. In this way the marriage of law and philosophy, which, as a systematic program, eluded Maimonides, could have been consummated, yielding for the history of Judaism a very different result from the one that followed their divorce. For understanding the philosophical modes of thought and also the philosophical problematic of the Mishnah – issues of mixtures, issues of the potential and the actual, for instance – should have meant that the law is part of, and expresses in its distinctive idiom of rules, the rules of a well-composed and clearly defined philosophical tradition.

Not only so, but the earliest intellectual critiques of the Mishnah recognized its fundamental Aristotelianism and rejected it, as I demonstrated in *Uniting the Dual Torah: Sifra and the Problem of the Mishnah.*[1] And, as I now am showing in its principal components, that philosophical tradition in which the Mishnah stands is the very tradition that so engaged Maimonides to begin with, which is the Aristotelian one. Had he understood that fact, he would have allowed Aristotle to teach him philosophy through the medium of law and its structure and system. For that is precisely what Judah the Patriarch did in his presentation of the Mishnah. That is to say, through the law of the social order that the Judaism of the Dual Torah set forth, Judah the Patriarch gave full and ample expression also, and at one and the same time, to philosophy and its principles and rules. What Maimonides wanted to do, Judah the Patriarch actually had accomplished a thousand years earlier – and Maimonides did not know it. That explains his mistake. When, therefore, we ask the deceptively simple question, how does the Mishnah relate to Scripture, we find ourselves addressing the most profound structural questions of the relationship of reason to revelation in the Judaism of the Dual Torah we know as normative, classical, and orthodox.

---

[1] In press at Cambridge University Press for publication in 1990.

12

The Mishnah's Philosophical Method: The Judaism of Hierarchical Classification in Greco-Roman Context

Address to the Société des études juives, Paris
January, 1990

The Mishnah, seen whole, presents a profoundly philosophical system, one that employs numerous cases to make a single general point. That proposition is that all things are one, complex things yield uniform and similar components, and, rightly understood, there is a hierarchy of being, to be discovered through the proper classification of all things. That philosophical representation of the theology of the one and singular God, from whom all being comes, comes to full expression in the Mishnah's massive and detailed account of the realm of nature: the rules that govern the ordering of all things in a cogent, ascending structure.

What marks the Mishnah's system as philosophical – and not theological – is its focus upon not merely how things are, but why they are the way they are, that is, upon the question of explaining by appeal to this-worldly and accessible rules what it means that things are this way, rather than some other. The Mishnah's philosophical method derives from the natural history of Aristotle and aims at the hierarchical classification of all things. It follows that the Mishnah's systemic statement, its philosophy of Judaism demonstrates that all things in place, in proper rank and position in the hierarchy of being, point to, stand for, one thing. I suppose that, in the context of Scripture, with its insistence that Israel's God is one and unique, we may take as the unarticulated premise a theological position, and, it would follow, identify as premise that fundamental and ancient affirmation of Israel.

But we deal with a composition that is everywhere systematically philosophical and only rarely, and then episodically, theological. Two-thirds of all tractates focus upon issues of philosophy, and scarcely a line of the Mishnah invokes the word "God" or calls upon the active presence of God. More to the point, the philosophy never addresses in philosophical terms such theological questions as the meaning and end of history, the nature of prophecy, nature and supernature, the being of God, miracles, and the like.[1] True, answers to these questions assuredly lie at, or even lay, the foundations for the philosophical structure. But the system and structure ask the questions philosophers ask, concerning the nature of things, and answer them in the way the philosophers answer them, through orderly sifting of data in the process of natural philosophy. The only point of difference is subject matter, but, after all, philosophers in the great tradition took up multiple questions; some worked on this, some on the other thing, and no single question predominated.

To identify we turn to the telos of thought in the Mishnah, I state the generative proposition of the Mishnah very simply: in the Mishnah, many things are made to say one thing, which concerns the nature of being: teleologically hierarchized, to state matters in simple terms. The system of the Mishnah registers these two contrary propositions: many things are one, one thing is many. These propositions of course complement each other, because, in forming matched opposites, the two provide a complete and final judgment of the whole. The philosophy of Judaism must be deemed ontological, for it is a statement of an ontological order that the system makes when it claims that all things are not only orderly, but ordered in such wise that many things fall into one classification, and one thing may hold together many things of a single classification.

For this philosophy rationality consists in hierarchy of the order of things. That rationality is revealed by the possibility always of effecting the hierarchical classification of all things: each thing in its taxon, all taxa in correct sequence, from least to greatest. And showing that all things can be ordered, and that all orders can be set into relationship with one another, we transform method into message. The message of hierarchical classification is that many things really form a single thing, the many species a single genus, the many genera an encompassing and well-crafted, cogent whole. Every time we speciate, we affirm that position; each successful labor of forming relationships

---

[1]The suspicious attitude toward miracles, expressed at M. Ta. 3:8 in the famous story about Honi the circle-drawer, forms a very minor footnote. Silences testify far more eloquently than occasional observations or pointed stories.

among species, e.g., making them into a genus, or identifying the hierarchy of the species, proves it again. Not only so, but when we can show that many things are really one, or that one thing yields many (the reverse and confirmation of the former), we say in a fresh way a single immutable truth, the one of this philosophy concerning the unity of all being in an orderly composition of all things within a single taxon.

To show how this works, I turn to a very brief sample of the Mishnah's authorship's sustained effort to demonstrate how many classes of things – actions, relationships, circumstances, persons, places – really form one class. This supererogatory work of classification then works its way through the potentialities of chaos to explicit order. It is classification transformed from the how of intellection to the why and the what for and, above all, the what does it all mean. Recognition that one thing may fall into several categories and many things into a single one comes to expression, for the authorship of the Mishnah, in diverse ways. One of the interesting ones is the analysis of the several taxa into which a single action may fall, with an account of the multiple consequences, e.g., as to sanctions that are called into play, for a single action. The right taxonomy of persons, actions, and things will show the unity of all being by finding many things in one thing, and that forms the first of the two components of what I take to be the philosophy's teleology.

Mishnah-tractate Keritot
3:9

A.   There is one who ploughs a single furrow and is liable on eight counts of violating a negative commandment:

B.   [specifically, it is] he who (1) ploughs with an ox and an ass [Deut. 22:10], which are (2,3) both Holy Things, in the case of (4) [ploughing] Mixed Seeds in a vineyard [Deut. 22:9], (5) in the Seventh Year [Lev. 25:4], (6) on a festival [Lev. 23:7] and who was both a (7) priest [Lev. 21:1] and (8) a Nazirite [Num. 6:6] [ploughing] in a graveyard.

C.   Hanania b. Hakhinai says, "Also: He is [ploughing while] wearing a garment of diverse kinds" [Lev. 19:19, Deut. 22:11).

D.   They said to him, "This is not within the same class."

E.   He said to them, "Also the Nazir [B8] is not within the same class [as the other transgressions]."

Here is a case in which more than a single set of flogging is called for. B's felon is liable to 312 stripes, on the listed counts. The ox is sanctified to the altar, the ass to the upkeep of the house (B2,3). Hanania's contribution is rejected since it has nothing to do with ploughing, and sages' position is equally flawed. The main point, for our inquiry, is simple. The one action draws in its wake multiple consequences. Classifying a single thing as a mixture of many things then forms a part of the larger intellectual address to the nature of mixtures. But it yields a result that, in the analysis of an action, far transcends the metaphysical problem of mixtures, because it moves us toward the ontological solution of the unity of being.

The real interest in demonstrating the unity of being lies not in things but in abstractions, and, among abstractions types of actions take the center stage. Mishnah-tractate Keritot works out how many things are really one thing. This is accomplished by showing that the end or consequence of diverse actions to be always one and the same. The issue of the tractate is the definition of occasions on which one is obligated to bring a sin-offering and a suspensive guilt-offering. The tractate lists those sins that are classified together by the differentiating criterion of intention. If one deliberately commits those sins, he is punished through extirpation. If it is done inadvertently, he brings a sin-offering. In case of doubt as to whether or not a sin has been committed (hence: inadvertently), he brings a suspensive guilt-offering. Lev. 5:17-19 specifies that if one sins but does not know it, he brings a sin-offering or a guilt-offering. Then if he does, a different penalty is invoked, with the suspensive guilt-offering at stake as well. While we have a sustained exposition of implications of facts that Scripture has provided, the tractate also covers problems of classification of many things as one thing, in the form of a single sin-offering for multiple sins, and that problem fills the bulk of the tractate.

Mishnah-tractate Keritot 1:1, 2, 7, 3:2, 4

1:1

A.   Thirty-six transgressions subject to extirpation are in the Torah...

1:2

A.   For those [transgressions] are people liable, for deliberately doing them, to the punishment of extirpation,

B.   and for accidentally doing them, to the bringing of a sin-offering,

C.   and for not being certain of whether or not one has done them, to a suspensive guilt-offering [Lev. 5:17] –

D.   "except for the one who imparts uncleanness to the sanctuary and its Holy Things,

E.   "because he is subject to bringing a sliding scale offering (Lev. 5:6-7, 11)," the words of R. Meir.

F.   And sages say, "Also: [except for] the one who blasphemes, as it is said, 'You shall have one law for him that does anything unwittingly' (Num. 15:29) – excluding the blasphemer, who does no concrete deed."

1:7

A.   The woman who is subject to a doubt concerning [the appearance of] five fluxes,

B. or the one who is subject to a doubt concerning five miscarriages
C. brings a single offering.
D. And she [then is deemed clean so that she] eats animal sacrifices.
E. And the remainder [of the offerings, A, B] are not an obligation for her.
F. [If she is subject to] five confirmed miscarriages,
G. or five confirmed fluxes,
H. she brings a single offering.
I. And she eats animal sacrifices.
J. But the rest [of the offerings, the other four] remain as an obligation for her [to bring at some later time] –
K. M'SH S: A pair of birds in Jerusalem went up in price to a golden denar.
L. Said Rabban Simeon b. Gamaliel, "By this sanctuary! I shall not rest tonight until they shall be at [silver] denars."
M. He entered the court and taught [the following law]:
N. "The woman who is subject to five confirmed miscarriages [or] five confirmed fluxes brings a single offering.
O. "And she eats animal sacrifices.
P   "And the rest [of the offerings] do not remain as an obligation for her."
Q. And pairs of birds stood on that very day at a quarter-denar each [one one-hundredth of the former price].

3:2
A. [If] he ate [forbidden] fat and [again ate] fat in a single spell of inadvertence, he is liable only for a single sin-offering,
B. [If] he ate forbidden fat and blood and remnant and refuse [of an offering] in a single spell of inadvertence, he is liable for each and every one of them.
C. This rule is more strict in the case of many kinds [of forbidden food] than of one kind.
D. And more strict is the rule in [the case of] one kind than in many kinds:
E. For if he ate a half-olive's bulk and went and ate a half-olive's bulk of a single kind, he is liable.
F. [But if he ate two half-olive's bulks] of two [different] kinds, he is exempt.

3:4
A. There is he who carries out a single act of eating and is liable on its account for four sin-offerings and one guilt-offering:
B. An unclean [lay] person who ate (1) forbidden fat, and it was (2) remnant (3) of Holy Things, and (4) it was on the Day of Atonement.
C. R. Meir says, "If it was the Sabbath and he took it out [from one domain to another] in his mouth, he is liable [for another sin-offering]."
D. They said to him, "That is not of the same sort [of transgression of which we have spoken heretofore since it is not caused by eating (A)]."

M. Ker. 1:7 introduces the case of classifying several incidents within a single taxon, so that one incident encompasses a variety of cases and therefore one penalty or sanction covers a variety of instances. That same conception is much more amply set forth in chapter two. There we have lists of five who bring a single offering for many transgressions, five who bring a sliding scale offering for many incidents, and the like, so M. 2:3-6. Then M. 3:1-3 we deal with diverse situations in which a man is accused of having eaten forbidden fat and therefore of owing a sin-offering. At M. 3:1 the issue is one of disjoined testimony. Do we treat as one the evidence of two witnesses. The debate concerns whether two cases form a single category. Sages hold that the cases are hardly the same, because there are differentiating traits. M. 3:2-3 show us how we differentiate or unify several acts. We have several acts of transgression in a single spell of inadvertence; we classify them all as one action for purposes of the penalty. That at stake is the problem of classification and how we invoke diverse taxic indicators is shown vividly at M. 3:2 in particular. Along these same lines are the issues of M. Ker. 3:3, 4-6: "There is he who carries out a single act of eating and is liable on its account for four sin-offerings and one guilt-offering; there is he who carries out a single act of sexual intercourse and becomes liable on its account for six sin-offerings," with the first shown at M. 3:4.

The recognition that one thing becomes many does not challenge the philosophy of the unity of all being, but confirms the main point. Why do I insist on that proposition? The reason is simple. If we can show that differentiation flows from within what is differentiated, – that is, from the intrinsic or inherent traits of things – then we confirm that at the heart of things is a fundamental ontological being, single, cogent, simple, that is capable of diversification, yielding complexity and diversity. The upshot is to be stated with emphasis. That diversity in species or diversification in actions follows orderly lines confirms the claim that there is that single point from which many lines come forth. Carried out in proper order – [1] the many form one thing, [2] one thing yields many – the demonstration then leaves no doubt as to the truth of the matter.

The upshot may be stated very simply. The species point to the genus, all classes to one class, all taxa properly hierarchized then rise to the top of the structure and the system forming one taxon. So all things ascend to, reach one thing. All that remains is for the theologian to define that one thing: God. But that is a step that the philosophers of the Mishnah did not take. Perhaps it was because they did not think they had to. But I think there is a different reason altogether. It is because, as a matter of fact, they were philosophers. And to philosophers, as I said at the outset, God serves as premise and principle (and whether or not it is one God or many gods, a unique being or a being that finds a place in a class of similar beings hardly is germane!), and philosophy serves not to demonstrate principles or to explore premises, but to analyze the unknown, to answer important questions.

What next? As we shall now see, among the philosophers of that time and place, which is to say, within important components of the philosophical tradition that sustained the Greco-Roman world, however arcane the subject matter of the philosophy of Judaism, the philosophers of Judaism can claim a rightful, and honored, place. I shall now show that among the philosophers, Judaism's philosophy can and should have been perceived not merely as philosophical, but, indeed, as philosophy. The basis for that claim is simple: whether or not philosophers can have understood a line of the document (and I doubt that they would have cared to try), the method and the message of the philosophy of Judaism fall into the classification of philosophical methods and messages of the Greco-Roman philosophical tradition. The method is like that of Aristotle, the message, congruent to that of neo-Platonism.[2] To state the upshot of the proposition at hand, Judaism's first system, the Mishnah's, finds its natural place within philosophy first because it appeals to the Aristotelian methods of natural philosophy – classification, comparison and contrast, – and the media of expression of philosophy – *Listenwissenschaft* – to register its position.[3]

As to method, can we classify the taxonomic method – premises and rules – of the sages in the same category as the method of Aristotle? This is the question that yields answers on the methodological context in which the philosophy of Judaism is to be located. And in this setting by "context" we mean something piquantly appropriate to our results: the classification of the philosophy. For, as I shall now show, our back-country philosophers in a fairly primitive way replicated the

---

[2]But here I restrict my presentation to the issue of the method of hierarchical classification. Elsewhere I treat the message, to which I merely allude in the present context.
[3]That proposition, on the essential unity of the hierarchical nature of all being, falls into the classification of philosophy, since it forms one important, generative premise of neo-Platonism. But here I concentrate on the issue of method, and the theological implications of the choices made by the Mishnah's philosophers.

188   Lectures on Judaism in the Humanities

method of Aristotle in setting forth the single paramount proposition of neo-Platonism.[4]

Having said that, I hasten to add this qualification. The issue is not one of direct connection. None conjures the fantasy and anachronism, of the Mishnah's authorship's tramping down a Galilean hill from their yeshiva to the academy in a nearby Greek-speaking town, Caesarea or Sepphoris, for example, there studying elementary Aristotle and listening to the earliest discourses of neo-Platonism, then climbing back up the hill and writing it all up in their crabbed back-country idiom made up of the cases and examples of the Mishnah.

But as a matter of fact, in its indicative traits of message and method, the Mishnah's philosophical system is a version of one critical proposition of neo-Platonism, set forth and demonstrated through a standard Aristotelian method.[5] And that is what an examination of the philosophical context will show us. But – I cannot overstress – these judgments rest upon not a claim of direct connection but an exercise of simple, inductive comparison and contrast, that is to say, of mere classification.[6] I propose now only in an entirely inductive

---

[4]I leave for Philonic scholarship the comparison of the Mishnah's neo-Platonism with that of Philo. Philo's mode of writing, his presentation of his ideas, seems to me so different from the mode and method of the Mishnah that I am not sure how we can classify as Aristotelian (in the taxonomic framework of natural philosophy, which seems to me the correct framework for the Mishnah's philosophical method) the principal methodological traits of Philo's thought. But others are most welcome to correct what is only a superficial impression. I think the selection for comparison and contrast of Aristotle and neo-Platonism, first method, then proposition, is a preferable strategy of analysis (and exposition, as a matter of fact), and I willingly accept the onus of criticism for not comparing and contrasting the method and message of Philo with those of the Mishnah. I mean only to suggest that the questions Wolfson's *Philo* raised may well be reopened, but within an entirely fresh set of premises and in accord with what I conceive to be a more properly differentiated and therefore critical reading of the data.
[5]And I need hardly add that the very eclecticism of the philosophy of Judaism places it squarely within the philosophical mode of its time. See J. M. Dillon and A. A. Long, eds., *The Question of "Eclecticism." Studies in Later Greek Philosophy* (Berkeley and Los Angeles, 1988: University of California Press).
[6]But I hasten to add that further studies of the Mishnah's philosophical context are bound to make much more precise any judgment about the philosophical context of the document and its system. For this initial account, it seems unnecessary to do more than argue, as I do, that the Mishnah's fundamental intellectual structure in its method and message fall into the classification, defined by circumstance and context, of philosophy. The method, I shall show, is standard for natural philosophy, exemplified by Aristotle, and the proposition proves entirely congruent to one principal conception of Middle Platonism, exemplified by Plotinus. At the same time, I point out, the

manner to classify the system by the indicative traits of philosophical systems. In that simple way I shall show that in one of the two fundamental aspects, – method, message – this system shares traits important to systems all deemed to be philosophical. Therefore this system by the criteria of philosophy and in the specific and explicit context of philosophy must be classified as philosophical. That is my simple argument. But it is fundamental to my purpose, which is to show that in the Mishnah's system, both as to mode of thought and as to message, we deal with a philosophy – philosophy in an odd idiom to be sure, but philosophy nonetheless.[7]

Let me ask the question in its simplest form: by appeal to the paramount taxic traits of Aristotelian method, can we classify the method as Aristotelian? If we can, then my purpose, which is to demonstrate that the Judaism of the Mishnah is a philosophy, will have been accomplished. That is as far as we can go: no further. But it suffices to accomplish the goal of demonstrating that, as to the method of classification, the Mishnah's is philosophical, in the way in which Greco-Roman philosophy, exemplified by Aristotle, is philosophical. True, we cannot show, and therefore do not know, that the Mishnah's

---

components of congruence, method and message alike, yield far more specific results. If we ask, does the Mishnah's theory of mixtures coincide with that of a specific philosophy of the larger tradition, the answer is, indeed so: the Stoic. But do other components of the Mishnah's metaphysics fit together with the rest of Stoic physics, e.g., theories of space and time? So too, if Middle Platonism will have found entirely familiar the Mishnah's keen interest in showing how one thing yields many things, in demonstrating a hierarchical unity of being through the ordering of all classes of things (that is to say, the ontological unity of things proven on the basis of the natural world), does that make the Mishnah's philosophy in general a form of Middle Platonism? If we ask about the concept of space or place, we look in vain for a familiar conception; cf. S. Sambursky, *The Concept of Place in Late Neoplatonism* (Jerusalem, 1982: The Israel Academy of Sciences and Humanities). My general impression is that when all is said and done, the philosophy of Judaism is far less abstract, even at its most abstract level, than other philosophy of the same tradition and temporal setting; as to the issue of space or place, my sense is that the Judaic philosophers were deeply concerned with *what* things are, not where they are; Jerusalem, for instance, is a profoundly abstract, taxic indicator. That conforms to the larger Aristotelianism of the system. Here, as I stress, I prove only that by the synchronic and even diachronic standards of philosophy, Judaism – method, message, if not medium – in this system is philosophical. These preliminary remarks are meant only to point the way toward a further range of inquiry into the philosophy of Judaism: the comparison and contrast in detail of that philosophy with other philosophies of the Greco-Roman tradition.
[7]And no less than Philo's philosophy was a philosophy. My sense is that these results when properly digested and refined as already noted must reopen the questions addressed by the great Harry A. Wolfson in his *Philo*.

philosophers read Aristotle's work on natural history or his reflections on scientific method, e.g., the Posterior Analytics,[8] we can compare our philosophers' method with that of Aristotle, who also, as a matter of fact, set forth a system that, in part, appealed to the right ordering of things through classification by correct rules.[9]

Now to the specific task at hand. A brief account, based upon the standard textbook picture, of the taxonomic method of Aristotle permits us to compare the philosophical method of the philosophy of Judaism with that of the methodologically paramount natural philosophy of the Greco-Roman world.[10] We begin with the simple

---

[8]I consulted Jonathan Barnes, *Aristotle's Posterior Analytics* (Oxford, 1975: Clarendon Press).

[9]And, as to proposition about the hierarchical ordering of all things in a single way, the unity of all being in right order, while we cannot show and surely do not know that the Mishnah's philosophers knew anything about Plato, let alone Plotinus's neo-Platonism (which came to expression only in the century after the closure of the Mishnah!), we can compare our philosophers' proposition with that of neo-Platonism. For that philosophy, as we shall see, did seek to give full and rich expression to the proposition that all things emerge from one thing, and one thing encompasses all things, and that constitutes the single proposition that animates the system as a whole.

[10]For this section I consulted the following:

Adkins, A. W. H., *From the Many to the One. A Study of Personality and Views of Human Nature in the Context of Ancient Greek Society, Values, and Beliefs* (Ithaca, 1970: Cornell University Press).

Allan, D. J., *The Philosophy of Aristotle* (London, New York, Toronto, 1952: Oxford University Press/Geoffrey Cumberlege).

Armstrong, A. H., "Platonism and Neoplatonism," *Encyclopaedia Britannica* (Chicago, 1975) 14:539-545.

Armstrong, A. H., "Plotinus," *Encyclopaedia Britannica* (Chicago, 1975) 14:573-574.

Bréhier, Émile, *The History of Philosophy. The Hellenistic and Roman Age* (Chicago and London, 1965: The University of Chicago Press). Translated by Wade Baskin.

Cherniss, Harold, *Selected Papers* (Leiden, 1977: E. J. Brill). Edited by Leonardo Tarán.

Feldman, Louis H., "Philo," *Encyclopaedia Britannica* (Chicago, 1975) 14:245-247.

Goodenough, Erwin R., *An Introduction to Philo Judaeus. Second Edition* (Lanham, 1986: University Press of America Brown Classics in Judaica).

Merlan, P., "Greek Philosophy from Plato to Plotinus," in A. H. Armstrong, ed., *The Cambridge History of Later Greek and Early Medieval Philosophy* (Cambridge, 1967: Cambridge University Press), pp. 14-136.

Minio-Paluello, Lorenzo, "Aristotelianism," *Encyclopaedia Britannica* 1:1155-1161.

Owens, Joseph, *A History of Ancient Western Philosophy* (New York, 1959: Appleton, Century, Crofts).

observation that the distinction between genus and species lies at the foundation of all knowledge. Adkins states the matter in the most accessible way, "Aristotle, a systematic biologist, uses his method of classification by genera and species, itself developed from the classificatory interests of the later Plato, to place man among other animals....The classification must be based on the final development of the creature..."[11] But to classify, we have to take as our premise that things are subject to classification, and that means that they have traits that are essential and indicative, on the one side, but also shared with other things, on the other. The point of direct contact and intersection between the Judaism's philosophy of hierarchical classification and the natural philosophy of Aristotle lies in the shared, and critical, conviction concerning the true nature or character of things. Both parties concur that there is such a true definition – a commonplace for philosophers, generative of interesting problems, e.g., about Ideas, or Form and Substance, Actual and Potential, and the like – of what things really are.[12]

But how are we to know the essential traits that allow us to define the true character of, e.g., to classify, things? And this is the point at which our comparison becomes particular, since what we need to find out is whether there are between Aristotle's and Judaism's philosophies only shared convictions about the genus and the species or particular conceptions as to how these are to be identified and organized. The basic convictions on both sides is this: objects are not random but fall into classes and so may be described, analyzed, and explained by appeal to general traits or rules. The generative point of comparison is the taxonomic interest in defining through classification. This definitive trait of natural philosophy is what we find in common between Aristotle's and the Mishnah's philosophical method, and the

---

Parker G. F., *A Short History of Greek Philosophy from Thales to Epicurus* (London, 1967: Edward Arnold (Publishers)).

Reale, Giovanni, *A History of Ancient Philosophy*. III. *The Systems of the Hellenistic Age* (Albany,1985: State University of New York Press). Edited and translated from the third Italian edition by John R. Catan.

[11]A. W. H. Adkins, *From the Many to the One. A Study of Personality and Views of Human Nature in the Context of Ancient Greek Society, Values, and Beliefs* (Ithaca, 1970: Cornell University Press), pp. 170-171.

[12]But only Aristotle and the Mishnah carry into the material details of economics that conviction about the true character or essence of definition of things. The economics of the Mishnah and the economics of Aristotle begin in the conception of "true value," and the distributive economics proposed by each philosophy then develops that fundamental notion. The principle is so fundamental to each system that comparison of one system to the other in those terms alone is justified.

points in common prove far more than those yielded by the general observation that both systems appeal to the identification of genera out of species. In fact, what philosophers call the dialectical approach in Aristotle proves the same approach to the discovery or demonstration of truth as that we find in the Mishnah. Owens sets the matter forth in the following language:[13]

> Since a theoretical science proceeds from first principles that are found within the thing under investigation, the initial task of the philosophy of nature will be to discover its primary principles in the sensible things themselves.

I cannot imagine a formulation more suited to the method of the Mishnah than that simple statement. For the Mishnah's philosophers compose their taxonomy by appeal to the indicative traits of things, rather than to extrinsic considerations of imposed classification, e.g., by reference to Scripture.[14] The philosophers whose system is set forth in the Mishnah appeal to the traits of things, deriving their genera from the comparison and contrast of those inherent or intrinsic traits.

If the parallels in method are clear, where do we find the difference between Aristotle's system and the Mishnah's? It is that the goal of Aristotle's system, the teleological argument in favor of the unmoved mover, and the goal of Judaism's system, the demonstration of the unity of being, are essentially contradictory, marking utterly opposed positions on the fundamental character of God and the traits of the created world that carries us upward to God. So we establish the philosophical character of the method of the Mishnah's system, only at the cost of uncovering a major contradiction: the proposition that animates the one system stands in direct opposition, as to its premises, implications, and explicit results, with the results of the other. Aristotle's God attained through teleological demonstration accomplished through the right classification of all things and the Mishnah's God, whose workings in the world derive from the demonstration of the ontological unity of all things, cannot recognize one another. And that is the case even though they are assuredly one.

Accordingly, we must ask ourselves, *cui bono?* Or more precisely, not to whose advantage, but rather, against whose position, did the Judaic philosophical system propose to argue? When we realize that at stake is a particular means for demonstrating the unity of God, we readily identify as the principal focus the pagan reading of the revealed world

---

[13]Joseph Owens, *A History of Ancient Western Philosophy*, pp. 309ff.
[14]And for that decision they are criticized by all their successors, chief among them, the authorship of Sifra. See my *Uniting the Dual Torah: Sifra and the Problem of the Mishnah* (Cambridge, 1990: Cambridge University Press).

of the here and the now, and, it must follow, Judaism as a philosophy stood over against the pagan philosophy of the world of its time and place. The fundamental argument in favor of the unity of God in the philosophy of Judaism is by showing the hierarchical order, therefore the unity, of the world. The world therefore is made to testify to the unity of being, and – to say the obvious with very heavy emphasis – the power of the philosophy derives from its capacity for hierarchical classification. When we compare the pagan and the Christian philosophical ontology of God, we see that it is the pagan position, and not the Christian one, that forms the target of this system. The Christian position is simply not perceived and not considered.

The comparison of the Judaic, Christian, and pagan systems of Middle Platonism seems to me made possible, in a very preliminary way to be sure, by Armstrong:

> The difference here between pagans and Christians...is a difference about the degree of religious relevance of the material cosmos, and, closely connected with this, about the relative importance of general, natural, and special, supernatural, divine self-manifestation and self-communication. On the one side, the pagan, there is the conviction that a multiple self-communication and self-revelation of divinity takes place always and everywhere in the world, and that good and wise men everywhere...have been able to find the way to God and the truth about God in and through rational reflection on themselves and on the world, not only the heavens but the earth, and the living unity of the whole. On the other side, the Christian, there is indeed a readiness to see the goodness and beauty of the visible cosmos as a testimony to God's creation...but the religious emphasis lies elsewhere. Saving truth and the self-communication of the life of God come through the Incarnation of God as a man and through the human...society of which the God-Man is the head, the Church....It is only in the Church that material things become means of revelation and salvation through being understood in the light of Scripture and Church tradition and used by God's human ministers in the celebration of the Church's sacraments. It is the ecclesiastical cosmos, not the natural cosmos, which appears to be of primary religious importance for the Christian.[15]

If God is revealed in the artifacts of the world, then, so pagans in general considered, God must be multiple. No, the philosophy of Judaism is here seen to respond. Here we find a Judaic argument, within the premises of paganism, against paganism. To state with emphasis what I conceive to be that argument: the very artifacts that appear multiple in fact form classes of things, and, moreover, these classes

---

[15]"Man in the Cosmos," A. Hilary Armstrong, *Plotinian and Christian Studies* (London, 1979: Variorum Reprints) No. XVII, p. 11.

themselves are subject to a reasoned ordering, by appeal to this-worldly characteristics signified by properties and indicative traits. Monotheism hence is to be demonstrated by appeal to those very same data that for paganism prove the opposite.

The medium of hierarchical classification, which is Aristotle's, conveys the message of the unity of being[16] in the this-worldly mode of discourse formed by the framers of the Mishnah. The way to one God, ground of being and ontological unity of the world, lies through "rational reflection on themselves and on the world," this world, which yields a living unity encompassing the whole. That claim, conducted in an argument covering overwhelming detail in the Mishnah, directly faces the issue as framed by paganism. Immanent in its medium, it is transcendent in its message. And I hardly need spell out the simple reasons, self-evident in Armstrong's words, for dismissing as irrelevant to their interests the Christian reading of the cosmos. To the Mishnah's sages, it is not (merely) wrong, it is insufficient.

And yet, that is not the whole story. For the Mishnah's sages reach into Scripture for their generative categories, and, in doing so, they address head-on a Christianity that Armstrong centers, with entire soundness, upon the life of the Church of Jesus Christ, God-Man.[17] We do well here to review Armstrong's language: "It is only in the Church that material things become means of revelation and salvation through being understood in the light of Scripture and Church tradition and used by God's human ministers in the celebration of the Church's sacraments."

The framers of the Mishnah will have responded, "It is in the Torah that material things are identified and set forth as a means of revelation."

Again Armstrong: "It is the ecclesiastical cosmos, not the natural cosmos, which appears to be of primary religious importance for the Christian."

To this the philosophers of Judaism reply, "It is the scriptural account of the cosmos that forms our generative categories, which, by

---

[16]which is Plato's and Plotinus's.

[17]That judgment does not contradict the argument of my *Uniting the Dual Torah: Sifra and the Problem of the Mishnah* (Cambridge, 1990: Cambridge University Press) concerning the Sifra's authorship's critique of the Mishnah's philosophers' stress upon classification through intrinsic traits of things as against through classes set forth solely by the Torah. I mean only to stress the contrast between appeal to Scripture and to nature, which I find in the philosophy of Judaism, and appeal to the ecclesiastical cosmos. This point registers immediately.

the power of intellect, we show to constitute an ordered, hierarchical unity of being."

So the power of this identification of "the ecclesiastical cosmos" is revealed when we frame the cosmos of the Mishnah by appeal to its persistent response to the classifications and categories of Scripture. If the Church as Armstrong portrays matters worked out an ecclesiastical cosmos, only later on producing the Bible as it did, for its part the philosophy of Judaism framed a scriptural cosmos, – and then read it philosophically in the way in which I have explained matters.

We may therefore identify three distinct positions on the reading of the natural world: the pagan, the Christian, and the Judaic. The one reads nature as a source of revelation. The other two insist on a medium of mediation between nature and intellect. For Christianity it is, as Armstrong says, ecclesiastical, and, as I claim, for Judaism, the medium of mediation of nature lies through revelation, the Torah.

Why the difference? There is a philosophical reason, which I deem paramount, and which explains my insistence that this Judaism is a philosophy, a philosophy – not a theology – in its message and its mode of thought. It is that by not merely appealing to the authority of Scripture, but by themselves analyzing the revealed truths of Scripture, that the intellects at hand accomplished their purposes. By themselves showing the order and unity inherent within Scripture's list of topics, the philosophers on their own power meant to penetrate into the ground of being as God has revealed matters. This they did by working their way back from the epiphenomena of creation to the phenomenon of Creation – then to the numinous, that is, the Creator. That self-assigned challenge forms an intellectual vocation worthy of a particular kind of philosopher, an Israelite one. And, in my view, it explains also why in the Mishnah philosophers produced their philosophy in the form that they chose.

For the form, so superficially unphilosophical in its crabbed and obsessive mode of discourse, proves in the end to form a philosophy. Judaism in the system of the Mishnah is philosophical in medium, method, and message. But then philosophy also is represented as, and within, the Torah in topic and authority. The union then of the Torah's classifications and topics, philosophy's modes of thought and propositions – that marriage produced as its firstfruits a philosophical Judaism, a Judaic philosophy: the Torah as Moses would have written it at God's instructions, were Moses a philosopher. But the offspring of the happy marriage was not to live long, and the philosophy of Judaism would soon give way to the theology of Judaism: theology, not philosophy, dictated the future for a thousand years.

13

Max Weber Revisited:
Religion and Society in Ancient Judaism

with Special Reference to the Late First and Second Centuries

The Sacks Lecture
Oxford University, 1981

A scholar's journey moves in ever-widening circles, down familiar paths towards frontiers of knowledge and across. For the study of religion in general, and Judaism as an example of the general, Max Weber laid out one road from the known even to the outer bounds of understanding. We do well again and again to walk on the road he laid out. There are two points of interest today in Weber's thought, one which serves to define my problem, and the other which shows the way in which I propose to solve it. First, Weber's interest in the relation between social stratification and religious ideas presents an enduring perspective for the analysis of the place of religion in society and of the relationship between religion and society. Second, Weber's mode of formulating ideal types for the purposes of analysis provides a model for how we may think about the castes, professions, and classes of society and the religious ideas they hold. The former is the fundamental issue. If we ask about whether we may discern congruence between the religious ideas to be assigned to a given group, described in gross terms as an ideal type, in ancient Israelite society, and the class status of that group, we use a mode of thought shaped by Weber in the analysis of a question raised by Weber.

It is in that sense alone that we revisit Weber. I do not propose to enrich the vast literature of interpretation of his writings, let alone discuss the enduring or transient value of his work on ancient Judaism, which is important only in the study of Weber. I shall simply take the road laid out by Weber, in order to cross frontiers of problems of interpretation not known to the world of learning in the time of Weber's *Ancient Judaism*, I mean, describing and explaining the character of Judaism as it took shape in the late first and second centuries. My purpose, stated simply, is to explore that paramount theme in Weber's great work, as expressed by Reinhard Bendix:

> In order to understand the stability and dynamics of a society we should attempt to understand these efforts in relation to the ideas and values that are prevalent in the society; or, conversely, for every given idea or value that we observe we should seek out the status group whose material and ideal way of life it tends to enhance. Thus, Weber approached the study of religious ideas in terms of their relevance for collective actions, and specially in terms of the social processes whereby the inspirations of a few become the convictions of the many (Reinhard Bendix, *Max Weber. An Intellectual Portrait* (New York, 1962: Doubleday), p. 259).

The question then is how to relate the religious ideas held by an important group of Jews in the late first and second centuries to the social world imagined by that group.

The group under discussion is that handful of sages who, from before 70, through the period between the second war against Rome, in 132-135, and down to the end of the second century, worked out the principal themes of Israelite life and law and produced the Mishnah, their systematic account of the way in which Israel, the Jewish people in the Holy Land, should construct its life.[1] Taking up, in succession, the holiness of the Land, the proper conduct of cult and home on holy days, the holiness of family life with special reference to the transfer of women from the father's house to the husband's bed, the stable conduct of civil life, the conduct of the cult on ordinary days, and the bounds of holiness in a world of cultic uncleanness, the Mishnah designed the formative categories of reality and designated their contents.

---

[1]Weber's formulation of the problem – the relationship of religious ideas to the group which held them – justifies our concentrating on a given book of the character of the Mishnah. First, we assume only that the Mishnah speaks for its authorities, with no presuppositions, at this point, about their prospective audience. Second, since the Mishnah to begin with is a collective document, carefully effacing the signs of individual authorship or authority, we are justified in deeming it to speak for a group. Third, as we shall now see, the Mishnah most certainly is a corpus of religious conceptions, framed, in some measure, through the medium of civil law to be sure. So it would be wrong to suppose that at hand is an exercise in treating a book as a religious community (!). Within the framework of Weber's paradigm, the Mishnah constitutes an ideal program for description and analysis of one suggestive aspect of the relationship between religion and society.

Our work is to generalize about fundamental religious perspectives and collective actions. Now it is not difficult to take up one teaching or another within that law code and speculate about who may have said it, for what material or ideal purpose, and as an expression of which social status or context. But that sort of unsystematic and unmethodical speculation is hardly worthy of the question presented to us by Max Weber, because in the end the answers are beside the point. We wish to ask how and why "the inspirations of a few" – the sages of the document under discussion and the people who stand behind the document – become "the convictions of the many." For that purpose, episodic speculation on discrete sayings is not really pertinent, even if it *were* to be subject to the controls and tests of verification and falsification.

Rather I wish to turn to a more fundamental matter, which is the mode of thought of the group as a whole. That mode of thought is revealed, in particular, in the way in which questions are formulated. For what is telling is the asking; what is revealing is how people define what they wish to know. If we may discover the key to the system by which questions are generated and by which the logic for forming and answering those questions is made to appear to be self-evident, and if we may then relate that mode of logic and inquiry to its social setting, then I believe we may claim to speak to that program of thought laid forth by Weber in his effort "to analyze the relation between social stratification and religious ideas" (Bendix, p. 258). In this regard, individual ideas, let alone the ideas of individual thinkers, are not important. The great classical historian, Harold Cherniss, says, "The historian is concerned to comprehend the individuality of a work of art only in order that he may eliminate it and so extract for use as historical evidence those elements which are not the creation of the author" (Harold Cherniss, "The Biographical Fashion in Literary Criticism," *University of California Publications in Classical Philology*, ed. by J. T. Allen, W. H. Alexander, and G. M. Calhoun, vol. XII, No. 15, pp. 279-292; quotation, pp. 279-280). We must do the same. That is, we are not helped to know the ideas of individuals or even the concrete and specific doctrines of the document. We wish, rather, to eliminate not only individuality, but also all specificity. So we turn to what is most general. That is, as I said, we want to discover the systemic motive behind asking a question, the power which generates and defines both problems and the logic by which they will be solved.

Let me now state the proposition of this lecture at the outset. The issues which occupy the Mishnah's philosophical mode of forming ideas and defining questions to be taken up will be seen to emerge from the social circumstance of the people of Israel in the Land of Israel. Specifically, the Mishnah's systematic preoccupation with sorting out uncertainties, with pointing up and resolving points of conflict, and with bringing into alignment contradictory principles, corresponds in thought to the confusion and doubt which then disordered Israelite social existence in the aftermath of defeat and catastrophe. In every line the Mishnah both expresses the issue of confusion in the wake of the end of the old mode of ordering life above and below, and also imposes order by sorting out confused matters. The mishnaic message is that Israel's will is decisive. What the Israelite proposes is what disposes of questions, resolves conflict, settles doubt. Everything depends upon Israelite will, whether this thing of which we speak be expressed in terms of wish, intention, attitude, hope, conception, idea, aspiration, or other words which speak of parts of the whole entity of heart and mind. So the medium is a sequence of problems of conflict and confusion, and the message is that things are what you will them to be. In a moment of deep despair and doubt such as the late first and second centuries, this appeal to the heart and mind of Israel penetrated to the depths of the dilemma.

I. The Mishnah in its Social Setting

The Mishnah presents a "Judaism," that is, a coherent worldview and comprehensive way of living. It is a worldview which speaks of transcendent things, a way of life expressive of the supernatural meaning of what is done, a heightened and deepened perception of the sanctification of Israel in deed and in deliberation. Sanctification means two things: first, distinguishing Israel in all its dimensions from the world in all its ways; second, establishing the stability, order, regularity, predictability, and reliability of Israel at moments and in contexts of danger, meaning instability, disorder, irregularity, uncertainty, and betrayal. Each topic of the Mishnah's system of Judaism as a whole takes up a critical and indispensable moment or context of social being. Through what is said in regard to each of the Mishnah's principal topics, what the system as a whole wishes to declare is fully expressed. Yet if the parts both severally and jointly give the message of the whole, the whole cannot exist without all of the parts, so well-joined and carefully crafted are they all together.

The critical issue in economic life, which means, in farming, is in two parts. First, Israel, as tenant on God's Holy Land, maintains the property in the ways God requires, keeping the rules which make the Land and its crops as holy. Second, at the hour at which the sanctification of the Land comes to form a critical mass, namely, in the ripened crops, comes the moment ponderous with danger and heightened holiness. Israel's will so affects the crops as to mark a part of them as holy, the rest of them as available for common use. The human will is determinative in the process of sanctification. Second, what happens in the Land at certain times, at Appointed Times, marks off spaces of the Land as holy in yet another way. The center of the Land and the focus of its sanctification is the Temple. There the produce of the Land is received and given back to God, the One who created and sanctified the Land. At these unusual moments of sanctification, the inhabitants of the Land in their social being in villages enter a state of spatial sanctification. This is expressed in two ways. First, the Temple itself observes and expresses the special, recurring holy time. Second, the villages of the Land are brought into alignment with the Temple, forming a complement and completion to the Temple's sacred being. The advent of the appointed times precipitates a spatial reordering of the Land, so that the boundaries of the sacred are matched and mirrored in village and in Temple. At the heightened holiness marked by these moments of appointed times, therefore, the occasion for an effective sanctification is worked out. Like the harvest, the advent of an appointed time, a pilgrim festival also a sacred season, is made to express that regular, orderly, and predictable sort of sanctification for Israel which the system as a whole seeks.

If for a moment we bypass the next two divisions, we come to the counterpart of the divisions of Agriculture and Appointed Times, that is, Holy Things and Purities. These divisions deal with the everyday and the ordinary, as against the special moments of harvest, on the one side, and special time or season, on the other. The Temple, the locus of continuous, as against special, sanctification, is conducted in a wholly routine and trustworthy, punctilious manner. the one thing which may unsettle matters is the intention and will of the human actor. The division of Holy Things generates its companion, the one on cultic cleanness, Purities. The relationship between the two is like that between Agriculture and Appointed Times, the former locative, the latter utopian, the former dealing with the fields, the latter with the interplay between fields and altar. Here too, once we speak of the one place of the Temple, we address, too, the cleanness which pertains to every place. A system of cleanness, taking into account what imparts uncleanness and how this is done, what is subject to uncleanness, and how that state is overcome – that system is fully expressed, once more, in response to the participation of the human will. Without the wish and act of a human being, the system does not function. It is inert. Sources of uncleanness, which come naturally and not by volition, and modes of purification, which work naturally and not by human intervention, remain inert until human will has imparted susceptibility to uncleanness, that is, introduced into the system, that food and drink, bed, pot, chair, and pan, which to begin with form the focus of the system. The movement from sanctification to uncleanness takes place when human will and work precipitate it.

The middle divisions, the third and fourth, on Women, on family law, and Damages, on civil law, finally, take their place in the structure of the whole by showing the congruence, within the larger framework of sanctification through regularity and the perfection of social order, of human concerns of family and farm, politics and workaday transactions among ordinary people. For without attending to these matters, the Mishnah's system does not encompass what, at its foundations, it is meant to comprehend and order. What is at issue is fully cogent with the rest. In the case of Women, attention focuses upon the point of disorder marked by the transfer of that disordering anomaly, woman, from the regular status provided by one man, to the equally trustworthy status provided by another. That is the point at which the Mishnah's interests are aroused: once more, predictably, the moment of disorder. In the case of Damages, there are two important concerns. First, there is the paramount interest in preventing, so far as possible, the disorderly rise of one person and fall of another, and in sustaining the *status quo* of the economy of the household Israel, the holy society in perfect stasis. Second, there is the necessary concomitant in the provision of a system of political institutions to carry out the laws which preserve the balance and steady state of persons.

The divisions which take up topics of concrete and material concern, the formation and dissolution of families and the transfer of property in that connection, the transactions, both through torts and through commerce, which lead to exchanges of property and the potential dislocation of the state of families in society, are both locative and utopian. They deal with the concrete locations in which people make their lives, household and street and field, the sexual and commercial exchanges of a given village. But they pertain to the life of all Israel, both in the Land and otherwise. These two divisions, together with the household ones of Appointed Times, constitute the sole opening outward toward the life of utopian Israel, that diaspora in the far reaches of the ancient world. This community from the Mishnah's perspective is not merely in exile, but unaccounted for; it is simply outside the system, for the Mishnah declines to recognize and take it into account. Israelites who dwell in the land of (unclean) death instead of in the Land simply fall outside of the realm and range of (holy) life.

Now if we ask ourselves about the sponsorship and source of special interest in the topics just now reviewed, we come up with obvious answers.

So far as the Mishnah is a document about the holiness of Israel in its Land, it expresses that conception of sanctification and theory of its mode which will have been shaped among those to whom the Temple and its technology of joining Heaven and holy Land through the sacred place defined the core of being, I mean, the caste of the priests.

So far as the Mishnah takes up the way in which transactions are conducted among ordinary folk and takes the position that it is through documents that transactions are embodied and expressed (surely the position of the relevant tractates on both Women and Damages), the Mishnah expresses what is self-evident to scribes. Just as, to the priest, there is a correspondence between the table of the Lord in the Temple and the locus of the divinity in the heavens, so, to the scribe, there is a correspondence between the documentary expression of the human will on earth, in writs of all sorts, in the orderly provision of courts for the predictable and just disposition of exchanges of persons and property, and Heaven's judgment of these same matters. When a woman becomes sanctified to a particular man on earth, through the appropriate document governing the transfer of her person and property, in heaven as well, the woman is deemed truly sanctified to that man. A violation of the writ therefore is not merely a crime. It is a sin. That is why the Temple rite involving the wife accused of adultery is integral to the system of the division of Women.

So there are these two social groups. But they are not symmetrical with one another. For one is the priestly caste, and the other is the scribal profession. We know, moreover, that in time to come, the profession would become a focus of sanctification too. The scribe would be transformed into the rabbi, locus of the holy through what he knew, just as the priest had been, and would remain, locus of the holy through what he could claim for genealogy. The tractates of special interest to scribes-become-rabbis and to their governance of Israelite society, those of Women and Damages, together with certain others particularly relevant to utopian Israel beyond the system of the Land – those tractates would grow and grow. Others would remain essentially as they were with the closure of the Mishnah. So we must notice that the Mishnah, for its part, speaks about the program of topics important to the priests. It does so in the persona of the scribes, speaking through their voice and in their manner.

Now what we do not find is astonishing in the light of these observations. It is sustained and serious attention to the matter of the caste of the priests and of the profession of the scribes. True, scattered through the tractates are exercises, occasionally important exercises, on the genealogy of the priestly caste, their marital obligations and duties, as well as on the things priests do and do not do in the cult, in collecting and eating their sanctified food, and other topics of keen interest to priests. Indeed, it would be no exaggeration to say that the Mishnah's system, seen whole is not a great deal more than a handbook of how the priestly caste wished to design its life in Israel and the world. And this is what makes amazing the fact that in the fundamental structure of the document, its organization into divisions and tractates, there is no place for a division of the Priesthood. There is no room even for a complete tractate on the rules of the priesthood, except, as we have seen, for the pervasive way of life of the priestly caste, which is everywhere. This absence of sustained attention to the priesthood is striking, when we compare the way in which the Priestly Code at Leviticus chapters one through fifteen spells out its triplet of concerns: the priesthood, the cult, the matter of cultic cleanness. Since we have divisions for the cult and for cleanness at Holy Things and Purities, we are struck by the absence of a parallel to the third division.

We must, moreover, be equally surprised that, for a document so rich in the importance lent to petty matters of how a writ is folded and where the witnesses sign, so obsessed with the making of long lists and the organization of all knowledge into neat piles of symmetrically arranged words, the scribes who know how to make lists and match words nowhere come to the fore. They speak through the document. But they stand behind the curtains. They write the script, arrange the sets, design the costumes, situate the players in their place on the stage, raise the curtain – and play no role at all. We have no division or tractate on such matters as how a person becomes a scribe, how a scribe conducts his work, who forms the center of the scribal profession and how authority is gained therein, the rights and place of the scribe in the system of governance through courts, the organization and conduct of schools or circles of masters and disciples through which the scribal arts are taught and perpetuated. This absence of even minimal information on the way in which the scribal profession takes shape and does its work is stunning, when we realize that, within a brief generation, the Mishnah as a whole would fall into the hands of scribes, called rabbis,[2] both in the Land of Israel and in Babylonia.

---

[2]But the title, "rabbi," cannot be thought particular to those who served as judges and administrators in small-claims courts and as scribes and authorities in the Jewish community, called "rabbis" in the talmudic literature and

These rabbis would make of the Mishnah exactly what they wished. Construed from the perspective of the makers of the Mishnah, the priests and the scribes who provide contents and form, substance and style, therefore, the Mishnah turns out to omit all reference to actors, when laying out the world which is their play.

The metaphor of the theater for the economy of Israel, the household of holy Land and people, space and time, cult and home, leads to yet another perspective. When we look out upon the vast drama portrayed by the Mishnah, lacking as it does an account of the one who wrote the book, and the one about whom the book was written, we notice yet one more missing component. In the fundamental and generative structure of the Mishnah, we find no account of that other necessary constituent: the audience. To whom the document speaks is never specified. What group ("class") generates the Mishnah's problems is not at issue. True, it is taken for granted that the world of the Mishnah expresses the sanctified being of Israel in general. So the Mishnah speaks about the generality of Israel, the people. But to whom, within Israel, the Mishnah addresses itself, and what groups are expected to want to know what the Mishnah has to say are matters which never come to full expression.

Yet there can be no doubt of the answer to the question. The building block of mishnaic discourse, the circumstance addressed whenever the issues of concrete society and material transactions are taken up, is the householder and his context. The Mishnah knows all sorts of economic activities. But for the Mishnah the center and focus of interest lie in the village. The village is made up of households, each a unit of production in farming. The households are constructed by, and around, the householder, father of an extended family, including his sons and their wives and children, his servants, his slaves, the craftsmen to whom he entrusts tasks he does not choose to do. The concerns of householders are in transactions in land. Their measurement of value is expressed in acreage of top, middle, and bottom grade. Through real estate critical transactions are worked out. The marriage settlement depends upon real property. Civil penalties are exacted through payment of real property. The principal transactions to be taken up are those of the householder who owns beasts which do damage or suffer it; who harvests his crops and must set aside and so by his own word and deed sanctify them for use by the castes scheduled from on high; who uses or sells his crops and feeds his family; and who, if he is fortunate, will acquire still more land. It is to householders that the Mishnah is

---

afterward. The title is clearly prior to its particularization in the institutions of the talmudic community.

addressed: the pivot of society and its bulwark, the units of production of which the village is composed, the corporate component of the society of Israel in the limits of the village and the land. The householder, as I said, is the building block of the house of Israel, of its *economy* in the classic sense of the word.

So, to revert to the metaphor which has served us well, the great proscenium constructed by the Mishnah now looms before us. Its arch is the canopy of heaven. Its stage is the holy Land of Israel, corresponding to heaven. Its actors are the holy people of Israel. Its events are the drama of unfolding time and common transactions, appointed times and holy events. Yet in this grand design we look in vain for the three principal participants: the audience, the actors, and the playwright. So we must ask why.

The reason is not difficult to discover, when we recall that, after all, what the Mishnah really wants is for nothing to happen. The Mishnah presents a tableau, a wax museum, a diorama. It portrays a world fully perfected and so wholly at rest. The one thing the Mishnah does not want to tell us is about change, how things come to be, or cease to be, what they are. That is why there can be no sustained attention to the caste of the priesthood and its rules, the scribal profession and its constitution, the class of householders and its interests. The Mishnah's pretense is that all of these have come to rest. They compose a world in stasis, perfect and complete, made holy because it is complete and perfect. It is an economy – again in the classic sense of the word – awaiting the divine *act* of sanctification which, as at the creation of the world, would set the seal of holy rest upon an again-complete creation, just as in the beginning. There is no place for the actors when what is besought is no action whatsoever, but only perfection, which is unchanging. There is room only for a description of how things are: the present tense, the sequence of completed statements and static problems. All the action lies within, in how these statements are made. Once they come to full expression, with nothing left to say, there also is nothing left to do, no need for actors, whether scribes, priests, or householders.

We have now to ask how the several perspectives joined in the Mishnah do coalesce. What the single message is which brings them all together, and how that message forms a powerful, if transient, catalyst for the social groups which hold it – these define the task in portraying the Judaism for which the Mishnah is the whole evidence. Integral to that task, to be sure, is an account of why, for the moment, the catalyst could serve, as it clearly did, to join together diverse agents, to mingle, mix, indeed unite, for a fleeting moment, social elements quite unlike one another, indeed not even capable of serving as analogies for one another.

One of the paramount, recurring exercises of the mishnaic thinkers is to give an account of how things which are different from one another become part of one another, that is, the problem of mixtures. This problem of mixtures will be in many dimensions, involving cases of doubt; cases of shared traits and distinctive ones; cases of confusion of essentially distinct elements and components; and numerous other concrete instances of successful and of unsuccessful, complete and partial catalysis. If I had to choose one prevailing motif of mishnaic thought, it is this: the joining together of categories which are distinct, the distinguishing among those which are confused. The mishnaic mode of thought is to bring together principles and to show both how they conflict and how the conflict is resolved; to deal with gray areas and to lay down principles for disposing of cases of doubt; to take up the analysis of entities into their component parts and the catalysis of distinct substances into a single entity; to analyze the whole, to synthesize the parts. The motive force behind the Mishnah's intellectual program of cases and examples, the thing the authorship of the Mishnah wants to do with all of the facts it has in its hand, is described within this inquiry into mixtures. Now the reasons for this deeply typical, intellectual concern with confusion and order, I think, are probably to be found here and there and everywhere.

For, after all, the basic mode of thought of the priests who made up the priestly creation legend (Gen. 1:1-2:4a) is that creation is effected through the orderly formation of each thing after its kind and correct location of each in its place. The persistent quest of the mishnaic subsystems is for stasis, order, the appropriate situation of all things.

A recurrent theme in the philosophical tradition of Greco-Roman antiquity, current in the time of the Mishnah's formative intellectual processes, is the nature of mixtures,[3] the interpenetration of distinct substances and their qualities, the juxtaposition of incomparables. The types of mixture were themselves organized in a taxonomy: a mechanical composition, in which the components remain essentially unchanged, a total fusion, in which all particles are changed and lose their individual properties, and, in-between, a mixture proper, in which there is a blending. So, concern for keeping things straight and in their place is part of the priestly heritage, and it also is familiar to the philosophical context in which scribes can have had their being. Nor will the householders have proved disinterested in the notion of well-marked borders and stable and dependable frontiers between

---

[3]I refer to S. Sambursky, *The Physics of the Stoics.*

different things. What was to be fenced in and fenced out hardly requires specification.

And yet, however tradition and circumstances may have dictated this point of interest in mixtures and their properties, in sorting out what is confused and finding a proper place for everything, I think there is still another reason for the recurrence of a single type of exercise and a uniform mode of thought. It is the social foundation for the intellectual exercise which is the Mishnah and its Judaism. In my view the very condition of Israel, standing, at the end of the second century, on the limns of its own history, at the frontiers among diverse peoples, on both sides of every boundary, whether political or cultural or intellectual – it is the condition of Israel itself which attracted attention to this matter of sorting things out. *The concern for the catalyst which joins what is originally distinct, the powerful attraction of problems of confusion and chaos, on the one side, and order and form, on the other – these form the generative problematic of the Mishnah as a system because they express in intellectual form the very nature and essential being of Israel in its social condition at that particular moment in Israel's history.* It is therefore the profound congruence of the intellectual program and the social and historical realities taken up and worked out by that intellectual program, which accounts for the power of the Mishnah to define the subsequent history of Judaism. That is why the inspirations of the few in time would become the convictions of the many. It is what Weber's questions generate for answers.

II. The Mishnah's Methods of Thought

Now that the tributaries to the Mishnah have been specified, we have to turn to those traits of style and substance in which the Mishnah vastly exceeds the flood of its tributaries, becomes far more than the sum of its parts. The Mishnah in no way presents itself as a document of class, caste, or profession. It is something different. The difference comes to complete statement in the two dimensions which mark the measure of any work of intellect: style and substance, mode of thought, medium of expression, and message. These have now to be specified with full attention to recurrent patterns to be discerned among the myriad of detailed rules, problems, and exercises, of which the Mishnah is composed.[4]

---

[4]Documentation for the general statements made in this section will be found in my *Judaism: The Evidence of the Mishnah* (Chicago, 1981: The University of Chicago Press).

Let us take up, first of all, the matter of style. The Mishnah's paramount literary trait is its emphasis on disputes about the law. Nearly all disputes, which dominate the rhetoric of the Mishnah, derive from bringing diverse legal principles into formal juxtaposition and substantive conflict. So we may say that the Mishnah as a whole is an exercise in the application to a given case, through practical reason, of several distinct and conflicting principles of law. In this context, it follows, the Mishnah is a protracted inquiry into the intersection of principles. It maps out the gray areas of the law delimited by such limns of confusion. An example of this type of "mixture" of legal principles comes in the conflict of two distinct bodies of the law. But gray areas are discerned not only through mechanical juxtaposition, making up a conundrum of distinct principles of law. On the contrary, the mishnaic philosophers are at their best when they force into conflict laws which, to begin with, scarcely intersect. This they do, for example, by inventing cases in which the secondary implications of one law are brought into conflict with the secondary implications of some other. Finally, nothing will so instantly trigger the imagination of the Mishnah's exegetical minds as matters of ambiguity. A species of the genus of gray areas of the law is the excluded middle, that is, the creature or substance which appears to fall between two distinct and definitive categories. The Mishnah's framers time and again allude to such an entity, because it forms the excluded middle which inevitably will attract attention and demand categorization. There are types of recurrent middles among both human beings and animals as well as vegetables. Indeed, the obsession with the excluded middle leads the Mishnah to invent its own examples, which have then to be analyzed into their definitive components and situated in their appropriate category. What this does is to leave no area lacking in an appropriate location, none to yield irresoluble doubt.

The purpose of identifying the excluded middle is to allow the lawyers to sort out distinct rules, on the one side, and to demonstrate how they intersect without generating intolerable uncertainty, on the other. For example, to explore the theory that an object can serve as either a utensil or a tent, that is, a place capable of spreading the uncleanness of a corpse under its roof, the framers of the Mishnah invent a "hive." This is sufficiently large so that it can be imagined to be either a utensil or a tent. When it is whole, it is the former, and if it is broken, it is the latter. The location of the object, e.g., on the ground, off the ground, in a doorway, against a wall, and so on, will further shape the rules governing the cases (M. Ohalot 9:1-14). Again, to indicate the ambiguities lying at the frontiers, the topic of the status of Syria will come under repeated discussion. Syria is deemed not wholly sanctified, as is the Land of Israel, but also not wholly outside of the frame of Holy Land, as are all other countries. That is why to Syria apply some rules applicable to Holy Land, some rules applicable to secular land. In consequence, numerous points of ambiguity will be uncovered and explored (M. Sheb. 6:1-6).

Gray areas of the law in general, and the excluded middle in particular, cover the surface of the law. They fill up nearly every chapter of the Mishnah. But underneath the surface is an inquiry of profound and far-reaching range. It is into the metaphysical or philosophical issues of how things join together, and how they do not, of synthesis and analysis, of fusion and union, connection, division, and disintegration. What we have in the recurrent study of the nature of mixtures, broadly construed, is a sustained philosophical treatise in the guise of an episodic exercise in ad hoc problem solving. It is as if the cultic agendum, laid forth by the priests, the social agendum, defined by the confusing status and condition of Israel, and the program for right categorization of persons and things, set forth for the scribes to carry out – all were taken over and subsumed by the philosophers who proposed to talk abstractly about what they deemed urgent, while using the concrete language and syntax of untrained minds. To put it differently, the framers of the Mishnah, in their reflection on the nature of mixtures in their various potentialities for formation and dissolution, shape into hidden discourse, on an encompassing philosophical-physical problem of their own choosing, topics provided by others.

In so doing, they phrased the critical question demanding attention and response, the question in dimensions at once social, political, metaphysical, cultural, and even linguistic, but above all, historical: the question of Israel, standing at the outer boundaries of a long history now decisively done with. That same question of acculturation and assimilation, alienation and exile, which had confronted the sixth century B.C. priests of the Priestly Code, from 70 to 200 was raised once more. Now it is framed in terms of mechanical composition, fusion, and something in between, mixtures. But it is phrased in incredible terms of a wildly irrelevant world of unseen things, of how we define the place of the stem in the entity of the apple, the affect of the gravy upon the meat, and the definitive power of a bit of linen in a fabric of wool. In concrete form, the issues are close to comic. In abstract form, the answers speak of nothing of workaday meaning. In reality, at issue is Israel in its Land, once the lines of structure which had emanated from the Temple had been blurred and obliterated. It is in this emphasis upon sorting out confused things that the Mishnah becomes truly mishnaic, distinct from modes of thought and perspective to be assigned to groups represented in the document. To interpret the meaning of this emphasis, we must again recall that the Priestly Code makes the point that a well-ordered society on earth, with its center and point of reference at the Temple altar, corresponds to a well-ordered canopy of heaven. Creation comes to its climax at the perfect rest marked by completion and signifying perfection and sanctification. Indeed, the creation-myth represents as the occasion for sanctification a perfected world at rest, with all things in their rightful place. Now the Mishnah takes up this conviction, which is located at the deepest structures of the metaphysic of the framers of the Priestly Code and, therefore, of their earliest continuators and imitators in the mishnaic code. But the Mishnah does not frame the conviction that in order is salvation through a myth of creation and a description of a cult of precise and perfect order, such as is at Gen. 1:1-2:4a. True, the Mishnah imposes order upon the world through lines of structure emanating from the cult. The verses of Scripture selected as authoritative leave no alternative.

Yet, the Mishnah at its deepest layers, taking up the raw materials of concern of priests and farmers and scribes, phrases that concern after the manner of philosophers. That is to say, the framers of the Mishnah speak of the physics of mixtures, conflicts of principles which must be sorted out, areas of doubt generated by confusion. The detritus of a world seeking order but suffering chaos now is reduced to the construction of intellect. If, therefore, we wish to characterize the Mishnah when it is cogent and distinctive, we must point to this persistent and pervasive mode of thought. For the Mishnah takes up a vast corpus of facts and treats these facts, so to speak, "mishnaically," that is, in a way distinctive to the Mishnah, predicable and typical of the Mishnah. That is what I mean when I refer to the style of the Mishnah: its manner of exegesis of a topic, its mode of thought about any subject, the sorts of perplexities which will precipitate the Mishnah's fertilizing flood of problem-making ingenuity. Confusion and conflict will trigger the Mishnah's power to control conflict by showing its limits, and, thus, the range of shared conviction too.

For by treating facts "mishnaically," the Mishnah establishes boundaries around, and pathways through, confusion. It lays out roads to guide people by ranges of permissible doubt. Consequently, the Mishnah's mode of control over the chaos of conflicting principles, the confusion of doubt, the improbabilities of a world out of alignment, is to delimit and demarcate. By exploring the range of interstitial conflict through its ubiquitous disputes, the Mishnah keeps conflict under control. It so preserves that larger range of agreement, that pervasive and shared conviction, which is never expressed, which is always instantiated, and which, above all, is forever taken for granted. The

Mishnah's deepest convictions about what lies beyond confusion and conflict are never spelled out; they lie in the preliminary, unstated exercise prior to the commencement of a sustained exercise of inquiry, a tractate. They are the things we know before we take up that exercise and study that tractate.

Now all of this vast complex of methods and styles, some of them intellectual, some of them literary and formal, may be captured in the Mishnah's treatment of its own, self-generated conflicts of principles, its search for gray areas of the law. It also may be clearly discerned in the Mishnah's sustained interest in those excluded middles it makes up for the purpose of showing the limits of the law, the confluence and conflict of laws. It further may be perceived in the Mishnah's recurrent exercise in the study of types of mixtures, the ways distinct components of an entity may be joined together, may be deemed separate from one another, may be shown to be fused, or may be shown to share some traits and not others. Finally, the Mishnah's power to sort out matters of confusion will be clearly visible in its repeated statement of the principles by which cases of doubt are to be resolved. A survey of these four modes of thought thus shows us one side of the distinctive and typical character of the Mishnah, when the Mishnah transcends the program of facts, forms, and favored perspectives of its tributaries. We now turn to the side of substance. What causes and resolves confusion and chaos is the power of the Israelite's will. As is said in the context of measurements for minimum quantities to be subject to uncleanness, "All accords with the measure of the man" (M. Kel. 17:11).

The Mishnah's principal message is that Israelite man is at the center of creation, the head of all creatures upon earth, corresponding to God in Heaven, in whose image man is made. The way in which the Mishnah makes this simple and fundamental statement is to impute power to the Israelite to inaugurate and initiate those corresponding processes, sanctification and uncleanness, which play so critical a role in the Mishnah's account of reality. The will of man, expressed through the deed of man, is the active power in the world. Will and deed – these constitute those actors of creation which work upon neutral realms, subject to either sanctification or uncleanness: the Temple and table, the field and family, the altar and hearth, woman, time, space, transactions in the material world and in the world above as well. An object, a substance, a transaction, even a phrase or a sentence, is inert but may be made holy, when the interplay of the will and deed of man arouses and generates its potential to be sanctified. Each may be treated as ordinary or (where relevant) made unclean by neglect of the will and inattentive act of man. Just as the entire system of uncleanness and holiness awaits the intervention of man, which imparts the capacity to become unclean upon what was formerly inert, or which removes the capacity to impart cleanness from what was formerly in its natural and puissant condition, so in the other ranges of reality, man is at the center on earth, just as is God in Heaven. Man is counterpart and partner in creation, in that, like God he has power over the status and condition of creation, putting everything in its proper place, calling everything by its rightful name.

So, stated briefly, the question taken up by the Mishnah is, What can a man do? And the answer laid down by the Mishnah is, Man, through will and deed, is master of this world, the measure of all things. Since when the Mishnah thinks of man, it means the Israelite, who is the subject and actor of its system, the statement is clear. This man is Israel, who can do what he wills. In the aftermath of the two wars, the message of the Mishnah cannot have proved more pertinent – or poignant and tragic. The principal message of the Mishnah is that the will of man affects the material reality of the world and governs the working of those forces, visible or not, which express and effect the sanctification of creation and of Israel alike. This message comes to the surface in countless ways. At the outset a simple example of the supernatural power of man's intention suffices to show the basic power of the Israelite's will to change concrete, tangible facts. The power of the human will is nowhere more effective than in the cult, where, under certain circumstances, what a person is thinking is more important than what he does. The basic point is that if an animal is designated for a given purpose, but the priest prepares the animal with the thought in mind that the beast serves some other sacrificial purpose, then, in some instances, in particular involving a sin offering and a Passover on the fourteenth of Nisan, the sacrifice is ruined. In this matter of preparation of the animal, moreover, are involved the deeds of slaughtering the beast, collecting, conveying, and tossing the blood on the altar, that is, the principal priestly deeds of sacrifice. Again, if the priest has in mind, when doing these deeds, to offer up the parts to be offered up on the altar, or to eat the parts to be eaten by the priest, in some location other than the proper one (the altar, the courtyard, respectively), or at some time other than the requisite one (the next few hours), the rite is spoiled, the meat must be thrown out. Now that is the case, even if the priest did not do what he was thinking of doing. Here again we have a testimony to the fundamental importance imputed to what a person is thinking, even over what he actually does, in critical aspects of the holy life (M. Zebahim 1:1-4:6, Menahot 1:1-4:5).

Once man wants something, a system of the law begins to function. Intention has the power, in particular, to initiate the processes of sanctification. So the moment at which something becomes sacred and so falls under a range of severe penalties for misappropriation or requires a range of strict modes of attentiveness and protection for the preservation of cleanness is defined by the human will. Stated simply: at the center of the mishnaic system is the notion that man has the power to inaugurate the work of sanctification, and the mishnaic system states and restates that power. This assessment of the positive power of the human will begins with the matter of uncleanness, one antonym of sanctification or holiness. Man alone has the power to inaugurate the system of uncleanness.

From the power of man to introduce an object or substance into the processes of uncleanness, we turn to the corresponding power of man to sanctify an object or a substance. This is a much more subtle matter, but it also is more striking. It is the act of designation by a human being which "activates" that holiness inherent in crops from which no tithes have yet been set aside and removed. Once the human being has designated what is holy within the larger crop, then that designated portion of the crop gathers within itself the formerly diffused holiness and becomes holy, set aside for the use and benefit of the priest to whom it is given. So it is the interplay between the will of the farmer, who owns the crop, and the sanctity inherent in the whole batch of the crop itself, which is required for the processes of sanctification to work themselves out.

In addition to the power to initiate the process of sanctification and the system of uncleanness and cleanness, man has the power, through the working of his will, to differentiate one thing from another. The fundamental category into which an entity, which may be this or that, is to be placed is decided by the human will for that entity. Man exercises the power of categorization, so ends confusion. Once more, the consequence will be that, what man decides. Heaven confirms or ratifies. Once man determines that something falls into one category and not another, the interest of Heaven is provoked. Then misuse of that thing invokes heavenly penalties. So man's will has the capacity so to work as to engage the ratifying power of Heaven. Let us take up first of all the most striking example, the deed itself. It would be difficult to doubt that what one does determines the effect of what one does. But that position is rejected. The very valence and result of a deed depend, to begin with, on one's prior intent. The intent which leads a person to do a deed governs the culpability of the deed. There is no intrinsic weight to the deed itself. Human will not only is definitive. It also provides the criterion for differentiation in cases of uncertainty or doubt. This is an overriding fact. That is why I insisted earlier that the principal range of questions addressed by the Mishnah – areas of doubt and uncertainty about status or taxonomy – provokes an encompassing response. This response, it now is clear, in the deep conviction of the mishnaic law, present at the deepest structures of the law, is that what man wills or thinks decides all issues of taxonomy.

To conclude: The characteristic mode of thought of the Mishnah thus is to try to sort things out, exploring the limits of conflict and the range of consensus. The one thing which the Mishnah's framers predictably want to know concerns what falls between two established categories or rules, the gray area of the law, the excluded middle among entities, whether persons, places, or things. This obsession with the liminal or marginal comes to its climax and fulfillment in the remarkably wide-ranging inquiry into the nature of mixtures, whether these are mixtures of substance in a concrete framework or of principles and rules in an abstract one. So the question is fully phrased by both the style of the mishnaic discourse and its rhetoric. It then is fully answered. The question of how we know what something is, the way in which we assign to its proper frame and category what crosses the lines between categories, is settled by what Israelite man wants, thinks, hopes, believes, and how he so acts as to indicate his attitude. With the question properly phrased in the style and mode of mishnaic thought and discourse, the answer is not difficult to express. What makes the difference, what sets things into their proper category and resolves those gray areas of confusion and conflict formed when simple principles intersect and produce dispute, is man's will. Israel's despair or hope is the definitive and differentiating criterion.

III. The Convictions of the Many

Passionate concern for order and stability, for sorting things out and resolving confusion, ambiguity, and doubt – these may well characterize the mind of priests, scribes, and householders. The priests, after all, emerge from a tradition of sanctification achieved through the perfection of the order of creation – that is the theology of their creation-myth. The scribes with their concern for the correspondence between what they do on earth and what is accorded approval and confirmation in Heaven, likewise carry forward that interest in form and order characteristic of a profession of their kind. But if I had to choose that single group for whom the system speaks, it would be neither of these. We noted at the outset that the scribe and the priest are noteworthy by their absence from the fundamental structure and organization of the Mishnah's documents. By contrast, the householder forms the focus of two of the six divisions, those devoted to civil law and family. Let us then reflect for a moment on the ways in which the householder will have found the Mishnah's principal modes of concern congruent with his own program. We speak now of the householder in a courtyard, for he is the subject of most predicates. He is the proprietor of an estate, however modest, however little. He also is a landholder in the fields, an employer with a legitimate claim against lazy or unreliable workers, the head of a family, and the manager of a small but self-contained farm. He is someone who gives over his property to craftsmen for their skilled labor, but is not a craftsman himself. He also is someone with a keen interest in assessing and collecting damages done to his herds and flocks, or in paying what he must for what his beasts do. The Mishnah speaks for someone who deems thievery to be the paltry, petty thievery ("Oh! the servants!") of watchmen of an orchard and herdsmen of a flock, and for a landowner constantly involved in transactions in real property.

The Mishnah's class perspective, described merely from its topics and problems, is that of the undercapitalized and overextended upper-class farmer, who has no appreciation whatsoever for the interests of those with liquid capital and no understanding of the role of trading in commodity futures. This landed proprietor of an estate of some size sees a bushel of grain as a measure of value. But he does not concede that, in the provision of supplies and sustenance through the year, from one harvest to the next, lies a kind of increase no less productive than the increase of the fields and the herd. The Mishnah is the voice of the head of the household, the pillar of society, the model of the community, the arbiter and mediator of the goods of this world, fair, just, honorable, above all, reliable.

The Mishnah therefore is the voice of the Israelite landholding, proprietary class (compare *Soviet Views of Talmudic Judaism. Five Papers by Yu. A. Solodukho in English Translation*, edited with a commentary by this writer (Leiden, 1973: E. J. Brill)). Its problems are the problems of the landowner, the householder, as I said, the Mishnah's basic and recurrent subject for nearly all predicates. Its perspectives are his. Its sense of what is just and fair expresses his sense of the givenness and cosmic rightness of the present condition of society. Earth matches Heaven. The Mishnah's hope for Heaven and its claim on earth, to earth, corresponding to the supernatural basis for the natural world, bespeak the imagination of the surviving Israelite burgherdom of the mid-second century Land of Israel – people deeply tired of war and its dislocation, profoundly distrustful of messiahs and their dangerous promises. These are men of substance and means however modest, aching for a stable and predictable world in which to tend their crops and herds, feed their families and workers, keep to the natural rhythms of the seasons and the lunar cycles, and, in all, live out their lives within strong and secure boundaries, on earth and in Heaven.

Now when we turn away from the Mishnah's imagined world to the actual context of the Israelite community after the destruction of the Temple in 70 and still later after Bar Kokhba, we are able to discern what it is that the Mishnah's sages have for raw materials, the slime they have for mortar, the bricks they have for building. The archaeological evidence of the later second and third century reveals a thriving Israelite community in Galilee and surrounding regions, a community well able to construct for itself synagogues of considerable aesthetic ambition, to sustain and support an internal government and the appurtenances of an abundant life. What that means is that, while the south was permanently lost, the north remained essentially intact. Indeed, it would be on the sturdy and secure foundations of that stable community of the northern part of the Land of Israel that Israelite life for the next three or four hundred years – a very long time – would be constructed.

So when the Mishnah's sages cast their eyes out on the surviving Israelite world, their gaze must have rested upon that thing which had endured, and would continue to endure, beyond the unimaginable catastrophe brought on by Bar Kokhba and his disruptive messianic adventure. Extant and enduring was a world of responsible, solid farmers and their slaves and dependents, the men and women upon the backs of whom the Israelite world would now have come to rest. They, their children, slaves, dependents could yet make a world to endure – if only they could keep what they had, pretty much as they had it – no more, but also no less. Theirs was not a society aimed at aggrandizement. They wanted no more than to preserve what had survived out of the disorderly past. That is why the Mishnah's is not a system respectful of increase. It asks no more than that what is to be is to be. The Mishnah seeks the perfection of a world at rest, the precondition of that seal of creation's perfection sanctified on the seventh day of creation and perpetually sanctified by the seventh day of creation.

But if the philosophers of Israelite society refer to a real world, a world in being, the values of which were susceptible of protection and preservation, the boundaries of which were readily discerned, they also defied that real world. They speak of location but have none. For Israelite settlement in the Land then was certainly not contiguous. There was no polity resting on a homogeneous social basis. All Israel had was villages, on a speckled map of villages of many peoples. There was no Israelite nation, in full charge of its lands or Land, standing upon contiguous and essentially united territories. This locative polity is built upon utopia: no one place. The ultimate act of will is forming a locative system in no particular place, speaking nowhere about somewhere, concretely specifying utopia. This is done – in context – because Israel wills it.

At the end, Weber's problem points the way for further inquiry: how do the inspirations of a few become the convictions of the many? For, we observe, while the Mishnah came into the world as the law book of a class of scribes and small-claims court judges, it in time to come formed the faith and piety of the many of Israel, the Jews at large, the workers and craftsmen. And these, it must be emphasized, were not landholders and farmers. They were in the main landless craftsmen and workers, but they took over this book of landholders and farmers and accepted it as the other half, the oral half, of the whole Torah of God to Moses at Mount Sinai.

That is to say, in somewhat less mythological terms, the Mishnah began with some one group, in fact, with a caste, a class, and a profession. But it very rapidly came to form the heart and center of the imaginative life and concrete politics, law, and society of a remarkably diverse set of groups, that is, the Jewish people as a whole. So the really interesting question, when we move from the account of Israelite religion and society in the first and second centuries, represented by the Mishnah, to religion and society in the third and fourth centuries, represented by the Talmuds, and in the fifth and later centuries, represented by the Midrashim, is how the Mishnah was transformed in social context from one thing into something else. If, as I said at the outset, we locate "the status group whose material and ideal way of life a given idea or value tends to enhance," then we must ask why that same idea or value served, as it did, to enhance a far wider and more encompassing group within Israelite society. We must investigate how it came about that, in time to come, Judaism, the worldview and way of life resting upon the Scriptures and upon the Mishnah and in due course upon the Talmuds, came to constitute the worldview and way of life of nearly all Israel.

For the difficult question before us is the truly historical one: the question of change, of why things begin in one place but move onward, and of how we may account for what happens. The weak point of sociology of religion, in Weber's powerful formulation, emerges from its strong point. If we begin by asking about the relevance of religious ideas to collective actions, we must proceed to wonder about the continuing relevance of religious ideas within a changing collectivity and context. If as Bendix says, Weber emphasizes the issue of how a given idea or value enhances the way of life of a "status group," then we must wonder why that given idea or value succeeds in maintaining its own free-standing, ongoing life among and for entirely other status groups and types of social groups. The history of Judaism from the formation of the Mishnah onward through the next four centuries, amply documented as is that period, provides an important arena for inquiry into yet another constituent of Weber's grand program. But this next set of questions will have to be taken up in another lecture. For the honor of the invitation to give this one, I thank my host, and for the gracious hospitality and hearing according to me on this visit, I thank you all.

14

From "Judaism" to "Torah": An Essay in Inductive Category Formation

The Kroland Coster Lecture
Hunter College, 1986

Categories dictate the intellectual processes of learning and so determine understanding: what we choose to learn, how we proceed to explain and make sense of it.[1] Our category tells us what we want to know, and, once we have selected our data, we find out also what we wish to know about it. The category *Judaism* defines what we study when we wish all together and all at once to describe what the Jews believe, or the Jewish religion, or similar matters covering religious ideas viewed as a system and as a whole. It therefore constitutes a philosophical category, an *-ism*, instructing us to seek the system and order and structure of ideas: the doctrine of this, the doctrine of that, in Juda-*ism*. We invoke the category, Judaism, when we wish to speak of the whole of Judaic religious existence. There are, as I shall argue, other categories, other words, to tell us how to select and organize and order data to instruct us on that same thing: all together, all at once to speak of the whole. But the category we select will guide us to data

---

[1] This lecture summarizes part of the introduction and of the final chapter of my *Ancient Judaism and Modern Category-Formation. "Judaism," "Midrash," "Messianism," and Torah in the Past Quarter-Century* (Atlanta, 1986: Scholars Press for Brown Judaic Studies), one of several books I published in celebration of the twenty-fifth year since the completion of my doctorate in Religion in Columbia University in November, 1960. Among the others is *Ancient Judaism and Contemporary Fundamentalism. The Past Twenty-Five Years* (Atlanta: Scholars Press for Brown Judaic Studies).

221

appropriate to that category, and, consequently, that "whole" of which we speak all together and all at once will not be the same "whole" that finds definition in a category in the classification of an -*ism*. Accordingly, the category in the classification of an -*ism*, in our case, Judaism, tells us what we collect and what we do not collect, how we arrange what we have assembled and so how we are to construe the relationships among data deemed relevant, that is to say, Judaic. Another category, in a different classification, will teach us another way of speaking of the whole all at once and all together. For example, a category in the classification of a central symbol, something that, in itself, encompasses the whole on its own authority and in its own framework, will produce a different picture: different data, assembled along distinct lines, producing a quite distinct and distinctive view of the whole. My argument favors a symbolic, and, in this context of a textual community, therefore canonical, as against a philosophical, definition. Why so? It is on the grounds that the symbolic definition of the definitive category derives from an inductive reading of data, while the philosophical one depends upon an extrinsic and deductive reading of the same data. So at issue in this argument is the appropriate principle of category formation.

I. Self-Evidence and Category Formation

Where to begin? It is with the fault of the category, "Judaism," because that category appears to many to constitute a given in the study of Juda-*ism*. Some claim in behalf of the category, "Judaism," the authority of self-evidence, the universal acknowledgement accorded by common sense. How else – they ask – select and organize data than by the category, *Judaism*. They maintain that that forms a self-evident category, based on the only rational formative process, which is, common sense. But, as I shall show, common sense supplies uncertain guidance indeed in telling us not only what are our categories but the principles that dictate their definition.

How shall I call into question the very self-evidence of the definitive, encompassing category, *Judaism*? And, second, how shall I identify a correct principle of category formation to yield on the basis of inductive inquiry an alternative category for the description of the whole, all at once and all together?

Let me violate all rules of rational discourse to show that the category, Judaism, does not enjoy the status of self-evidence. Specifically, I shall argue from an anecdote. Why adduce a mere anecdote in evidence in a serious argument? Because people think the present categories, beginning with Judaism, self-evident. There is no other. But as I shall now suggest, There is nothing self-evident about them. If I can point to one instance, plausible on the face of it, in which the present category formation does *not* prove self-evident, then choices open up. Nothing any longer may then demand the status of mere common sense. Why not? Because of the very character of a claim of self-evidence. For something to prove self-evident it must commonly make sense. A plausible exception, therefore, forms an insuperable obstacle, just as much as does a single exception to the claim of uniqueness. That is, if I claim something is unique, e.g., as to its species, or even as to its genus, then nothing else can form part of its species, or even its genus. Once we can find a plausible counterpart of parallel or equivalent, then what is alleged to be unique no longer is unique. To cite anecdotal evidence then constitutes a valid mode of argument against claims of self-evidence and common sense, just as a single exceptional case invalidates the claim of uniqueness.

As to plausible categories other than the received ones, therefore, I invoke the exception that comes to me from my grandmother.[2] My grandmother, who spoke Yiddish and came from somewhere near Koretz, in the province of Volhynia, in the northwestern part of the Ukraine, provides the unanswerable argument. She too sought language to speak of the whole all at once and all together, that is, to define the things she lived for. She did not use the word we use when speaking of the things of which we speak when we wish to speak of when we say, *Juda - ism*. She used a different word, which in fact referred to different things. Her category of definition, serving for her speech as does the category, *Judaism*, serves ours, namely, to refer to the whole, all in all, taken all together, therefore instructed her to speak of different things. Her categories and ours, which are supposed to refer to the same data in the same social world, in fact encompass different data from those taken in by ours in our speaking, categorically, of *Judaism*. So do different categories imposed on the same corpus of facts turn out to organize different worlds in different ways.

The difference? When my grandmother wished to invoke a category that included everything all together and in correct proportion, she used the word-category, *Torah*. And so did many centuries of Jews before her. Our category falls into the classification of

---

[2] I choose my grandmother because, in discourse among scholars on the definition and character of Judaism, a fair number of colleagues, specializing in subjects other than in the study of Judaism, or in aspects of Jewish data other than the study of religions, invoke arguments from what their parents or grandparents happened to tell them. So what my bubbee told me forms a valid counterargument in the court of I-think-you-think.

a philosophical or ideological or theological one, a logos: a word. Her category fell into the classification of a symbol, that is, a symbol that in itself encompassed the whole of the system that the category at hand was meant to describe. The species -ism falls into the classification of the genus, logos, while the species, Torah, while using words, transcends words. It falls into a different classification, a species of the genus symbol. How so? It is an object, a classification, an action – an everything in one thing, and that is the power and effect, therefore the definition, of a symbol.

Our -ism category, by contrast, does not invoke an encompassing symbol but a system of thought, as I shall explain presently. So today for a sentence meant to define everything all at once, we resort to the word-category, Judaism. By contrast, my grandmother resorted to a symbol-category, Torah. Why does this matter? It is because in fact the two categories do not correspond, though they are meant to function in the same way, and do run parallel to one another. So Torah as a category serves as a symbol, everywhere present in detail and holding all the details together.[3] Judaism as a category serves as a statement of the main points: the intellectual substrata of it all. If we uncover no such uniform substrate, we have problems – unless we use our ingenuity to find what is not there. How may we test this proposition? It is by appeal to common language usage, that is, to self-evidence. How in fact do people use language?

The conception of Judaism as an organized body of doctrine, as in the sentence, Judaism teaches, or Judaism says, derives from an age in which people further had determined that Judaism belonged to the category of religion, and, of still more definitive importance, a religion was something that teaches or says. That is to say, Judaism is a religion, and a religion is (whatever else it is) a composition of beliefs. In Protestant theological terms, one is saved by faith. But the very components of that sentence, one – individual, not the people or holy nation, saved – personally, not in history, and saved, not sanctified, faith – not mitzvot – in fact prove incomprehensible in the categories constructed by Torah.[4] In fact in the Torah one cannot make such a statement in that way. We have rather to speak as our subject of Israel, not one, to address not only individual life but all of historical time, so

---

[3]That is why I called my prime textbook, The Way of Torah, and its companion reader, The Life of Torah. But I see other ways to compose an introduction to Judaism and am now experimenting with one of them. My tentative title says it all: From Testament to Torah.

[4]My more sustained critique of the Protestant definition of religion and its effects upon the academic study of religion is in my "Theological Enemies of Religious Studies, Religion, in press for 1986.

saved by itself does not suffice, further to invoke the verb, the category of sanctification, not only salvation, and to speak of *mitzvot*, not of faith alone. So the sentence serves for Protestant Christianity but not for the Torah. If, according to the Protestant theological category, I want to study a religion, I study what people believe. So of course Judaism, for its part, will also teach things and lay down doctrines, even dogmas. But the category, faith, the work of constructing the system of thought of which the category is composed – these do not serve the study of the data we refer to, all in all, as Judaism.

Now, to revert to my grandmother, who in this setting serves as our native speaker: for my bubbee the counterpart of the statement, *Judaism teaches*, can only be, *the Torah requires*, and the predicate of such a sentence would be not, *...that God is one*, but, *...that you say a blessing before eating bread*. The category, *Judaism*, encompasses, classifies and organizes, *doctrines:* the faith, which, by the way, an individual adopts and professes. The category, *Torah*, teaches what "we," God's holy people, are and what "we" must do. The counterpart to the statement of Judaism, "God is one," then is, "...who has sanctified us by his commandments and commanded us to..." The one teaches, that is, speaks of intellectual matters and beliefs, the latter demands – social actions and deeds of us, matters of public consequence – including, by the way, affirming such doctrines as God's unity, the resurrection of the dead, the coming of the Messiah, the revelation of the Torah at Sinai, and on and on: "we" can rival the Protestants in heroic deeds of faith. So it is true, the faith demands deeds, and deeds presuppose faith. But, categorically, the emphasis is what is: *Torah* on God's revelation, the *canon*, to Israel and its social way of life, *Judaism* on a system of *belief*. That is a significant difference between the two categories, which, as I said, serve a single purpose, namely, to state the thing as a whole.

Equally true, one would (speaking systematically) also *study Torah*. But what one studied was not an intellectual system of theology or philosophy, rather a document of revealed Scripture and law. That is not to suggest that my grandmother did not believe that God is one, or that the philosophers who taught that Judaism teaches ethical monotheism did not concur that, on that account, one has to say a blessing before eating bread. But the categories are different, and, in consequence, so too the composites of knowledge. A book *on* Judaism explains the doctrines, the theology or philosophy, of Judaism. A book *on* Judaism explains the doctrines, the theology or philosophy, of Judaism. A book *of* the holy Torah expounds God's will as revealed in "the one whole Torah of Moses, our rabbi," as sages teach and embody God's will. I cannot imagine two more different books, and the reason is that they represent totally different categories of intelligible discourse and of knowledge. Proof, of course, is that the latter books are literally unreadable. They form part of a genuinely oral exercise, to be cited sentence by sentence and expounded in the setting of other sentences, from other books, the whole made cogent by the speaker. That process of homogenization is how *Torah* works as a generative category. It obscures other lines of structure and order. True, the two distinct categories come to bear upon the same body of data, the same holy books. But the consequent compositions – selections of facts, ordering of facts, analyses of facts, statements of conclusion and interpretation and above all, modes of public discourse, meaning who says what to whom – bear no relationship to one another, none whatsoever. Indeed, the compositions more likely than not do not even adduce the same facts or even refer to them.

How is it that the category I claim imposed, extrinsic, and deductive, namely, "Judaism," has attained the status of self-evidence? The reason, as I shall argue in a moment, is that the principles of category formation rest on social foundations, and categories serve because they are self-evident to a large group of people. In the case at hand, therefore, Judaism serves because it enjoys self-evidence as part of a larger set of categories that are equally self-evident. In all of these categories, religion constitutes a statement of belief, so religions form a body of well-composed -*isms*. So whence the category, "Judaism"? The source of the categorical power of "Judaism" derives from the Protestant philosophical heritage that has defined scholarship, including category formation, from the time of Kant onward. From the nineteenth century forward in universities a prevailing attitude of mind, particularly in the academic study of religion, has identified religion with belief, to the near exclusion of behavior. In the hands of academic scholars religion has tended to identify itself with faith, so religion is understood as a personal state of mind or an individual's personal and private attitude. In the classroom, after all, it is to attitudes of mind that we gain most ready access. Other matters lead us far beyond the walls of the lecture room. But the reason for the prevailing conviction is not merely adventitious: we study the data where they are convenient to us, hence, ideas in books. The reason for the categorical power of religion is theological, deriving from the Protestant character of universities, and the reason for the self-evidence of that category is social, deriving from the character of the societies in which religion is studied. When we study religion, the present picture suggests, we ask about not society but self, not about culture and community, but about conscience and character.

So when we study religion, we tend, in the aggregate, to speak of individuals and not groups: faith and its substance, and, beyond faith, the things that faith represents: faith reified, hence, religion. Let me give as example of what I mean the observations by William Scott Green, as follows:

> The basic attitude of mind characteristic of the study of religion holds that religion is certainly in your soul, likely in your heart, perhaps in your mind, but never in your body. That attitude encourages us to construe religion cerebrally and individually, to think in terms of beliefs and the believer, rather than in terms of behavior and community. The lens provided by this prejudice draws our attention to the intense and obsessive belief called "faith," so religion is understood as a state of mind, the object of intellectual or emotional commitment, the result of decisions to believe or to have faith. According to this model, people have religion but they do not do their religion. Thus we tend to devalue behavior and performance, to make it epiphenomenal, and of course to emphasize thinking and reflecting, the practice of theology, as a primary activity of religious people....The famous slogan that "ritual recapitulates myth" follows this model by assigning priority to the story and to peoples' believing the story, and makes behavior simply an imitation, an aping, a mere acting out.[5]

Now as we reflect on Green's observations, we of course recognize what is at stake. It is the definition of religion, or, rather, what matters in or about religion, emerging from Protestant theology and Protestant religious experience. For when we lay heavy emphasis on faith to the exclusion of worlds, on the individual rather than on society, conscience instead of culture, when we treat behavior and performance by groups as less important and thinking, reflecting, theology, and belief as more important, we simply adopt as normative for academic scholarship convictions critical to the Protestant Reformation.

For my grandmother, and a hundred generations of Jews before her, the categories of the Protestant Reformation scarcely served in helping her to define the whole all at once and all together. She resorted to a different category from faith, meaning ideology, theology, or philosophy, a category deriving from the way of life and worldview represented, symbolized, by the Torah: intrinsic, inductive, self-evident. And so did her Russian and Ukrainian Orthodox neighbors, and so did her Polish Roman Catholic neighbors not far away. To that entire universe of human civilization, the nation, the language, the religion, the way of life, clothing, food, occupation – everything stood for one thing, and one thing stood for everything, whether the cross, whether the Torah, whether (I suppose) the hammer and the sickle. The Torah stood for the Jewish language, the Jewish food, the Jewish garments, the Jewish occupation, the Jewish way of treating other

---

[5]Personal letter, January 17, 1985.

people, and on and on and on: the whole, all at once, all together. What has a mere -*ism* to do with all of that!

II. The Importance of the Correct Category and the Right Generative Principle of Category Formation

Why, in the study of ancient Judaism, do I find it necessary to pursue the rather abstract question of category formation? The reason is that the issue of category formation dictates the character of learning. So the matter is urgent. Until we have explained the answer to the question of why we want to know what we investigate, that is, the principle of category formation that tells us what we want to know and what we do not want to know, we labor without learning at all. We pursue unexamined careers of collecting and arranging, like the cavemen who went hunting and gathering. We compile information for a purpose we cannot specify, sort out data the cogency of which we cannot explain. What question, therefore, does the analysis of category formation answer? It is what we want to know, how we propose to find out, and why, to begin with, we ask.

Nothing in learning derives from nature, that is, the nature of the data. All things come from nurture and therefore culture, that is, the social exercise of learning. Each of the categories we invoke to impart meaning and order to our minds comes from somewhere. Categories so deeply mark our minds that they appear to us to be self-evident. That, indeed, indicates the effect of a category. But, as I have shown, each category finds self-evidence solely in its large social context, therefore forms a construct, not a given, of learning. Therefore categories, and the principle of category formation that generated them, ultimately express an aspect of culture, serve political or economic expediency, or even introduce into the processes of intellect the effects of consciousness and conscience – what our Gallic masters call *interiority* – as I shall explain presently. I have now to make these allegations stick.

III. The Social Construction of Categories

Categories take form in the context not of the unconstrained mind but of the social intellect: the imagination formed, made plausible, by society, culture, politics – that is to say, context and circumstance. What we want to know society tells us we should find out. How we shall find out what we want to know culture explains. And beyond the two lies the social compact that imparts sense and acceptance to the facts we think we know and to the categories that legislate the rules of comprehension and collective understanding. These are common sense and self-evidence. They in the end form the criteria for description.

Description lends order and meaning to discrete pieces and bits of information, so forming the beginning of comprehension, of knowledge. So what we want to know, that is, the categories of knowledge, and how we find it out, namely, through selecting appropriate data and analyzing them, come to us as the gifts and givens of our social world. Our context provides the technology of finding things out, identifying sources we want to study and determining how to read them, also specifying sources we ignore and explaining why they contain only gibberish. All these, when brought to the surface and examined, testify to the formation of the categories of our minds, the structure and construction of all knowledge. So category formation forms the critical component of consciousness and defines the structure of understanding.

To give a simple example of the centrality of social reality in the definition of how we shall undertake category formation, I point to a case far away from the recognition of *Judaism* as a category. Rather, I refer to the recognition of *the* Maori as a social entity and – more to the point – as an organizing category of learning. In turning to far-off New Zealand, I want to know why that remote society falls into two parts, Maori and Pakeha (European), and, more especially, who first discovered that the Maori are *te Maori* – that is, *the Maori,* a social entity, a group – and why the discovery that various groups form *te Maori* mattered. To frame the question simply: Did Maori know they were *the Maori,*[6] and, if not, who told them? The parallel question: did my grandmother know that the Torah was Judaism, and if not, why did her grandson have to find out? What we shall see is that just as "Judaism" is the invention of philosophers, so the Maori as a category is the invention of people pressed to make sense of an unknown world. The answer to that question follows:

> In attempting to describe *the* Maori and his culture, we are creating a stereotype that did not exist; for there was no one typical Maori but many Maories; no one Maori culture but regional and tribal varieties of culture. Moreover, most observers were expert in the culture of only one or two areas, though they often passed off that information as representative of the Maori people as a whole. Even the name, Maori, is an abstraction, created in the nineteenth century. Cook called them Indians, though the name New Zealanders was soon applied. Maori (ordinary) was first recorded about 1800 as an adjective in the phrase *tangata maori,* an ordinary person, as contrasted with *tangata tupua,* a

---

[6]The counterpart: did my grandmother know that she "practiced" or "believed in" Judaism? And if not, how and why did my father find out? And why did I take up the questions? We enter deeply into the history of the Jews in America when we study ancient Judaism. And when our Israeli counterparts do the same, they too would do well to ask some rigorous questions about their own intellectual roots.

230   *Lectures on Judaism in the Humanities*

supernatural being, as the Europeans were first thought to be. By the
1830 Maori was being used occasionally as a proper noun, but it did
not come into general use as such until about the 1860s. Since then it
has been used retrospectively to describe the early inhabitants.[7]

In fact when the Europeans came, New Zealand consisted of two dozen
different groups (social entities), at war among themselves, unaware
that, as a whole, they formed a distinct society or nation or culture-
group. They were no more a "the" – *"the* Maori," (*te Maori)* – than "the
Jews believed in and practiced Judaism" – in that order. The category in
either case derived from the imagination of hard-pressed outsiders,
seeking to make sense of an unknown world, to which known categories
did not apply.

All the aboriginal inhabitants of New Zealand knew they had in
common was that they lived on the same islands. When Europeans
came, *te Maori* therefore were not *te Maori.* That is to say, the diverse
social entities of the two islands shared the same planet, just as much
as we share the same planet with Ethiopians or Peruvians, without
regarding ourselves as part of a single entity (short of the human race,
and that category bears slight consequence, beyond a rather trivial
sentimentality). Were explorers from a distant galaxy to come and call
us all "the weirdos," the sense – the self-evident appropriateness of
the name – would strike us as no different from the self-evident
appropriateness of the name Maori, when applied to the twenty-four
perpetually warring groups ("nations"? "tribes"?) of the North and
South Islands. Someone from the moon might as well have appeared on
the Somme in 1916 and announced that the French and the Germans
formed (under God) one indivisible nation. Such a statement, in that
circumstance, would not likely have enjoyed universal self-evidence.
Whatever the diverse Maori called themselves, they saw differences
where outsiders saw sameness, and, in consequence, they fought
unceasing wars, living out their lives in stockades. So, descriptively
speaking, the generative category, Maori, derived from elsewhere. To
them it was not only not self-evident, it made no sense at all.

But under other circumstances, at a different time, and for a fresh
purpose, the categorical self-evidence of *Maori* struck the Maori quite
forcefully. So even to the Maori *te Maori* became a self-evident
category. But it was not because of the character of the data to which

---

[7]M. P. K. Sorrenson, *Maori Origins and Migrations* (Auckland, 1979: Aukland
University Press and Oxford University Press), pp. 58-59. My dear colleague,
Ernest S. Frerichs, and I stumbled on the book when visiting the Auckland
Museum, and he found it first, so to him goes the credit for seeing it. But it is in
the writing of Jonathan Z. Smith that both of us developed our interest in the
Maori/Pakeha relationship as an example of the problem of the outsider.

the category applied. In fact the category proved contingent on circumstance: politics and interest, things not of the mind at all. So much for context and self-evidence! As Sorrenson says, *maori* meant ordinary, that is, the normal, *us*, as against the extraordinary, *them*, the supernaturals. But that is not what the word means now. Then it was a mode of organizing unfamiliar experience by distinguishing natural from supernatural data. Now it serves as a political category, classifying for racial purposes a diverse and mixed population. So do categories form and reform, now supernatural, now political, now economic, in response to changing circumstance. When the New Zealand government today asks incoming travellers whether they are Maori, it does not mean to raise a theological question: are you ordinary or supernatural? And the question the government does address travellers remains one of classification. But the category has shifted, *and therefore also the facts.*

IV. The Circumstantial Character of Categories and of Their Formation

Knowing consists in more than merely following the intellectual equivalent of the rules of syntax for language. Knowing always rests on selection among the things that are there to be known, as everyone knows. We may choose to ignore, as the Australian aborigines did when the Europeans came, or we may choose to recognize and take charge, like the Maori in New Zealand, who carefully constructed a myth to account for their ownership of the land and much else:

> Maoris had their own purposes to serve in reciting and recording oral traditions, myths, and legends. Above all there was the vital question of establishing titles not land, since genealogies showing descent from Maui and the commander of the ancestral canoe from Hawaiki could be used to establish a charter to land....Far from dying out as the Europeans expected, Maori traditions, myths, and legends, including those elaborated in the nineteenth century, have continued as a vital part of what is still very much an oral culture.[8]

The Maori created categories in response to circumstance, and the categories then dictated the kinds of information they would collect or invent, as circumstance required.[9]

---

[8]Sorrenson, pp. 84-85.

[9]Indeed, I wonder whether the prehistoric, traditional tale, first told to be sure in the later nineteenth century, for the primeval or prehistoric migration by great canoe may in time turn out to be a restatement, with exquisite irony, of the (by-then-well-known) fact of the First Fleet. bringing the original settlers to Australia. But that is not our problem.

Understanding the categories that dictate what we want to know and how we shall find it out defines our problem. Yet, as is clear, I find much to learn in a field so alien, so distant, to the one at hand. For where on the face of the earth can we go further from the Near East and Europe, and what age can we located, beyond our own, more remote from that of the Jews of late antiquity, in the firs through the seventh centuries, than nineteenth-century New Zealand. And how astonishing then is it to know, as Sorrenson says:

> The ethnographers nearly always found in Maori culture what they expected to find; their expectations were kindled by the prevailing anthropolitical theories of their day. In this respect the ethnographic record on the Maori is a fairly faithful reproduction of changing fashions in anthropology....Description which purported to be of the Maori as he was at the time of Cook were often considerably influenced by the condition of contemporary Maoris.[10]

What conclusion do I draw from this observation? It is that theologically motivated anachronism flourishes, not only in the study of the history of the Jews and Judaism in antiquity, but also in anthropology.

In fact *everything* we know, we know because, to begin with, we require knowledge of one sort, rather than some other. And our context, that is to say, our circumstances in society and among the cultural groups of our own country, or our country among the countries of our region, and on upward, tells us what we need to know and why. In the study of social groups, for example, before recording facts, we know that the facts concern the social group at hand, and not some other. So we start with a definition of traits that distinguish a social group. The consequence is simple. If you have those traits, you are in the group, and if you do not, you are not in the group. I know the traits before I know the group that is defined by them, so to speak. That is why, as Sorrenson says, observers see what they anticipate seeing, and their expectations come from what they have already seen: the categories established in their minds.

The history of knowledge monotonously reminds us that people see what they expect to see, rarely noticing merely everything there is to see. In Sydney, I was told, when the ships of Captain Cook's fleet appeared at Botany Bay, the aborigines, farming on the shore, simply did not see them all: they just did not *see* them. Not expecting such a sight, their eyes – so people report – perceived nothing at all. Whether or not the story is true, I cannot say. But it does conform to the rule that we see what we expect to see. In broader terms, we perceive through

[10]Sorrenson, p. 58.

analogies, think in metaphors, interpret and understand the unknown in terms of the known – all this because there is no alternative.

Let me conclude with a simple example of these facts of learning and life. Describing the formation of knowledge about the Maori peoples of New Zealand, Sorrenson[11] further states:

> For most European observers were not content to record what they heard and saw; they had to interpret their information and above all to answer intriguing questions about the ultimate origin of the Maori and their coming to New Zealand....Europeans' answers to these questions and interpretations of Maori culture were profoundly influenced by the prevailing philosophies of man and the latest scientific techniques....The idea that mankind had diffused from a single point, usually in the Middle East or India, offered a starting point for interpretation. Comparative techniques in physical anthropology, culture, philology, and myths and legends offered means of proving ancient racial connections and of tracing the footsteps of primitive men, including the migrations of Polynesians. Darwinism offered a way of stretching the existing chronologies....There is no need to expand further on the absurdities of the Semitic or Aryan Maori theses – both were attempts to apply the conventional wisdom of the day to the problem of the origin of the Polynesians....But it is worth pausing briefly to ask why the Maori was so favorably regarded: to be considered a Semite, when most other colored people were designated as Hamites; and, in the later nineteenth century, to be awarded the ultimate accolade of an Aryan ancestry like that of the Anglo-Saxon colonists?....This was part of the wider ideal of an embryonic New Zealand nationalism. Nations are based on historical myths and New Zealand by the late nineteenth century was in the process of inventing hers.

So at the foundations of the category, *the Maori,* we uncover that demonic trinity, diffusionism, racism, and Social Darwinism! But as to the generative cause of the formation of that category, we uncover something considerably more within our range of understanding: the need of a new society, coming into existence out of the sherds and remnants of an older set of societies, to explain itself and its future.[12] And so too when it comes to "Judaism," "Midrash," and "The Messianic Doctrine of Judaism." What counterparts to such discredited ideas as diffusionism, Social Darwinism, or racism lie in the deep archaeology of these categories, of course, we cannot say. I see none. Nor do we know

---

[11]Sorrenson, p. 82.

[12]The invention of the Maori formed into a single category all of the (to themselves diverse) populations extant on the islands at the beginning of European-descended settlement. Today, I have the impression, the Maori assist the European New Zealanders to accept their situation at the end of the earth and to let go of the long cord that binds them to "home," that is, "England."

the human circumstances that made Jews look for a Judaism when they wanted to speak of the whole, all at once and all together, of their system.[13] But, to conclude, *Judaism* surely rests on a distinctive view of what we study when we study religion.

V. How Categories take Shape
An Inductive Approach

Now that we recognize the adventitious, indeed circumstantial character of categories, we need hardly dwell upon the distinction between inductive and deductive category formation. That distinction seems to me self-evident. Such categories as *te Maori* and *Judaism* emerge when outsiders find it necessary to resort to available, therefore extrinsic rules of order and description in order to characterize the whole, all together and all at once. The alternative, an inductive principle of category formation, will emerge from the data to be characterized. In the present case, the question that yields an inductive principle of category formation is simple: how do the data "describe themselves," so to speak.[14]

A study of the history of category formation in the study of ancient Judaism carries us not into the first six centuries of the Common Era (A.D.) and off to the Land of Israel ("Palestine"), but to nineteenth and twentieth century Europe and America. There we should expect to find out where and why people determined that *Judaism* constituted a

---

[13]In his classic work, *The Uprooted*, Oscar Handlin argues that it was in America that the diverse immigrant groups discovered their shared nationality, e.g., as Italians. In Italy, if you asked, what are you and where do you come from, the answer would come as: from a village, such-and-so, in the province of X. In America, the *you* became Italian. So too the Jews of Eastern Europe described themselves by reference to village, near town, in province X. I never knew the name of my grandmother's village, all the more so that of the first Jacob Neusner, nor the name of their family, only "near Koretz," in the "government of Volhynia in the Ukraine. Jewish? Of course, so what? That did not count as a point of differentiation, therefore of category formation. In America the immigrants gained that other identification, Jews, as a group, Italians as a group. More to the point, the category made a difference. The self-consciousness that forces definition intellectually also expresses the power of homogenization working on internal points of distinction and differentiation within the social group. Wilfred C. Smith correctly has taught us that it is the outsider who names a religion, e.g., Hinduism. And, I would add, and as much to the point, it is the experience of *being the outsider* that in the perception of the participant names the group. But what are the "insides" to which the participant is outsider?

[14]Wilfred C. Smith's observation therefore is not the end, but only the beginning, of the matter. For knowledgeable people do come along and they are not outsiders to the data. And they too have their contribution to make.

principal category for identifying information, organizing it, and lending it proportion, sense, meaning, and even significance. The category therefore dictates the rules of description, determines the issues for analysis, and governs the hermeneutical alternatives explored in the interpretation of data. None is teased out of the data it is meant to categorize. All come from without – some from far away indeed. An account of modern and contemporary consciousness among Jews would certainly tell us much about the formation of these categories, as expressions of what proved self-evident in the unfolding consciousness of the social group at hand.

My purpose, however, is not to explore the modern and contemporary history of how Jews and outsiders formed the category *Judaism* and so identified data they determined would form *Judaism*. What I wish to pose is a different question. It is an inquiry intimate to, generated by, the data I study, which is to say, the documents provided in late antiquity and from then to now preserved by Jews as God's revelation to Israel.

Specifically, I am trying to learn how to form appropriate categories for the description of *those* data, for the analysis of *those* data, and for the interpretation of *those* data. So my exercise in the study of category formation begins not in abstract and philosophical reflection on nineteenth and twentieth century philosophy but in a particular body of the (to me) givens: the writings of the ancient sages, there alone. My study of category formation therefore appeals to a particular authority: data already identified. It is inductive in a peculiar and curious way: I already know the limns and limits of my category,[15] and now I wish to find out what further categories have applied and whether they fit. My category is the canon of writings universally regarded by Jews from antiquity to the present day as Torah. My question is whether any other category than Torah applies. My answer is that none does. Specifically, such *-isms*, such categories as *Judaism* violate the limns and borders of the one category that forms from within the data and not outside of it. Those other categories, I shall try to show, therefore do not apply. That, sum and substance, is the argument at hand: that the only useful categories for the analysis of data derive from the data, in the case at hand, the analytical categories for the Torah inductively derive from the Torah.

---

[15]Presently, I confront the circularity of the present statement and show how to emerge from it.

VI. Canon, that is, Torah, as an Inductive Category

An inductive approach to category formation requires that we take up the pieces of evidence one by one and propose by sorting out those data long lines they themselves dictate to find out what they mean. But an inductive approach presents us with its own circularity. Let me explain this circularity and how I propose to emerge from it, for this is the heart of the problem. How shall I know what data to select for organization in categories if to begin with I do not know what data I wish to organize and categorize? So knowing what I have to form into categories tells me the principles of category formation. But if I already know what data demands categorization, then do I not already have my categories? That circularity confronts us first of all in our quest for a principle of category formation intrinsic to the data and not extrinsic to them. My problem is to point to an initial and generative category external to the data yet (paradoxically) intrinsic to them. Lacking such a principle of selection and organization outside of the data I propose to describe, analyze, and interpret, I find myself at the same impasse at which I have located others. To restate matters as clearly as I can:

(1)   We can know nothing without categories that permit classification, yielding the possibility of describing facts, analyzing them, and interpreting them.

(2)   We wish to generate those categories out of the data themselves, rather than imposing categories external to the data, that is, we seek an inductive, rather than inductive, principle of category formation.

(3)   But how do we know what data we wish to categorize and classify, if not through some principle of category formation that tells us one set of data belongs within the system, another set outside?

So that is the circularity from which I have now to seek to emerge. Let us stipulate at the outset that all data – all forms of evidence, in writing, in stones, in material culture, in reference in all writings – pertaining to people regarded as Jews, and no data associated with people not regarded as Jews, to begin with require categorization for purposes of description, analysis, and interpretation. I believe philosophers will find that specification reasonable. But how, then, to begin the work of differentiation, if so external a category as just now specified tells me more merely that

(1)   *everything in* is in and

(2)   *everything out* is out?

Better the dreaded circularity with which we began. My responsibility, then, is to propose a category external to the data and yet appropriate to them.

I find that generative principle for category formation in the matter of – to state with heavy emphasis – *the diverse institutional media by which the data are mediated from antiquity to the present.*

I refer to the differentiation among data imposed by the simple fact that some materials come to us in one medium, some in another. Some data reach us through the mediation of the diverse Christian churches. Some come to us through the continuous process of tradition of the Judaic religious institution, the synagogue, and its associated, and continuing institutions, e.g., the master-disciple circle, the school, and the like. Some data come to us by the happy accident of being preserved in the earth and dug up. These facts of transmission differentiate. How so? The third group of data – that produced by archaeology – bears no relationship to the first or the second, since, by definition, no one knew about it until it was dug up. It forms a single group. The materials preserved by, respectively, church and synagogue scarcely overlap. The former constitute one distinct group, the latter, another. And, further, that latter group – the writing preserved by the synagogue – constitutes not library but a canon. That is to say, the synagogue preserved the writing of late antiquity, where and when it did, because the group that kept the materials and copied them and handed them on and treasured them regarded them as holy, a statement of God's will to Israel: Torah. So that set of data stands quite distinct from the other two. Consequently, I claim an objective set of facts, external to the character and quality of the data, and yet enormously consequential in making differentiations among the data.

Accordingly, some data come to us (1) through the enduring institutions of the West, and synagogue and the church. Some data come to us (2) accidentally, through survival in caves. Some data come to (3) us in the form of writing, some data come to us (4) in the form of surviving buildings, artifacts, and other evidences of material culture. The one set differs from the other, and that in the merely advantageous sense just now specified: the medium of preservation and transmission. What is preserved and transmitted by people falls into (1) one gross category, what is preserved and transmitted by accident of nature falls into (2) another. And the people who did the preserving break up into (3, 4) distinct and scarcely intersecting groups as well.

Precisely what comes down to us from the Jews of late antiquity and how does it reach us? As is clear, the answer to the second question covers both: we have evidence in the media, material artifacts of archaeological provenience and writings of various kinds. The former then form one category, the latter another. As to the latter, the media for the preservation of documents – deliberate or accidental – once more supply us with our criterion for differentiation. What Judaism in its later history preserved as holy – that is, the canon of Judaism from late antiquity to the present – we must treat as distinct from what others than Jews preserved. The distinction – the definition of the generative category – therefore derives from circumstance and from without.

So we can indeed generate differentiating categories, variables that derive from the data themselves. Do these distinctions make a difference? For reasons already suggested, it makes a difference to know that (some) outsiders found materials worth saving. And, along these same lines and critical to the argument: it also makes a difference to know that (some) Jews found materials worth saving.[16] Some writings of Jews reaches through the medium of the copyists of the churches, others through the serendipity of preservation in dry caves. Some books come down to us only through the medium of the synagogue. And those for that – adventitious – reason form one distinct corpus of data – for reasons of a nearly physical, and essentially material character.

So, in my judgment, the simplest category at hand is how – by what medium materials reached us. The items that come to us through institutions under Jewish auspices, therefore from the synagogue, fall together into one group, and that is *because of traits of all these items and none of the others.* When we can point to traits characteristic of one set of data and not characteristic of another, we have found an appropriate category, and that category inductively derives from data.

I speak of course, of what later on became known as the Torah, that is, the canon of the Judaism that defined and preserved these books as a canon (not, for example, as a library).[17] The other data find their points of cogency elsewhere; they do not form our problem here. And, to proceed, once the books that for clear and distinct reasons fall together into a group define the broadest perimeters of our category, the mode of

---

[16]We do not know whether or not Jews thought so too, since we have these writings only from institutions under Christian auspices. If there were groups of Jews who cherished these books and also saved them, they did not succeed in handing on their holy books to the present generation.

[17]I work on the distinction between canon and library in *The Oral Torah. An Introduction* (San Francisco, 1985: Harper & Row), and on the distinction between a composition and a scrapbook or anthology in *The Integrity of Leviticus Rabbah* (Atlanta, 1985: Scholars Press for Brown Judaic Studies). These distinctions bear their own importance to my larger argument, but not here.

subdividing that encompassing category also is defined. From the canon, we divide by the same principle of category formation as has led to the recognition of the canon as the principal category, namely, by the books that make up the canon. These categories then find definition in the books that the canon for its part preserved one by one (not as part of an undifferentiated mass) – and so on down to the very sentences.

So I claim to move from the mass of evidence, delimited in a gross and completely external way, to the formation of categories that we recognize on inductive and external grounds. That is to say, on the basis of a descriptive and external approach to the diverse data that Jews of late antiquity produced, we locate a direct road to the categories formed by the canon and its components. These then define and constitute the categories, and so, I claim, the principle of category formation derives from an inductive examination of the entire corpus of evidence, divided to being with only among the media by which the evidence was preserved and transmitted to us, divided at the second level by the criteria themselves dictated by media internal to the first of the subdivisions of the data we chose to take up: the canon of that Judaism that preserved and handed on these books and not other books. And so the process proceeds.

VII. Describing a System Whole:
The Canonical Principle in Category Formation and How It Works

The limns of documents then generate, form, and define our initial system of categories, that is, the document to being with is what demands description, then analysis by comparison and contrast to the other documents, then interpretation as part of the whole canon of which it forms a part.[18] Now to the rules of description, which is to say, of category formation along the lines of the canonical principle of category generation.

Documents stand in three relationships to one another and to the system of which they form part, that is, to Judaism, as a whole. When we understand these relationships, we shall grasp not only the premise of this paper, but the future of the study of Judaism in its formative centuries, therefore, also, of the study of the Christianity that took shape in the same context and circumstance.

---

[18]I hasten to add, I do not take the canon to be a timeless category, as my analysis of the Mishnah and its associates indicated. Quite to the contrary, the canon itself takes shape in stages, and these form interesting categories for study. So things are considerably more complicated than I can presently explain.

Autonomy: Each document, it is clear, demands description, analysis, and interpretation, all by itself. Each must be viewed as autonomous of all others.

Connection: Each document also is to be examined for its relationships with other documents that fall into the same classification (whether that classification is simply "Jewish" or still more narrowly and hence usefully defined).

Continuity: Each document is to be allowed to take its place as part of the undifferentiated aggregation of documents that, all together, constitute the evidence of a Judaism, in the case of the rabbinic kind, the canon of the Torah.

How so?

Autonomy: If a document reaches us within its own framework as a complete book with a beginning, a middle, and an end, we do not commit an error in simple logic by reading that document as it has reached us, that is, as a book by itself.

Connection: If, further, a document contains materials shared verbatim or in substantial content with other documents of its classification, or if a document explicitly refers to some other writings and their contents, then we have to ask the question of connection. We have to seek the facts of connectedness and ask for the meaning of those connections.

Continuity: In the description of a Judaism, we have to take as our further task the description of the whole out of the undifferentiated testimony of all of its parts. For a Judaism does put together a set of once discrete documents and treat them as its canon. So in our setting we do want to know how a number of writings fit together into a single continuous and harmonious statement.

That is the point at which we do describe and analyze a Judaism. We therefore take up the task of interpreting that Judaism in the relationship between its contents and the context in which it makes its statement. In taking up the question of the harmony of the canon, whether of the rabbinic sources represented in this book by the Mishnah, or of the courses comprising the Pseudepigrapha, or of the writings of the Essenes of Qumran, or even of the Maccabean historians, we ask a theological question. And, in our context, that question elicits enormous interest: what after all was the Judaism of the Maccabean historians, or of the Essenes of Qumran, or of the authorship represented by Mark, or by the Mishnah?

By seeing the several components of the canons of the Judaisms of antiquity in sequence, first one by one, then one after the other in an orderly progression and sequence, and, finally, all together all at once, we may trace the histories of Judaisms. We may see a given document come into being on its own, in its context and circumstance. So we interpret the document at its site.

Since many documents relate to others prior to themselves or are brought into relationship to later writings, the issue of connectedness and connection demands attention. And, finally, all together and all at once, a given set of documents does form a whole, a canon, a frame that transcends the parts and imparts proportion, meaning, and harmony to the parts – a Judaism (to resort to the "self-evident" category).

What do I hope to accomplish in the accurate description, to begin with through categories of its own devising, of a Judaism? The answer derives from the work on the systemic analysis of Mary Douglas. Her stress is upon the conception that, "each tribe actively construes its particular universe in the course of an internal dialogue about law and order."[19] So, she says,

> Particular meanings are parts of larger ones, and these refer ultimately to a whole, in which all the available knowledge is related. But the largest whole into which all minor meanings fit can only be a metaphysical scheme. This itself has to be traced to the particular way of life which is realized within it and which generates the meanings. In the end, all meanings are social meanings.[20]

If I seek to state the large issues of that culture precisely as they are expressed through minute details of the way of life of those who stand within its frame, I have to start with the correct categories that encompass all the extant data of the culture at hand. These interrelate and define a coherent system. So at stake in category formation is systemic description.

For once we have discerned the system which the compositors and framers of the books at hand evidently meant to create, we have the task before us of comparing that system to other systems, yielded both by Judaisms in their various stages and by other religious and cultural systems, in quite different contexts. For a system described but not juxtaposed to, and compared with, other systems has not yet been interpreted. Until we realize what people might have done, we are not going to grasp the things they did do. We shall be unable to interpret the choices people have made until we contemplate the choices they rejected. And, as is clear, it is the work of comparison which makes

---

[19]Mary Douglas, *Implicit Meanings: Essays in Anthropology* (London: Routledge & Kegan Paul, 1975), p. 5.
[20]p. 8.

that perspective possible. But how do we compare systems?[21] In fact, whenever we try to make sense for ourselves of what alien people do, we are engaged in a work of comparison, that is, an experiment of analogies. For when we are trying to make sense for ourselves of what alien people do, we are engaged in a work of comparison, that is, an experiment of analogies. For we are trying to make sense specifically by comparing what we know and do to what the other, the alien culture before us, seems to have known and to have done. For this purpose we seek analogies from the known to the unfamiliar. I am inclined to think the task is to encompass everything deemed important by some one group, to include within, and to exclude from, its holy book, its definitive text: a system and its exclusions, its stance in a taxonomy of systems. For, on the surface, what they put in they think essential, and what they omit they do not think important.

VIII. Challenges to the Canonical Principle of Category Formation

Now in consequence of the theory at hand, we begin by describing, analyzing, and interpreting the documents, not ideas held in a variety of documents. Our category derives not from *Judaism* but from *Torah*, that is, canon. But when we take up as our generative category a single book or document deriving from Jews of ancient times, without making theological judgments about whether the authors were "loyal" or "normative" or "authentic," we do something genuinely new. It is not only new, it also is secular. When we take up not a whole canonical, or official, literature but only a single book or document, and further, when we avoid judgments about normative or authentic or classical Judaism as against the heterodox or heretical kind, we set aside theological issues. Rather, we address descriptive and anthropological ones. That approach to the study of ancient Jewish writings still surprises believers of one kind or another.

When, furthermore, we approach the canon of that form of Judaism that did emerge as normative from late antiquity and did define the outlines of the history of the Judaism that was normative from the seventh to the nineteenth century, we commit a still more remarkable act. For, if some concede that all Jewish texts do not attest to a single Judaism, few grasp that to begin with we cannot treat as unified and harmonious all the texts preserved by rabbis from antiquity to the present time, that is, the canon, or, in common language, "rabbinic" or "Canon of Judaism in late antiquity" or simply "Judaism." Our work is

---

[21]Much that is called "comparative religions" compares nothing and is an exercise in the juxtaposition of incomparables. But it does not have to be that way.

to test, not to affirm at the outset, the premise that all books of the official canon of rabbinic Judaism form a single whole and harmonious "Torah." That fundamental dogma of the faith demands demonstration through the evidence itself. And the test must be a simple one. It is a test of description, analysis, and interpretation of the documents of the canon of Judaism, read, first, one by one, then, second, as connected to one another, and, third and finally as part of a single and harmonious system, a Judaism, thus a continuity. That test begins with my work and stands at its elementary stages even now. So, to return to the main point, when we take up a single book or document in the canon of Judaism as we know it, or in the canon of any other Judaism, and when we propose to describe, analyze, and interpret that book in particular, we violate the lines or order and system that have characterized earlier studies of these same documents. Not only so, but we open our question in quite different way from earlier efforts to describe matters such as doctrine or belief. How so?

Until now canonical texts as testimonies to a single system and structure, that is, as I said, not to *"a Judaism"* or to a component of some larger Judaism, but it is, that is, to *"Judaism."* What sort of testimonies texts provide of course varies according to the interests of the scholars, students, and saints who study them. Scholars look for meanings of words and phrases or better versions of a text. For them, all canonical documents serve equally well as a treasury of philological facts and variant readings. Students look for the sense of words and phrases and follow a given phrase hither and yon as their teachers direct their treasure hunt. Saints study all texts equally, looking for God's will and finding testimonies to God in each component of the canon, in the case of Judaism, in each component of "the one whole Torah of Moses, our rabbi." And that is how it should be, for students, scholars, and saints within Judaism.

Among none of these circles, however, will the discrete description, analysis, and interpretation of a single text make sense. Why not? Because for them all texts ordinarily form a single statement in common, "Torah" in the mythic setting, "Judaism" in the philosophical and theological one. From that perspective people correctly expect each document to make its contribution to the whole, to Judaism. If, therefore, we wish to know what "Judaism" or "the Torah" teaches on any subject, we simply open all the books equally. We draw freely on sayings relevant to that subject whenever they occur in the entire canon of Judaism. Guided only by the taste and judgment of the great "sages of the Torah" or, in formally secular circumstances, Orthodox Judaic professors at seminaries or ethnic-nationalist ones at universities, as they have addressed the question at hand, we do not merely describe "Judaism," we also declare dogma.

In the view of persons in these classifications, composites of sayings on a single topic (in our example, "Judaism," meaning "what the Jews believe") drawn from diverse books in no way violate the frontiers and boundaries that distinguish one part of the canon from some other part of the same canon. Why not? The theological conviction defines the established approach. Frontiers and boundaries stand only at the outer limits of "the whole Torah of Moses our rabbi." Within the bounds, "there is neither earlier nor later," that is to say, temporal (therefore all other differentiating) considerations do not apply.[22] If temporal distinctions make no difference, no others do either. For people who want to study in an inductive way the formation of Judaism in late antiquity as well as the setting in which Christianity took shape, however, the analysis of the literary evidence of the Jewish canon requires a different approach from the received orthodox-scholarly one.

IX. The Integrity of a Document in the Canon of Judaism

To describe and analyze documents one by one violates the lines of order and system that have characterized all earlier studies of these same documents. But the hermeneutical issue directed by the system – hence, as I have argued, the canon and its components – overall defines the results of description, analysis, and interpretation. Simple logic makes self-evident the proposition that, if a document comes down to us within its own framework, as a complete book with a beginning, middle, and end, in preserving that book, the canon presents us with a document on its own and not solely as part of a larger composition or construct. So we too see the document as it reaches us, that is, as autonomous.

If, second, a document contains materials shared verbatim or in substantial content with other documents of its classification, or if one document refers to the contents of other documents, then the several documents that clearly wish to engage in conversation have to address one another. That is to say, we have to seek for the marks of

---

[22]That view characterizes historians as much as theologians, historians of events, persons, or institutions and movements as much as historians of theology. These people just collect and arrange everything they find on the topic they have chosen and then make up history. That the younger and supposedly secular generation does the same sort of collecting and arranging – but now by collecting things attributed to a single authority, without differentiating where and when and by whom the attribution is made – is the burden of my *Ancient Judaism and Contemporary Fundamentalism*.

connectedness, asking for the meaning of those connections. It is at this level of connectedness that we labor. For the purpose of comparison is to tell us what is like something else, what is unlike something else. To begin with, we can declare something unlike something else only if we know that it is like that other thing. Otherwise the original judgment bears no sense whatsoever. So, once more, canon defines context, or, in descriptive language, the first classification for comparative study is the document, brought into juxtaposition with, and contrast to, another document.

Finally, since the community of the faithful of Judaism, in all of the contemporary expressions of Judaism, concur that the documents held to be authoritative constitute one whole, seamless "Torah," that is, a complete and exhaustive statement of God's will for Israel and humanity, we take as a further appropriate task, if one not to be done here, the description of the whole out of the undifferentiated testimony of all of its parts. These components in the theological context are viewed, as is clear, as equally authoritative for the composition of the whole: one, continuous system. In taking up such a question, we address a problem not of theology alone, though it is a correct theological conviction, but one of description, analysis, and interpretation of an entirely historical order.

In my view the various documents of the canon of Judaism produced in late antiquity demand a hermeneutic altogether different from the one of homogenization and harmonization, the ahistorical and anti-contextual one definitive for contemporary category formation. As I showed in the opening unit of this paper, it is one that does not harmonize but that differentiates. It is a hermeneutic shaped to teach us how to read the compilations of exegeses first of all one by one and in a particular context, and second, in comparison with one another.

X. From "Judaism" to *Torah*

Let us conclude with the point with which we began, the difficulty attached to generating categories for the present purpose out of theological or philosophical concepts. Why *Torah*, a literary principle of category formation, not *Judaism*, a theological one? To answer that question, we briefly turn to the greatest work ever published in any language[23] under the title *Judaism*, namely, George Foot Moore,

---

[23]E. E. Urbach, *The Sages, Their Concepts and Beliefs* (Jerusalem, in Hebrew, 1969, English, 1975: The Magnes press) provides much valuable information but lacks intellectual cogency. It has not enjoyed a particularly favorable reception, and, in English, it has made no impact on method. It has generated

Judaism. The Age of the Tannaim (Cambridge, 1927: Harvard University Press). Here we shall gain access to the main problem with the category at hand. The critical problem of definition is presented by the organizing category, "Judaism." Moore does not think definition is needed. But we now know that it is. Explaining what we propose to define when we speak about "Judaism" is the work of both contemporary philosophy of religion and history of religion. Moore fails to tell us also of whom he wishes to speak. So his repertoire of sources for the description of "Judaism" in the "age of the Tannaim" is awry. He makes use of sources which speak of people assumed to derive from a much later or a much earlier time. What generates this error is a mistake in category formation.

Specifically, Moore had to confront the problem of dealing with a category asymmetrical to the evidence. An essentially philosophical construct, "Judaism," is imposed upon wildly diverse evidence deriving from many kinds of social groups and testifying to the state of mind and way of life of many sorts of Jews, who in their own day would scarcely have understood one another, for instance, Bar Kokhba and Josephus, or the teacher of righteousness and Aqiba. So for Moore "Judaism" is a problem of ideas, and the history of Judaism is the history of ideas abstracted from the groups that held them and from the social perspectives of said groups. This seems to me a fundamental error, making the category "Judaism" a construct of a wholly fantastic realm of thought: a fantasy, I mean. In this regard matters are admirably summed up in Arthur Darby Nock's inquiry about the matter of "Gnosticism." He wanted to know where are the Gnostic churches, who are the Gnostic priests, and what are the Gnostic church's books and doctrines.[24] What he meant was to point out that what we have are rather specific evidences of a single genus, the Gnostic one, e.g., of Manichaeism or Mandaism and now, of Nag Hammadi. Out of the agglutination and conglomeration of these diverse social groups and their writings scholars (not Jonas alone) formed (I should say invented) that higher idea, that *"the"* – the Gnostic religion. That the forms the counterpart of the *-ism*-izing of Juda-, thus: *Judaism*.

From a philosophical viewpoint the intellectual construct, Gnosticism, may bear scrutiny. From a historical viewpoint, it does not. The reason is that the *-ism* of *Gnostic-*, as much as the counterpart, the

---

no studies beyond itself, no major books continuing its lines of inquiry. It marks the end, not the beginning, of research in its model.

[24]Arthur Darby Nock. *Essays on Religion and the Ancient World*, ed. Zeph Steward (Oxford, 1972: Clarendon Press), I, 444-51, in his review of Hans Jonas, *The Gnostic Religion*.

-ism of the *Juda-, ism*-izes too facilely. That is to say, Moore and other systematic theologians who have studied *Judaism* join together into harmonies data that derive from quite diverse groups at different times, and that were produced and preserved under different circumstances. So little is proved and much assumed. If we propose to present a cogent picture of how data deliver a single message, then the harmony and unity of the data demand demonstration. Before we know that the data derive from a single category, we can hardly undertake to form those data into a cogent statement about that category, describing, e.g., its ideas, analyzing its positions in comparison to the positions of other, related groups, interpreting those ideas in a still larger context. None of these routine activities of intellect can begin without a clear demonstration that the *it* – the *-ism* – is an *it* to begin with, and not a *them*. History, rightly done, must err on the side of radical nominalism, as against the philosophical power for tolerance of something close to pure realism. In invoking these categories of medieval philosophy for analogical purposes, I mean only to explain why, for the present purpose, *"Juda"* + *"ism"* do not constitute self-evident, let alone definitive, categories. So, as I said, Judaism constitutes a category asymmetrical to the evidence adduced in its study. The category does not work because the principle of formation is philosophical and not historical. And to begin with historical category formation, we start with the sources at hand: once more, the canon, or, in mythic terms, the Torah.

Second, Moore's work to begin with is not really a work in the history of religions at all – in this instance, the developmental and formative history of a particular brand of Judaism. His research is in theology. It is organized in theological categories, That hardly presents a surprise, since Moore quite naturally took as the work of describing a religion the task of spelling out its ideas. For religion is faith, conviction, as the received datum, in theological words the tradition of salvation by faith, had taught him. This bias again derives from the faulty generative principle of category formation: religion is belief, and the categories therefore are those of systematic theology.

What Moore constructed therefore is a static exercise in dogmatic theology, not an account of the history of religious ideas and – still more urgent – their unfolding in relationship to the society of the people who held those ideas. Moore in no way describes and interprets the religious worldview and way of life expressed, in part, through the ideas under study. He does not explore the interplay between that worldview and the historical and political context of the community envisioned by that construction of a world. To state matters in the present context, my grandmother would not have understood Moore's picture of "Judaism," even if it had been translated into Yiddish.

But from our perspective, Moore's kind of classification, his "Judaism," and the continuators of that mode of description and analysis, prove equally alien. Why so? We who want to understand not only religions but religion ask ourselves a different set of questions, those that ask about religion as a social fact, a force in the shaping of human events. So far as history of religion, (as distinct from histories of religions) attends to the material context of ideas and the class structure expressed by ideas and institutions alike, so far as ideas are deemed part of a larger social system and religion systems are held to be pertinent to the given political, social, and economic framework which contains them, Moore's account of dogmatic theology to begin with has nothing to do with religious history. His picture of Judaism bears no relationship to the history of Judaism in the first two centuries of the Common Era. So much for *Judaism* and for the principle of category formation that yields *Judaism*. As soon as we speak of Judaisms, not Judaism, we see the flaw and understand the hopeless impasse to which we have come in the Protestant ascendancy in the study of religion. The principle of category formation derives from the wrong generative conception and premise.

This in conclusion brings us to the contrary principle of category formation. Again I state with emphasis: it is this:

> *The one that commences with the sources, that is, in the case at hand, with the canon or the Torah – that is, with an inductive inquiry originating in the data subject to categorization.*

How do we proceed to form categories out of that principle of inductive formation out of data? One route to the interpretation of a system is to specify the sorts of issues it chooses to regard as problems, the matters it chooses for its close and continuing exegesis. When we know the things about which people worry, we have some insight into the way in which they see the world. So we ask, when we approach the canon of Judaism in late antiquity, about its critical tensions, the recurring issues which occupy its great minds. It is out of concern with this range of issues, and not some other, that the canon of Judaism in late antiquity defines its principal areas for discussion. Here is the point at which the great exercises of law and theology will be generated – here and not somewhere else. This is a way in which we specify the choices people have made, the selections a system has effected. When we know what people have chosen, we also may speculate about the things they have rejected, the issues they regard as uninteresting or as closed. We then describe the realm of thought and everyday life which they do not deem subject to tension and speculation. It is on these two sides – the things people conceive to be dangerous and important, the things they set into the background as unimportant and uninteresting – which provide us with a key to a Judaism – that is to say, the culture of a community or, as I prefer to put it, to the system constructed and expressed by a given group of people.

The central issues, those questions which generate insight worth sharing and understanding worth having, therefore, find definition in these terms: what does the canon of Judaism in late antiquity, viewed item by item, by its components and then as a whole, define as its central problems? How does the canon of Judaism in late antiquity perceive the critical tensions of its world? We want to describe the solutions, resolutions, and remissions the category of the canon poses for these tensions. We propose to unpack and then to put back together again the worldview of the canon as a whole, but first document by document. When we can explain how this system fits together and works, then we shall know something worth knowing, which is how to describe, analyze, and interpret *the Torah.*

Epilogue

15

The Power of Imagination

The O. C. Tanner Lecture in Humanities
Utah State University, Logan, February 23, 1989

The power of the human imagination, expressed in the human will, attitude, and intentionality, for nearly two hundred years has competed with explanations of human action that dismiss imagination, will, attitude, intentionality altogether. These explanations treat what is intangible as inconsequential, on the one side, or merely subsidiary and contingent, on the other. Accordingly, they dismiss imagination as an effect of interest, maintaining that what we want to have happen is shaped by considerations entirely unrelated to that want. Or these explanations treat humanity as itself incapable of an act of will and beyond all reach of intentionality. Therefore what we want is shaped by what we do not want and do not even acknowledge.

The first of the two modes of dismissing as null the power of imagination is exemplified by marxist theories of action, which appeal to economic and especially class interest to explain matters of not only the political economy but also the house of intellect and sensibility in which we live. The second, which regards us as creatures shaped, distorted really, by internal forces beyond our control, is exemplified by freudian theories of personality, which treat as beside the point matters of character and conscience, and, it must follow, understand imagination outside of the framework of intentionality, attitude, and will.

There comes a time, in the unfolding of debate, to stand stock still and say, No, that is not how things are. And that we do when we invoke for purposes of argument facts that stand outside of the frame of argument. We have come to that point in debates on the power of imagination, of humanity to form an attitude in which the place of intentionality proves paramount, in which we center attention once again, in explaining who we are and what we do, upon what we want. That is to say, it is time to speak of responsibility, to invoke our power to make decision, and, above all, to explain our actions in light of our intentionality, our perceptions in the illumination of our imagination. And this is that time.

The day has come to say, we are not only what others make of us, or what inner powers over which we have no control make of us, or of what our class interests make of us. We are what we make of ourselves, by force of our conscience and character, our individuality and our sense of responsibility. And these are formed – conscience, character, individuality, responsibility – by imagination. For that is what comes to the fore and comes first of all: our sense within of what lies beyond. Our capacity to imagine a world and go out and make that world takes pride of place in explaining what we are and the world we make: so I wish to maintain.

The negative arguments, against the marxist theory of humanity and the freudian theory of humanity which typify the theories that deny to imagination and the inner life all autonomy, all power of uncontingent action, are familiar. No marxist economy has accomplished its goals. But the mixed economies of the West, which provide ample space for individual initiative along with shared action on the part of uncoerced groups (e.g., corporations), have gained much and lost nothing. Freudian theories of personality, well represented in public life for nearly a century now, have opened many doors and brought to the surface much that lay hidden. But they no longer find themselves asked to explain – and explain away – that entire range of reality that, a generation ago, in some circles at least, they were asked to do. That is to say, psychology now enjoys all due honor and respect, but it no longer pronounces on questions beyond its range of data and tested hypothesis to an awe-struck audience.

But the positive arguments in favor of the free imagination of humanity have yet to gain a hearing. And, at the beginning of the counterattack upon the view that we are what others make of us, or what society or class interest makes of us, or what forces beyond our control make of us, let me invoke a single powerful example, which will show us the shape and structure of the coming argument. It is the example of religion. And I have chosen that example not because I am a religious person, though I am in believing in God and providence, but because religion has found itself identified by these competing explanations of human action as the principal opponent.

That is why through the nineteenth century and down to our own day, every theory of humanity that sought a hearing for itself reached its climax with its attack upon religion as a competing, and contrary, theory of who we are and what we mean. Marx, after all, chose not to explain but to explain away religion as an opiate for the masses, a medium of social control of slaves by masters, or of masters by slaves (as Nietzsche improved upon matters). Freud, for his part, found a place for religion within his account of the unfolding personality, and that place accorded to religion no autonomous standing but only a contingent role in the neurotic personality.

I need hardly, in this context, rehearse the language made familiar by common culture, "wish-fulfilment," "fantasy," for example. And these, I repeat, represent mere examples of a two-hundred-year campaign against religion – in this context, representing the imagination of humanity, the quest for what lies within and beyond the everyday. That campaign began in the Enlightenment, found its generals, each leading his own army on his own front, everywhere it looked for them, and throughout the arts and humanities promoted that view of humanity that in mere detail Freud and Marx for their part represented: we are there not to be explained, but to be explained away. And, I must emphasize, it was not only Freud and psychology, not only Marx or sociology and political science and economics. It was also the humanities practiced as expressions of a secular humanism that engaged in the long-term attack upon religion, and, therefore, the autonomous will, the free-ranging imagination. If I mention, after all, such areas of humanistic learning as philosophy, on the one side, and history, on the other, I call to mind fields of battle against the possibility that religion explains reality.

But religion explains a greater range of everyday reality than philosophy and history, economics, sociology, psychology, and politics, on the other. Proof of that simple proposition lies not in the distant past of the rise of Islam and the Christian Crusades, on the one hand, or the building of the Christian civilization of Europe or the Buddhist civilization of the Orient, on the other. Proof comes from the here and the now. I invoke only these places to make my point: Sri Lanka, Ireland, Canada, Belgium, Jerusalem, Baghdad, and Teheran. True, the point is then a negative one. Religion forms a powerful force for human action against humanity, for the nurture of hostility and the legitimation of homicide. But explain Ireland without religion, or the Middle East without religion, or India and Pakistan and Sri Lanka without religion, or the struggle for Belgium and the Netherlands and the politics of Italy and Canada without religion? It simply cannot be done. Religion is what they call in the social sciences an independent variable. And for us in the humanities, the appeal to religious belief as an autonomous force in the framing of culture and sensibility, in the shaping of mind and intellect, in the structure and system of imagination bears the same force.

One may argue that religion then bears a heavy burden of responsibility for the human condition, and indeed it does. But that is not to the point. For when we seek to find our way toward the twenty-first century – and that is the task of the hour and the purpose of our learning – then we have to turn to ask how religion, in its concrete embodiment of the works of imagination and will, has done its work. And dismissing religion as contingent, a dependent variable, no longer yields that guidance that we must have in making sense of human action and in making something out of the human condition.

For at stake is not whether or not religion is a good thing. It is, what religion is? and what makes up the human imagination and will that religion embodies? The answer to the first question is simple. Religion forms a world-creating realm of power, and that means, so I maintain, that it is within our mind and imagination that the world takes shape. First we dream, then we do. And our dreams are ours, or come from somewhere beyond this place, and from some force beyond the tangible.

Let me give three concrete instances of what I regard as that simple fact. First, the State of Utah, built as it was by decision, born as it was in the mind and imagination of Joseph Smith and Brigham Young. First they dreamed, then they went and did. Second, the entirety of the civilization of Latin America, which, as much of the place-names indicate, is the formation of a particular kind of Christian, a Roman Catholic Christian engaged (as the founders of my native New England were engaged), in the creation of a Christian civilization in the New World. They went from Spain and Portugal to found Christian, by which they meant, Catholic, civilization, and they were mostly priests and religious. And they did precisely what they planned to do: but first came the plan. Third, the State of Israel, born as it was in the imagination of a Jewish journalist of meagre religious roots in the anti-Semitic Vienna of the 1890s, realized as it was at the very moment at which the Jewish People passed beyond the gates of hell. That was an act of not only supererogatory imagination, it was, still more, a statement of defiance of despair. Whence such power in the realm of the unconscious, and where in class interest such a thing takes place, I cannot say.

That is why I maintain that there is simply no coping with the world today without the intellectual tools for understanding religion, not as a theory of another world, but as a power and force in the shaping of this world. Events in Iran and Afghanistan, as to Islam, Azerbaijan and Armenia as to Islam and Christianity, Latin America and Poland, as to Roman Catholic Christianity, the State of Israel and the USA, as to Judaism, only illustrate that simple fact that most (though not all) of humanity does what it does by reason of religious conviction. And since public policy falls silent before that fact, it is time to reenter discourse with issues long dormant on the relationship between religious systems and the world of politics and of economics, psychology and sociology.

To do so, let me call attention to two cases that seem to me to demonstrate the power of imagination, in particular, the religious imagination, to form culture and frame politics. The one shows us how religions change – and then change the world. The other defines for us a range of thought and speculation that seems to me productive. To show how religions change and then, in that sequence, change the world, I wish to invoke the case of Roman Catholic Christianity in its relationship with the Jewish People and with Judaism. In every account of the history of the Jews in Christian Europe and the Western hemisphere, Roman Catholic power and policy find a principal role in explaining the Jews' condition. Since that condition is always (and generally with good reason) represented as uncertain and frequently as pitiable, Catholic power and policy are implicitly credited with considerable influence over the making of the world. But in our own time, when, we are asked to assume, religion, including Roman Catholic Christianity, is no longer a force, we hear little about that same matter.

When we examine the issues of Christian-Jewish relationship, however, we discover an interesting fact. From World War II onward, the Roman Catholic Church has totally and completely reconsidered its relationship with the Jews and also with Judaism. Formerly it was at best humanitarian toward the Jews, showing a patronizing and condescending willingness, sometimes, to let them breathe. And, as to Judaism, that attitude uniformly yielded the dismissal of Judaism as a road to salvation. So many important books have traced the long history of Roman Catholic hostility toward Judaism and also toward the Jews that we must stipulate the facts. Less celebrated is the news that, in the past two generations, since before World War II, the Roman Catholic Church has affirmed Jewry as the enduring people of God, and has affirmed Judaism as a work of God. This is not in theory only or mainly. It is in liturgy and homily, where the Church lives in the hearts of the people.

As evidence let me point to something very current, which is the paper called, "God's Mercy Endures Forever: Guidelines on the Presentation of Jews and Judaism in Catholic Preaching," issued in September 1988 by the Committee on the Liturgy of the National

Conference of Catholic Bishops. The operative sections of that report advise Catholic preachers on appropriate ways to read those events and Scriptures that have in times past kindled hatred for "the Jews" and contempt for Judaism, the Passion Narratives, for example. Throughout, the guidelines insist upon "respect for the continuing validity of God's covenant with the Jewish people and their responsive faithfulness, despite centuries of suffering, to the divine call that is theirs." The document reaffirms the earlier (1985) language, which I quote, "Attentive to the same God who has spoken, hanging on the same word, we have to witness to one same memory and one common hope in him who is master of history." Commenting on the development of a new doctrine of "Israel," Eugene J. Fisher comments [in *Fifteen Years of Catholic-Jewish Dialogue. Teologia e Filosofia* (Vatican, 1988: Libreria Editrice Lateranense), 11:243], "One can...discern in the cautiousness of each of these steps taken on an official Catholic level not only the seriousness with which the topic is approached by the magisterium but...an indication of the 'irreversibility' of the process itself."

But does it all make a difference? Fisher's own studies of Catholic textbook presentation of Jews and Judaism have shown that, in the aggregate, it does. The teaching about the Jews has taken hold, in the American Church at any rate. Opinion surveys of Roman Catholic opinion have yielded the interesting result that Roman Catholics today bear a far lower quotient of hostility toward Jews and Judaism than Jews do about Roman Catholics and their religion. That is to say, measured by concrete opinions people hold and things they say they are prepared to do or not do, Roman Catholic opinion stands well past the frontiers of tolerance and condescension. It today affirms, respects, esteems, what formerly was despised and humiliated. That is a change. It is a change in imagination, framed in religious teaching, and, studies are telling us, it is a change with concrete implications for the shape of society and the character and configuration of culture.

So we see how religions change – and then change the world. But so what? What broader conclusions are we to draw for the role of religion in the definition of culture, which is to say, for the power of imagination to make the world? To answer that question I turn to the writings of another Roman Catholic intellectual, in addition to Eugene Fisher. He is Professor, Doctor, and Father Andrew M. Greeley, who in a single career has made his mark on both the social study of religion and also on the world of the imagination conveyed by fiction. Greeley's sociology, with stress on demographic study of ethnicism, has demonstrated that religion forms an independent variable that explains other things, but is not explained by those other things: a power and a force in the world on its own. His fiction, which is deeply Catholic in its formation and message, has evoked a deep response in Protestants and Jews, as well as Catholics. Dismissed by uncomprehending or indifferent people as merely "steamy," though the fiction treats sex only in the context of love and always with a chaste respect for the feminine, Greeley's novels, like his sociology, convey a religious message about religion.

He is therefore an appropriate source for the framing of a humanistic program of study of religion. It is not one to affirm the particular truths of a particular religion; that would be a program of theological study of religion that we, in the humanities, cannot sustain. We cannot sustain it because we cannot share it without regard to those particular sources of truth that we affirm, each for himself or herself, and that, therefore, distinguish one from another within the common corps of humanistic learning. It is a program of intellect – study here in the University, thought and reflection long after we have gone on to other chapters of our lives – that seems to me appropriate and plausible. And, when we consider what is at stake, we realize the remarkable fit between the issue, does the human imagination matter? and the possibilities of the critical intellect to face that issue.

To be quite specific, Greeley wants to know whether Protestants' power of imagination is different from Catholics' power of imagination. Can we show that there is a difference between how Protestants conceive the world and how the Catholics do? That seems to me a fundamental question, and one that, if answered in the affirmative, does yield the result that religion makes a difference, forms that independent variable to which I referred at the outset. In asking this question, of course, Greeley carries forward the inquiry of Max Weber into *the Protestant ethic and the spirit of Capitalism,* but he does so in a different and original way. Since the issue is imagination and the power of imagination, Greeley sets matters out in the following language:

> Protestants are expected to be individualist because of an imagination of society as 'sinful and God-forsaken.' Catholics are expected to be communitarian because of an imagination of society as sacramental, that is, revelatory of God.

This "expectation" or hypothesis is then framed in terms of research in the following way:

> The research question is whether the analogical/communitarian imagination can persist in a world of industrialization, modernization, urbanization, and homogenization. The issue was tested against data from seven nations (35 variables) with the null hypothesis that denominational background does not predict value orientation.

That is to say, if the theory is wrong, then when we study the opinion of various groups, Protestant and Catholic, we shall find that the fact that someone is Protestant does not help us predict values or opinions that that person will hold. Greeley found that the "null hypothesis" was false; there are meaningful and substantive differences that can be explained only by appeal to religious difference, specifically, the different imaginations nurtured by Protestantism in Protestants, by Catholicism in Catholics. For the USA, Greeley further tested the null hypothesis "that differences in religious imagery could not account for some of the variance between Protestants and Catholics on value measures." This too he found to be false. Greeley draws this conclusion from his analysis:

> The old, the archaic, the communal manages to survive, especially when that matter is religious.

Greeley points out that that is not how things were expected to come out. At the time that social science was taking shape, toward the end of the last century, people in Europe saw a change from the organic society to the mechanical society, from the organic community to the association. "The Protestant ethic, broadly defined as the 'individualist' ethic, was replacing the Catholic ethic, broadly defined as the 'communal' ethic." But that is not how things have happened, at least, not yet. Industrialism has not eliminated differences between Protestants and Catholics. Why has that not happened? The reason Greeley gives is this:

> World views...are, in their origins and their raw, primal power, tenacious and durable narrative symbols that take possession of the imagination early in the socialization process and provide patterns of meaning and response that shape the rest of life.

So, Greeley says,

> The theory of different imaginations of society, encoded in different stories of God's relationship with the world...can explain the durability of separate world views among Protestants and Catholics. The differences will disappear only when Protestants become more likely to picture God as present in the world, and Catholics more likely to picture Her as absent from the world.

But this will happen, I should imagine, when the Pope moves to Temple Square. Accordingly, Greeley's evidence suggests, religion forms that independent variable that social scientists invoke to explain things.

Shall we then reject the theory of humanity implicit in marxian economics or in freudian psychology? Only when that theory explains data that lie beyond its method, provoking in us a sense of nonsense, that is to say, of dissonance. Control of the means of production explains much about economic behavior, but it cannot tell us what a poem means or why it was written. And shall we turn the clock back to the age before Freud insisted that there is a realm of being beyond the verbal and the rationally explained? Only when that theory of humanity is asked to tell us how Mozart wrote Don Giovanni, or why selflessness endures on earth, or how love works. We find ourselves dismissing class interest without the corrective of Marx, even though we explain too much through marxism; we explain, account for, too little when we pretend Freud did not accomplish what he did, even though we not only explain, we explain away, through freudianism. In both cases religion proves the point. In religion we act in a way that is indifferent to our class interest. In religion we form relations in a manner not shaped wholly or mainly by those patterns of relationship formed in our infancy and shaped by sexuality. Religion seen as mere class interest imputed to God's authority, or interpreted as only a neurotic response, is explained away. But the facts deny such dismissal.

When I ask whether the imagination still matters, or whether we cannot now explain how we think in terms of what we want – class interest – or how we feel – psychological impulse, here I find an answer. Imagination still matters, and it matters a great deal. Imagination has the power to shape the world, and imagination is not shaped by the world of the here and now, but the world of long ago and far away imparts its shape and structure to that here and now.

That is why I say, it is time to stand back and say "no" to the representation of the human condition as shaped by forces wholly beyond ourselves, and "yes" to that representation of the human condition that affirms us in the image and after the likeness of God, who creates. When we create, as all of us do in one way or another, we act freely, out of our inner world of imagination, to make a world: like God.

Index

Scripture(s) 8, 43-47, 81, 82, 92, 119, 120, 124, 149, 153-156, 159, 165, 167-169, 171-177, 179, 181, 184, 192-195, 211, 218, 225, 258

Scroggs, Robin 36

Siddur 122

Sifra 82, 179, 192, 194

Silberman, Lou H. 63

Simeon b. Gamaliel 170, 185

Simeon b. Shatah 149, 152, 156

Sin-offering 184-186

Sinai 46, 48, 75, 81, 82, 176, 218, 225

Sklare, Marshall 52, 53, 58

Smith, Jonathan Z. 36, 80, 113, 143, 144, 230

Smith, Wilfred C. 234

Social Darwinism 233

Sociologist 52, 58, 125

Sociology 5, 11, 20, 22, 54, 58, 67, 93, 115, 130, 135, 136, 218, 255, 257-259

Sociology of Religions 20

Socrates 67

Solomon 43, 169

Soloveichik, Joseph Dov 119, 122

Sorrenson, M. P. K. 230-233

State of Israel 19, 37, 51, 55, 256, 257

Stonehenge 134, 136

Structuralism 23, 143, 147, 159-162

Structuralist 147, 154, 160

Structuralist (post-) 147

Study of religion(s) 4, 6, 15, 17, 20-29, 31, 33-35, 37, 40, 48, 55, 68-

70, 73, 75-79, 83, 87, 92, 98, 130, 144, 197, 223, 224, 226, 227, 248, 258, 259

Synagogue 237, 238

Tabernacles 172

Talmud(s), talmudic 39, 64, 67, 74, 75, 81, 103, 116, 119, 120, 122, 133, 137, 138, 144, 145, 151, 154, 204, 218

Talmud of Babylonia 137

Talmud of the Land of Israel 39

Talmudic Judaism 81, 216

Tanakh 103, 120

Targumim 124

Taxonomy 83, 161, 183, 192, 207, 215, 242

Taxonomy/Taxonomies of systems 80, 83, 242

Temple 10, 44, 47, 76, 78-80, 136, 148-152, 158, 159, 161, 173, 201, 203, 210-212, 217, 260

Tent of the corpse 174

Theology 27, 33-35, 37, 39, 54, 57, 74, 81, 107, 108, 113-116, 118-124, 126-130, 144, 177, 178, 181, 195, 215, 225, 227, 244, 245, 247, 248

Torah 37-44, 46-48, 57, 58, 60-62, 65, 73-76, 81, 82, 84, 85, 92, 114, 115, 119-122, 126-129, 152, 155, 158, 163, 165, 167, 170, 173, 176-179, 184, 192, 194, 195, 218, 221, 223-227, 229, 235-238, 240, 242-245, 247-249

Trachtenberg, Joshua 151

Tracy, David 113, 126

Tradition 9, 23, 30, 34, 42, 46, 54, 60, 65, 69, 71, 74-76, 81, 83, 84,